Holiest Wars

Holiest Wars

*Islamic Mahdis, Their Jihads,
and Osama bin Laden*

TIMOTHY R. FURNISH

Foreword by Michael Rubin

PRAEGER

Westport, Connecticut
London

Library of Congress Cataloging-in-Publication Data

Furnish, Timothy R., 1960-
  Holiest Wars : Islamic Mahdis, their Jihads, and Osama bin Laden / Timothy R. Furnish ;
foreword by Michael Rubin.
    p. cm.
  Includes bibliographical references and index.
  ISBN 0–275–98383–8 (alk. paper)
  1. Mahdism—History of doctrines. 2. Jihad. 3. Islamic fundamentalism. 4. War—Religious
aspects—Islam. 5. Terrorism—Religious aspects—Islam. 6. Islam—21st century.
I. Title.
  BP166.93.F87   2005
  297.2′4—dc22   2004028295

British Library Cataloguing in Publication Data is available.

Library of Congress Catalog Card Number: 2004028295
ISBN: 0–275–98383–8

First published in 2005

Praeger Publishers, 88 Post Road West, Westport, CT 06881
An imprint of Greenwood Publishing Group, Inc.
www.praeger.com

Printed in the United States of America

The paper used in this book complies with the
Permanent Paper Standard issued by the National
Information Standards Organization (Z39.48–1984).

10 9 8 7 6 5 4 3 2 1

Contents

Foreword		vii
Acknowledgments		ix
Chapter 1	What Is Mahdism and Where Does It Come From?	1
Chapter 2	Mahdist Movements throughout History	30
Chapter 3	Counter-Mahdist Rationales and Policies	72
Chapter 4	The Virtual Mahdi Today	87
Chapter 5	Modern Muslim Anti-Mahdists	130
Chapter 6	Conclusion: Who Will Be the Next Mahdi?	150
Subject Index		169
Index of Important Arabic Terms		176
Index of Qur'anic Citations		177
Index of Biblical Citations		179

Foreword

Every year the world grows smaller. The September 11, 2001, terrorist attacks illustrate how the West is no longer immune from radical movements and ideologies that arise across oceans, in desert tents and mountain schools thousands of miles away. Islamic history is long and rich. The first schisms developed over succession disputes in the wake of the prophet Muhammad's death. Division begat division as theological movements fractured, coalesced, and reinterpreted Islamic doctrine.

Over the course of centuries few theological movements have provoked as much violent reaction and counterreaction in Islamic societies as have Mahdist movements. From India to Tunisia, every few generations an individual lifts a banner and claims that he is the Mahdi, the figure who will usher in divine government and just rule. Some Mahdis lead only rag-tag bands of followers, and others command large armies. Today would-be Mahdis command networks of terrorists who use the Internet and threaten society at large.

Too many academics indulge in the luxury of political correctness. With a wave of the hand, they can dismiss the uncomfortable notion of a clash of civilizations. True, many citizens in the Islamic world want nothing better than to enjoy liberty, freedom, and democracy. But as Timothy Furnish rightfully points out, within Islamist and, more specifically, Mahdist discourse, "Christian powers" and the United States are interminable foes. Perhaps they are at the fringe of Islamic discourse, but with massacres of schoolchildren in Russia, assassinations in the Netherlands, and the murder of morning commuters in Madrid, it is imperative to study problems rather than wish them away.

Furnish has assembled the definitive work on this important phenom-enon. With rich historical detail, he shows how Mahdis have risen to chal-lenge societies. In 1880 in Sudan a charismatic figure named Muhammad Ahmad declared himself Mahdi. In a brief and bloody uprising, he cap-tured and decapitated the British governor-general, establishing a short-lived state that was independent, even if it lacked divine rule. Other movements are less successful. When a would-be Mahdi named Mehmet challenged Mustafa Kemal Atatürk, the founder of the Turkish Republic, it was Mehmet's head that ended up perched on pole. More recently, Furnish examines the bloody Mahdist movement that shook Saudi Arabia to its core in late 1979. He does not fall into the trap of examining trees while ignorant of the forest. His insights on similar movements in the Judeo-Christian tradition provide helpful perspective.

Furnish is not just a historian, though. A former army linguist, soldier, interrogator, and chaplain, he brings a wealth of experience and perspec-tive that many lifelong academics never achieve. He has not only studied Middle Eastern society but also lived it. Unlike many instant experts, he reads and understands the languages of the Middle East; not just Arabic, but Persian and Turkish as well. His research is based on more than just books in dusty archives. Today radical Islamists do not just publish books or write tracts as they did until just a decade ago. They now publish web-pages and send emails to bulletin boards. Furnish has exposed this world and conducted perhaps the most thorough study of the use of the Internet by "virtual Mahdis" and violent Jihadis.

Like any true historian Furnish analyzes the past to elucidate the pres-ent and speculate about the future. The societal discontent afflicting the Islamic world, the corruption of autocratic societies, and growing radical-ization have led many Muslims to speculate that a new Mahdi might soon emerge. Many members of al-Qaeda speculate that billionaire terrorist Osama bin Laden might be their man. However, a new charismatic figure might emerge and seek to justify his claim with a spectacular attack on the United States, Europe, or Israel. *Holiest Wars: Islamic Mahdis, Their Jihads, and Osama bin Laden* is the right book at the right time.

Michael Rubin
American Enterprise Institute and *Middle East Quarterly*

Acknowledgments

The genesis of this book lies in my doctoral dissertation on Islamic escha-tology and Mahdism at Ohio State. The crux of that study was com-pressed and refashioned into the article "Bin Ladin: The Man Who Would Be Mahdi" (in the spring 2002 issue of *Middle East Quarterly*). That short article, to borrow a line from J.R.R. Tolkien, then "grew in the telling" into this book on Mahdis and their jihads.

For that I have a number of people to thank. Jim Dunton of the Center for Strategic and International Studies read my article and contacted me about turning it into a book through Praeger. My editor there, Heather Staines, and her editorial assistant Alex Andrusyszyn, have been extremely helpful and patient with my first-time-author questions and blues. Dr. Dona Straley, Mid-dle East librarian, and Mr. Pat Visel, assistant Middle East librarian, have for the past year helped me fill in any research blanks with invaluable resources from the ample collection at the Ohio State University. Dr. Michael Rubin of the American Enterprise Institute was kind enough to read the entire manu-script and offer invaluable constructive criticism. My wife, Davina, let me take the first half of summer 2004 off from teaching in order to write the bulk of the book and she reassured me I would get it done—even when I doubted. And my sons, Tad and Ty, supplied enough hugs to keep me going through the museless periods (of which there were more than a few).

A note on transliteration of Arabic into English: a simplified version of the Online Computer Library Center system is utilized herein. This will undoubtedly displease purists of the scholarly persuasion, but it will make Arabic terms more palatable to nonspecialists, for whom this book is intended. In this vein, Osama bin Laden will be employed, although the correct transliteration is Usama bin Ladin.

CHAPTER 1

What Is Mahdism and Where Does It Come From?

INTRODUCTION

One man's messiah is another man's heretic, as well as a potential usurper of the ruling regime, should such a figure emerge within a society where political grievances can don religious garb. Such messianic revolutions—many abject failures, but some wildly successful—have occurred numerous times in the Islamic world over the 14 centuries since it came into existence. These seldom-studied movements are the topic of this book. And Islamic messianic insurrections are qualitatively different from mere fundamentalist ones such as bedevil the world today, despite their surface similarities. In fact, Muslim messianic movements are to fundamentalist uprisings what nuclear weapons are to conventional ones: triggered by the same detonating agents, but far more powerful in scope and effect.

Currently there is no self-proclaimed Mahdi in the mainstream Islamic world—not yet—but the importance of the belief among Muslims is evidenced, for example, by the name applied to the armed faction that until recently followed Muqtada al-Sadr in Iraq: *jaysh al-mahdi*, "the army of the Mahdi." Before his putative acquiescence to the new political order in Iraq al-Sadr proclaimed that his armed struggle against American forces was on behalf and in anticipation of the Mahdi's arrival. Even more ominously for America and the West, are the indications that at least some Muslims are willing to consider the possibility that Osama bin Laden might be the Mahdi. Al-Sadr's declared and Bin Laden's as-of-yet undeclared Mahdist missions would strike no chords among Muslims unless they had a long history of legitimate Mahdist belief underlying them.

Islam is the world's second-largest religion in numbers of adherents: its 1.3 billion trails only Christianity with 2 billion.[1] It is also the newest of the world's major religions, founded some six centuries after Jesus. The Muslim prophet Muhammad died, according to tradition, in 632 CE. (The Islamic calendar, however, starts not with Muhammad's birth or death but with the early Muslim community's flight to Medina to escape Meccan persecution in 622 CE: this flight is the *hijrah*, and dates after it are designated AH.)[2] Islam, which means "submission" to *Allah*—"the god" in Arabic—as the only true deity, claimed not to be a new religion but, instead, God's final corrective revelation to humanity after errors had crept into the originally pristine monotheisms of the Jews and the Christians. Muslims place Muhammad in the chain of prophets that includes the likes of Noah, Moses, and David, as well as `Isa, "Jesus." Allah's revelations to humanity were given through Muhammad and written down after his death as the Qur'an.[3] Not surprisingly, Islam shares a great deal of material and beliefs with both Judaism and Christianity, including that of a "messiah."

The central messianic figure in Islam is al-Mahdi, "the rightly guided one," who will come near the end of historical time in order to usher in a worldwide Islamic state with the help of the returned prophet Jesus. The Mahdi is not referred to anywhere in the Qur'an, but he is mentioned in a number of hadiths, or "traditions," which are sayings attributed to the prophet Muhammad. In terms of designation Jesus actually holds the more ostensibly messianic title in Islam in that he is referred to as al-Masih in the Qur'an,[4] likely a cognate to the original ancient Hebrew term mashiakh, or "anointed one"[5]: a political-military leader who would restore the kingdom of Israel.[6] As such, the term mashiakh applied to rulers in ancient Hebrew society, such as King David, and to the expected political and military deliverer of the Jewish people after the destruction of the kingdoms of Israel and Judah in 722 and 586 BCE by the Assyrians and neo-Babylonians, respectively. The early Christian church changed the understanding of messiah from a political restorer to the suffering and resurrected Jesus, attaching to him the surname "Christ"—Greek for "the anointed one." When the Qur'an was redacted and written down, traditionally said to have been in the seventh century CE, a number of passages describing Jesus as al-Masih were included, perhaps emulating the Christian title applied to Jesus.[7] This usage seems to be little more than respectful labeling, however, or perhaps pious imitation, largely devoid of the Christian sense of the word "messiah." For all intents and purposes the Mahdi is the more relevant messianic figure in Islamic thought and history. Perhaps most important, his is the role more easily appropriated by a self-appointed Islamic revolutionary exhibiting what Westerners would call a messiah complex. For example, it is relatively easy to claim to be fulfilling that aspect of Mahdist tradition that declares the Mahdi will be an Arab, but it is rather more problematic to descend from on high onto the minaret of a mosque in Damascus, which is how the relevant traditions have Jesus making his divine comeback. Mahdism, then, is actually the more correct term in an Islamic context for what we in the West often refer to as a Muslim messianic movement.[8]

This audacious adoption of the mantle of the Mahdi has been attempted numerous times in Islamic history. This book deals with eight of the most prominent such movements within the Sunni Muslim world: those of Ibn Tumart (d. 1130), Ibn Abi Mahallah (d. 1613), and Muhammad Amzian (d. 1879) in North Africa; Muhammad Jawnpuri (d. 1505) and Ahmad Barelwi (d. 1831) in India; Muhmmad Ahmad (d. 1885) in Sudan;

Mehmet (d. 1930) in Turkey; and most recently, Muhammad al-Qahtani (d. 1979), proclaimed the Mahdi by his better-known brother-in-law, Juhayman al-Utaybi (d. 1980), in Saudi Arabia.

Why these eight? I chose them based on three criteria: each was overtly Mahdist, did not transform into a new religious movement, and was not Shi`i. Regarding explicit claims to the *Mahdiyah*, "status of the Mahdi," both Muslim and Western writers and historians have often erroneously called certain charismatic religious rebels Mahdis when in fact they had never claimed the title. Examples of this mislabeling include Usman don Fodio (d. 1817), founder of the Sokoto Caliphate in what is now Nigeria; Sayyid Muhammad al-Mahdi[9] al-Sanusi (d. 1902), chief of the Sanusiyah Sufi (Muslim mystical) order that fought the Italians in present-day Libya; Ali Shamil (d. 1871), leader of the Muslim fight against the Russians' bloody annexation of Chechnya and environs; and Muhammad b. Abd Allah Hassan (d. 1920) the so-called Mad Mullah who rallied the Somalis to fight British imperialism.[10] None of these men ever claimed to be the Mahdi. All indeed declared *jihad*, or "holy war," against their enemies, and all were Muslim mystics (Sufis) of one kind or another. Although declaration of jihad and involvement in some aspect of mystical Islam may both be necessary, they are insufficient to constitute Mahdism on their own. Doing some of the things the Mahdi will do is not the same as actually appropriating the title and attempting to fit the role. Only one of these prototypical jihads came anywhere near such a level of hubris, and that was Usman don Fodio's. He seems to have considered himself the *mujaddid*, or "renewer" believed by many Muslims to come every century to reinvigorate the Islamic world.[11] However, the mujaddid is at best, to use a sports analogy, Triple A baseball, whereas the Mahdi is definitely major league. Sometimes someone makes the leap from mere mujaddid to Mahdi, however. Of the eight Sunni Mahdist claimants and their movements examined herein, four did so: Sayyid Muhammad Jawnpuri of India and, on the other end of Eurasia in Morocco, Ibn Abu Mahallah, both of whom took full advantage of the turnover of the tenth century, and thus the first millennium, of Islam in 1591 CE; Muhammad Ahmad in Sudan, who leveraged his Mahdist claims by pointing out that the Islamic year 1300 AH (1882 CE) was nigh; and Juhayman al-Utaybi and Muhammad al-Qahtani, who likewise exploited the advent of 1400 AH (1979 CE) to kick off their ill-fated Mahdist coup attempt in Saudi Arabia. But since the massive self-confidence (or self-deception) required of a mahdi is much higher than that of a relatively humble mujaddid, Mahdism is relatively rarer.

There have been instances in Islamic societies where movements that began as ostensibly Mahdist ones transformed into new religious movements, divorcing themselves eventually from their Muslim roots and thereby vitiating their claim to be Mahdist within the Muslim fold. Three prominent examples here are the Ahmadis (or Qadiyanis), the Deendar

Anjuman, and the Baha'is. The Ahmadis were founded by Ghulam Ahmad (d. 1908) in the Qadiyan region of India. Originally a Muslim, he eventually declared himself a combination of the Mahdi, Jesus, and an avatar (manifestation) of the Hindu god Krishna.[12] His followers, who claim to number about 10 million worldwide, are not considered Muslims by anyone but themselves. The Deendar Anjuman was started by Siddiq Hussain (d. 1952), who strongly implied he was the Mahdi and devoted himself to syncretistic missionary work in an attempt to convert the Hindus of India to Islam. This group still exists, its numbers uncertain, but its membership still active in the subcontinent.[13] Perhaps the most well known Mahdist group that converted into a totally separate religion is that of the Baha'is, cofounded by Ali Muhammad (d. 1850), known as "the Bab" (gateway), and his disciple Baha'ullah (d. 1892) in Iran. The former claimed to be standing in for the Mahdi, whom Shi`is refer to as the Hidden Imam; but after his death Baha'ullah claimed the Bab was indeed himself the Mahdi. Baha'is today number perhaps 6 million worldwide and constitute a new religion,[14] the leadership's protestations of still being the consummation of Islam notwithstanding.

An examination of Baha'ism's Shi`i roots broaches the topic of why this work deals only with Sunni Mahdist movements. Shi`is, or "Shi`ites" as they are often called in the Western press, have their origins in a disagreement within the early Muslim commmunity over who could succeed Muhammad as political and military leader, though not as prophet, for that role ceased with his death in 632 CE. The majority, who came to be known as the Sunnis and today make up about 85 percent of the world's 1.3 billion Muslims, believed this *caliph,* or "successor," should be chosen by consensus. The minority argued that only a descendant of Muhammad through his closest male relative, his cousin and son-in-law Ali, could lead the religion and growing empire of Islam. In Arabic they were called the *shi`at `Ali,* "faction of Ali"—hence collectively Shi`ah,[15] individually Shi`i(s).

Ali became the fourth caliph in 656 CE but was killed in 661. A dynasty from Damascus known as the Umayyads (al-Umawiyah) took over and politically neutralized Ali's two sons Hasan and Husayn by bribing the former and, in 680, killing the latter and his small band of supporters at Karbala. (This is the so-called martyrdom of Husayn, commemmorated, often bloodily, by Shi`is on the 10th of the month of Muharram.) Afterward the defeated Shi`is never acknowledged the Sunni caliphs as legitimate; instead, they postulated that the true leadership of the Islamic community was passed down from Ali to his sons Hasan and Husayn and thereupon to the latter's descendants, each of whom they referred to as the *Imam.*[16] This line of imams continued for years until the Imam went into a state of *ghaybah,* "hiddenness" or "occultation"—that is, until he withdrew from public life into a transcendent state whence this now Hidden

Imam will someday emerge as the Mahdi, the deliverer of the Islamic community in its hour of dire need. The sects of Shi`ism disagree as to just exactly through which descendent of Ali the line of legitimate Imam(s) should be traced. For example, "Seveners" or Isma'ilis terminate the line of imams with Isma'il, the seventh imam (as well as believe that the Aga Khan is his heir); the Zaydis, or "Fivers," do the same with the fifth imam, Zayd; the largest bloc of the world's Shi`ah, the "Twelvers" of today's Iran and Iraq, continue the line through other descendents of Ali to Muhammad al-Mahdi, the twelfth imam.[17] All Shi`ah groups do, however, agree that a Hidden Imam will reveal himself, before the Last Days, as *al-Mahdi al-Muntazar*, the "Awaited Mahdi" who will not only create a worldwide, socioeconomically just Islamic state (a point on which they agree with the Sunnis) but also rebuke the Sunnis for their stubborn refusal to admit their historical mistake of rejecting the Shi`i Imams.[18]

For two major reasons my analysis is limited to Sunni Mahdist movements and largely steers clear of Shi`i ones. First, even among scholars there is a stereotype that Mahdism is chiefly a Shi`i phenomenon, whereas in reality throughout Islamic history most Mahdist movements have sprung from the brows of charismatic Sunni holy men with an axe to grind against a usually Islamic regime. I began correcting this misperception with my doctoral dissertation[19] and in this work again take up the gauntlet. Second, more than a millennium after the twelfth imam went mystically missing, the original political nature of the disagreement between Sunnis and Shi`is has taken on many quite complex religious, philosophical, and indeed metaphysical aspects, so much so that one really needs be a specialist in a specific branch of Shi`ism[20] and in Farsi, the Persian language, in order to do justice to the Hidden Imam-as-Mahdi. As an Arabist and a historian, therefore, I decided to concentrate on what I know best: Arabic sources and history.

Of course, Sunni and Shi`i belief systems regarding the Mahdi show some degree of overlap, the most important aspects of which are covered later in this book. But the focus herein is on Sunni Mahdism—its history, opposition to it, its modern manifestations, especially as articulated in modern Arabic books and websites on the topic, and whether there might be on the horizon anyone with the hubris to attempt to seize the mantle of the Mahdi, be his name Osama bin Laden or otherwise. The aim is to provide something lacking in both scholarship and the popular arena: a historical overview of Sunni Mahdism movements and a look at the continuing relevance of belief in the Mahdi in the Sunni world today. This book may serve as a modest beginning in rectifying the unfortunate deficiency within the field that "no comprehensive study of the whole range of Mahdi themes and historical movements exists."[21]

Scholarship and popular works on the Muslim world and its movements prior to the September 11, 2001, attacks almost totally ignored the

Mahdist aspects of Islam. Even today, while a few scholars deal with the theological roots of Mahdism, their provenance in Hadith, and their working out in the first few centuries of Islamic history,[22] none has undertaken a comprehensive study of Mahdist claimants and movements across space and time, much less made an analysis that includes the modern era. The relatively few "September 10"[23] scholars and analysts who did bother to examine the revolutionary potential of modern Islam mostly focused on Muslim fundamentalism. In the post-9/11 world an increasing number of terrorism experts and writers on religion have begun to hazard an exploration of the eschatological or apocalyptic dimensions of Islam,[24] yet none has heretofore systematically scrutinized the Arabic works by modern Sunni believers in the Mahdi. No one has made the connection between ancient Islamic traditions and modern Sunni beliefs in the coming of the Mahdi and also read modern Sunni Arabic books on the topic. In sum, experts on Mahdism and Islamic eschatology study the early period of Islam[25] almost exclusively, whereas modern analysts and experts largely dismiss Mahdism as an Islamic anachronism or as purely a Shi`i phenomenon.

This work should prove a first step in remedying this situation. The present analysis combines a historical study of the major Mahdist movements with an examination of a significant number of books and websites in the Arab world on the topic of the Mahdi. This study aims to demonstrate that belief in the Mahdi is firmly grounded in Islam and, perhaps more important, continues to serve as a motivation and beacon of hope for many Muslims today.

Such an analysis must begin by defining terms. In particular, the usual suspects of End Time lingo—"eschatology," "apocalyptic," "utopian," "millenarian or millennial," and "chiliastic"—must be rounded up and inspected for suitability. Although many writers on religious topics use these words interchangeably, the terms have distinctly different shades of meaning.

Apocalyptic means "forecasting the ultimate destiny of the world: prophetic; foreboding imminent disaster or final doom; terrible; wildly unrestrained; grandiose; ultimately decisive; climactic,"[26] and its derivative *apocalypticism*, "a doctrine concerning an imminent end of the world and an ensuing general resurrection and final judgment."[27] *Eschatology* is "a branch of theology concerned with the final events in the history of the world or of mankind; a belief concerning death, the end of the world, or the ultimate destiny of mankind."[28] *Utopian* relates to "having impossibly ideal conditions, especially of social organization; proposing or advocating impractically ideal social and political schemes; impossibly ideal; visionary; one that believes in the perfectability of human soceity."[29] Finally, *millennialism* and *millennarianism* both have to do with "belief in the millennium of Christian prophecy; belief in a coming ideal society and especially one created by revolutionary action."[30]

Which of these, if any, is appropriate to use in an Islamic context? David Cook, probably today's foremost expert on Islamic hadiths dealing with the end of time, maintains that one should differentiate the eschatological from the apocalyptic, seeing the former as mainly the province of the Qur'an itself in passages that deal with the end of history and the Last Judgment,[31] and the latter a proper designation for those Muslim hadiths that pertain more to the events leading up to, but not acutally encompassing, The End.[32] This is a trenchant point, but the problem is that *apocalyptic* carries a connotation for most modern Western readers, Christian or not, of, well, apocalyptic images: mushroom clouds and the four supernatural horsemen tend to spring to mind, for example. Anyone who has ever declared himself the Mahdi would not have been thinking in such terms, or even their twelfth-, sixteenth-, or nineteenth-century equivalent; a Mahdi wants, not to usher in the end of the world, but to fix the world's problems on Islamic terms. History will go on for considerable time after the Mahdi takes over; not only will he reign for five, seven, or nine years, the actual End Time could come over a century later.[33] And *eschatological* is a problematic term, too, when applied to Mahdism. Not only does history go on post-Mahdi, but Islamic eschatology encompasses several major figures in addition to the rightly guided one. So *Muslim eschatological movement*, as an alternative term for Mahdism, doesn't really do justice to the concept.

Considering that one of the Mahdi's major tasks will be the reordering of global society along more just socioeconomic lines, *utopian* might be a better adjective for such movements. However, whereas all Mahdist movements are utopian in large measure, not all utopian movements, even in Islam, are Mahdist. Islamic fundamentialist factions, for example, are utopian in their belief that a comprehensive application of Islamic law, or *shari`ah*, and a return to the praxis of the early community of the prophet Muhammad's time, will create an ideal society. But many Islamic fundamentalists believe such an Islamic utopia can be achieved through their own efforts and jihad, without the presence of the Mahdi.[34]

Millennarian and *millennial* are two other terms often used to describe Mahdist movements. Both derive from the Latin term for "1,000" and more specifically from the Christian idea of the 1,000-year reign of the returned Christ on earth.[35] Such is also true for the related term *chiliastic*, in vogue prior to the year 2000 but rarely employed now. It also refers to 1,000 but derives from the Greek. Islam normally attaches little importance to millennial time periods, and so any of these terms is rather inaccurate when applied to Mahdist movements. In fact, since in Islam the tradition about the aforementioned mujaddid or renewer has Muhammad predicting such a one to come every 100 years, *centennialism* might be an apt term for Islamic renewal movements. But only half of the eight self-proclaimed Mahdis whom this book examines came at the beginning of an Islamic century. Mahdist claims cannot by their very nature be limited to such junctures, nor indeed have they been historically. So, besides conjuring up images for historically minded Americans of 1876, the term *centennialism* is frankly inadequate to describe the provenance and power of a Mahdist movement.

In short, although a movement centered around a charismatic Muslim leader who considers himself the fulfillment of religious traditions about the coming of "the rightly guided" one does have characteristics in common with Christian as well as other religions' apocalyptic, eschatological, utopian, and millennial movements,[36] the best term for such an Islamic movement and its attendant belief system is, simply, Mahdism.

THE ZOROASTRIAN, JEWISH, AND CHRISTIAN ROOTS OF MAHDIST TRADITIONS

Why would beliefs about a messiah-like figure develop in Islam and become codified in traditions, when the Qur'an itself says nothing of such a figure? The influence of Judaism and Christianity on the matter of the term *al-Masih* in Islam, already broached, is further elaborated upon here. But first a less well known religious influence upon Islam, at least in matters eschatological, should be mentioned: Zoroastrianism.

The first major empire conquered by the Arab Muslims, in the seventh century CE, was that of Sasanian Persia (centered on modern Iran). The Persians at that time adhered neither to Judaism nor Christianity but to the teachings of *Zartusht*, or "Zoroaster," a Persian prophet who lived probably in the first millennium BCE and created a religion that was, for all practical purposes, dualistic. Zoroastrians believed in two gods: a good one, Ahura-Mazda, and a bad one, Ahriman. Their religion sported a number of characteristics that arguably influenced Judaism and Christianity, as well as Islam: a distinct heaven and hell, angels and demons, and judgment. In particular, Zoroastrian eschatology posits a cyclical cosmic history of 3,000-year dispensations and the appearance of a messianic or saviour figure, a *saoshyant*, at the end of time. What is particularly interesting about Zoroastrianism in this regard is that the messianic figures, Usedar and Pisyotan, come in tandems. One ushers in the other's millennial reign.[37] After Zoroastrian Persia's conquest by the Arab Muslims in 651 CE, this idea of the messianic avenger who would come to rescue his people provided hope for the dwindling numbers of Zoroastrians.[38]

By virtue of its conquest of Sasanian Persia, the developing religion of the Muslims came into contact with two major eschatological ideas that very likely later manifested themselves within Islam: the hidden-yet-returning deliverer, which would predominate in Shi`ism's ideas of the occulted Imams; and the division of labor between the deliverer and his precursor or helper, an eschatological paradigm in both Shi`i and Sunni Islam that is reflected in the respective End Time tasks apportioned to the Mahdi and Jesus. Even taking into account the hazards of the post hoc, ergo propter hoc fallacy, these Islamic parallels with Zoroastrian eschatology are difficult to ignore.

Even so, Zoroastrian antecedents are not sufficient to explain Mahdism. As aforementioned, Judaism and Christianity also influenced Islam. Throughout most of Jewish history any prophet, priest, or ruler could be anointed as a sign of God's favor and thus wear the mantle of *mashiakh*.[39] Eventually, however, the term came to be applied specifically to David, second ruler (after Saul) of the united kingdom of Israel from about 1000 to 961 BCE, and his descendants, including the predicted future Messiah. This Messiah would be an individual historical figure who would restore not only the good fortune but also the political autonomy of the Jewish people.

Over the centuries, as various factions have developed within Judaism, different views of the future Messiah have also evolved, a process similar to that undergone later by Muslims regarding the Mahdi. Orthodox Jews still look to the future for the Messiah; indeed, some within this fold of Judaism think the state of Israel has advanced the time of the messianic advent. In this they ironically share a viewpoint with conservative and fundamentalist Christian denominations that think the reestablishment of the Jewish homeland in 1948 presages the return of Jesus. Others in the Orthodox Jewish community have always considered Zionism and even modern Israel itself illegitimate in that the Messiah was not involved in the movement to reestablish a Jewish homeland. The American Conservative and Reform Jewish movements, in contrast, downplay the actual historical manifestation of the Messiah. They do this either by dispensing with him as a historical figure altogether, substituting instead a "mood of universal ethical regeneration,"[40] or by calling for what is in effect a demessianization of Judaism. In the final analysis, however, the fact remains that historically, and certainly in pre-Islamic times, the Jewish idea of a messiah has been important and a crucial influence on its two monotheistic children, Christianity and Islam.

Christian messianism is, of course, distinct from its forefather Jewish version. The early church transformed the idea from that of a political-military leader who would throw off the occupier's yoke for the Jewish people to that of a crucified and resurrected spiritual savior for all humanity: Jesus Christ.[41] Christians also believe that 40 days postresurrection Jesus ascended to heaven, whence he will return eventually. Christian interpretations of this Second Coming and its ultimate ramifications fall into three broad categories, commonly called amillennial, premillennial, and postmillennial. All three views reference the 1,000-year reign of Christ on earth predicated in Revelation 20. Amillennialists hold that there will not be a literal, historical millennial rule by the returned Jesus. Premillennialists maintain that Christ will return before this utopian millennium begins, and that after it is over will come the other eschatological events described in the last book of the Christian Bible: the release of the 1,000-year-incarcerated Satan; the gathering of the masses of Gog and Magog for their assault on God's people; the final defeat of of Satan, Gog and Magog, the False Prophet and the Beast, and their consignment to the Lake of Fire and, ultimately, the creation of a new heaven and earth.[42] Postmillennialists believe that human societies will grow progressively better and better by following Christianity and that at some point a utopian millennium will commence, at the end of which Christ will return. Different Christian denominations tend to fall into one or another of these categories: Lutherans are officially amillennial, for example; whereas Baptists, especially Southern ones, are predominantly premillennial, as seemingly are the writers of the *Left Behind* bestsellers. And although almost all Christian denominations agree that Jesus will return someday, as avowed in the Apostle's, Nicene, and Athanasian creeds, they do differ on several points: whether Christ's return will accompanied by a "Rapture," or taking up of all Christians bodily to heaven;[43] and perhaps more important, when this return will occur and what will be the world political, social, and economic situation that will precede it. For despite Jesus' own admonitions that not even he knew when that time would come,[44] Christians have throughout history, especially whenever a new millennium dawns, exerted great efforts to predict his Second Coming.

Mahdism shares some characteristics with Jewish and Christian messianism, but there are also significant points of departure. Unlike Jewish and Christian messianic figures, the Islamic one cannot be found in the religion's holy scriptures: the Qur'an says nothing of the Mahdi, whereas the Hebrew Bible[45] and the Christian New Testament[46] both mention their respective Messiahs (the latter, of course, numerous times). The Mahdi, as we shall see, appears in traditions attributed to the prophet Muhammad. Mahdism is more akin to Jewish messianism than it is to the Christian variety in that both the Mahdi and the still-to-come Jewish Messiah are primarily political-military leaders whose tasks will be accomplished within the framework of human history. Jesus, in contrast, is in his returned state the second person of the Godhead and operates largely outside the space-time continuum. Mahdism also shares with Jewish messianism a belief that one of the major emphases of the Mahdi or Messiah will be collective socioeconomic justice, rather than salvation of individual souls as in the Christian formulation. It is true that Islam is the only world religion besides Christianity that officially and canonically includes Jesus—though as a great prophet, not as the Son of God,—and fully expects his return, albeit as a Muslim. Nonetheless, the actual messianic figure in Islam, the Mahdi, has more in common with Jewish ideas of the Messiah than with Christian ones. And just as a significant number of Christians comb the Bible and the front pages of the newspapers attempting to ascertain if Jesus' return is nigh, a growing number of Muslims, including Sunnis, have begun a similar effort vis-à-vis the Mahdi by trying to read the Qur'an and the relevant traditions in light of early-twenty-first-century events.

THE ISLAMIC TRADITIONS ABOUT THE MAHDI

Background on Traditions in Islam

For Muslims two authoritative poles of religious reference exist: the Qur'an, of course, and the Sunnah plus the *Hadith* (Arabic plural *Ahadith*). The Sunnah is the customary practice of the Islamic community as derived from the actions and words of the prophet Muhammad (d. 632 CE/10 AH). Hadiths are narrative accounts of the these same actions and pronouncements, rather like "hearsay" records of what Muhammad did and said.[47] Hadiths are not the word of God in the sense that the Qur'an is, but they are of only slightly lesser importance. They were almost certainly orally transmitted for some time before being redacted in the first few centuries of Islamic history. A specialized field of hadith criticism and analysis developed as a means of sorting the wheat of legitimate traditions—that is, ones that ostensibly truly went back to Muhammad—from the chaff of forgeries.

Two aspects of individual hadiths became the focus of scholarly criticism within the early Islamic world: the *matn* (plural *mutun* or *mitan*), or "text," and the *isnad* (plural *sanad*), or "chain of transmission." A matn might well be rejected on the grounds that it seemed to contradict the Qur'an. But the focus of hadith criticism was channeled into investigating the isnads rather than the matns. The number, credibility, and seamlessness of the transmitters became more important than what the tradition actually said. And so as long as a hadith text did not actually contradict the Qur'an, it had a shot at being accepted by at least some segment of the early Islamic community, especially if what it said proved useful in some manner, usually political. Hadiths were ranked into three categories based on the trustworthiness of their chains of transmission going back to the Prophet: *sahih*, "sound"; *hasan*, "good"; and *da`if*, or "weak." This categorization was largely worked out by Muhammad b. Idris al-Shafi`i (d. 820 CE), who had been disturbed by the proliferation of questionable, even downright false, traditions in his time and developed the gauge of isnad legitimacy as a means of differentiating spurious hadith from acceptable ones. If a consensus of scholars agreed a particular hadith was acceptable, then it was deemed so for the entire Islamic world.[48]

By the end of the ninth century CE two major compilations of Islamic traditions existed. One had been assembled by Isma`il al-Bukhari (d. 870 CE and the other by Muslim b. al-Hajjaj (d. 875), and these two earliest collections are to this day considered the most authoritiative ones. Within a half-century four more Sunni collections of traditions would be put together: those of Ibn Majah (d. 887), Abu Da'ud (d. 888), al-Tirmidhi (d. 892), and al-Nasa'i (d. 915). To this day these six collections are for Sunnis the six canonical anthologies of traditions. Of these six, only Abu Da'ud, Ibn Majah, and al-Tirmidhi contain sections on the Mahdi. Indeed, the lack of Mahdist hadiths in al-Bukhari and Muslim, as well as the Qur'an's silence on the topic, is one of the major objections adduced by Muslim opponents of Mahdism, as we shall see.

The Shi`ah, for their part, have their own collections of hadiths, which they use in addition to the Sunni ones: those of al-Kulayni (d. 940 CE), those of al-Qummi (d. 991), and two of al-Tusi (d. 1067).[49] That separate collection, as well as their different historical experience from Sunnis, gave rise to a discernibly different view of the Mahdi among Shi`is than among the majority Sunnis[50]—an issue largely beyond the scope of this book.

The arena of Hadith became a propaganda battlefield upon which the divisions in the early Islamic movement were fought, often simultaneously with actual armed conflict. The Umayyad dynasty, which took the reins of the Islamic empire after the killing of Caliph Ali in 661 CE, faced opposition from two sides: from the *Khawarij*, or "Kharijis," puritanical Sunnis who would accept as legitimate ruler only a perfect Muslim;[51] and from Shi`i groups. In particular, Shi`i discontent with Umayyad rule was exploited by the Abbasids, who were named after Muhammad's uncle Abbas and not coincidentally trumpeted the need for the caliphate to be returned to the Prophet's family.[52] This movement began in Khurasan (today eastern Iran and western Afghanistan) around 745 and conquered the Umayyads by 750. Two good examples of specific hadiths that might have been fabricated and wielded as propaganda weapons are the claim that the caliphate should be restricted to the prophet Muhammad's family and, even more specifically, the allegation that Muhammad predicted a righteous army coming from the East, bearing black banners. Both alleged traditions were seized upon and made part of the Abbasid movement, the former rhetorically and the latter literally—for when their armies headed West to overthrow the Umayyads, the Abbasid regiments carried black flags.[53]

Were such traditions simply made up? A number of influential Western scholars of Islam have wondered just that. Ignaz Goldziher, in the late nineteenth century, said that both the Umayyads and some of their nascent Shi`ah opponents did not simply exploit extant traditions but went so far as to engage in wholesale fabrication of them, a process known in Arabic as *tadlis* or *wad`*.[54] Whereas Goldziher argued that actual matns, or texts, were falsified in order to support a certain religious or political position, Joseph Schact maintained, in the mid-twentieth century, that it was not so much that the texts themselves were invented as it was their chains of transmission that were spuriously traced back to Muhammad.[55] More recently G.H. Juynboll has attempted to uphold the integrity of these links to prophetic utterances, with limited success.[56] Jacob Lassner, in a rather postmodern vein, argues that in the propaganda aspect of the war between the Umayyads and the Abbasids the truth of the traditions being hurled back and forth was not really the primary issue, even for the second-century AH Islamic community[57]—a tacit admission that some of the hadiths were probably fictitious. John Burton prefers not to think of hadiths as fabricated but to see them as the early Islamic world's first attempts at Qur'anic exegesis.[58] However, he does not disprove the fabrication thesis. Further, there is a problem with his viewpoint regarding the doctrine concerning the Mahdi: it is not Qur'anic at all, but derives entirely from Hadith. It's difficult to see how an idea that is not found in the Muslim scripture can be an example of exegesis thereof. Finally, Daniel Brown has documented the tentative beginnings of a trend in modern Islam that advocates gimlet-eyed criticism of the actual texts of traditions, rather than merely of their legitimizing filaments allegedly going back to the Prophet.[59] His observation that "the tradition literature serves as a sort of vast museum of Muslim ideas to which modern Muslim thinkers could go for evidence to support their argument"[60] could also be extended back a millennium or more and applied to Muslim society at that time. Rather than a museum of ideas, however, the mass of hadiths amounted to more of a shopping center, with a saying of the Prophet available off the shelf as a legitimizing agent for just about any position.

By the late ninth century CE (the late third century AH), a number of traditions about the Mahdi had been validated by their inclusion in the anthologies of three compilers.[61] Abu Da'ud is perhaps the most prestigious of the three. His surname was al-Sijistani, which meant he was probably from that region of eastern Persia (Iran), although he spent much of his life in Basrah (today southern Iraq). Ibn Majah was from Qazvin, in northwestern Persia, but most of his collection came from Egypt and Syria. And al-Tirmidhi, although originally from modern Tajikistan in Central Asia, also gathered traditions from the central Islamic lands, such as Iraq and the Hijaz (the western coastal strip of Arabia that includes the two Muslim holy cities of Mecca and Medina).

Why did these three compilers include Mahdist traditions, but al-Bukhari and Muslim did not? No one really knows. Considering that seven out of the eight historical Sunni Mahdist movements surveyed in this work, as well as the two most successful, erupted on the geographical peripheries of the Islamic world (two in Morocco, two in India, and one each in Algeria, Sudan, and Turkey), it is tempting to theorize that such movements gestate there more easily than in the heartland (Arabia, Syria, Egypt, and Iraq). In this view the origins of Abu Da'ud, Ibn Majah, and al-Tirmidhi on the margins of Islamic civilization may have predisposed them to a greater degree of sympathy toward Mahdism in general and its supporting traditions. However, the greatest hadith-compiler himself, who left any traditions about the Mahdi on the ninth-century version of the editing room floor, was himself from the Central Asian periphery of the Islamic world, as his name al-Bukhari ("of Bukhara," in modern Uzbekistan) attests. It seems likely, then, that other sympathies or factional proclivities—religious, political, or a combination thereof—entered into the calculus of whether to include material on the Mahdi as legitimate traditions. We may never know what these were. What we do know is that three of the six Sunni anthologies of hadith tell of the Mahdi.

The Traditions about the Mahdi

Following are the traditions describing the status, role, and appearance of the Mahdi, sans the often laboriously long chain of hearsay transmission linking the saying to the prophet Muhammad.[62]

ABU DA'UD, KITAB AL-MAHDI [BOOK OF THE MAHDI][63]

The Prophet said: "Even if only one day remains, God will lengthen this day until He calls forth a man from me, or from the family of my house, his name matching mine and his father's name matching that of my father. He will fill the Earth with equity and justice just as it had previously been filled with injustice and oppression. He [God] will not destroy or annihilate the world until the Arabs possess a man from the family of my house, whose name matches my name."

The Prophet said, "The world would not continue, but for that day wherein God will send a man from the family of my house,[64] filling the world with justice as it had been filled with injustice."

The Messenger of God said: "The Mahdi will be from my family, from the descendants of Fatimah."[65]

The Messenger of God said: "The Mahdi, like me, will have a distinct forehead, a hooked nose, and will fill the earth with equity and justice just as it had previously been filled with injustice and tyranny, and he will reign seven years."

The Prophet said: "There will be strife upon the death of a caliph and a man from the people of Medina will emerge and flee to Mecca. Some of the people of Mecca will come and drag him out against his will and swear loyalty to him between the corner and the building near the Ka`bah.[66] An army from Syria will move against him but God will cause it to be swallowed up in the desert between Mecca and Medina. When the people see this, the factions of Syria and the Iraq will come and swear loyalty to him between the corner and the building near the Ka`bah. Then there will appear a man whose maternal uncles are from Kalb.[67] He will send an army which they will defeat; this will be the battle of Kalb. Those who do not receive the spoils of Kalb will be disappointed. He will distribute the wealth and implement the Sunnah of the Prophet[68] among the people and establish Islam upon the Earth. He will remain seven years, then die and the Muslims will pray for him." Abu Da'ud editorializes that other versions of this tradition say "nine years."

The Prophet said (regarding the swallowed-up army): "They will be swallowed up but he will be raised on the Day of Resurrection according to his intentions."

The Prophet said: "A man from Wara' al-Nahr[69] will emerge, calling himself al-Harith b. Harrath. In his vanguard will be a man calling himself Mansur. He will pave the way for the family of Muhammad, just as the Quraysh[70] had done for the Messenger of God. Every believer must support and follow him."

IBN MAJAH, KITAB AL-FITAN [BOOK OF STRIFES], CHAPTER 34, "EMERGENCE OF THE MADHI"[71]

The Prophet said: "I am of the Ahl Bayt[72], for whom God has chosen the Hereafter over the world. Truly the family of my house will suffer affliction and banishment and expulsion afterwards, until a people comes from the East bearing black banners. They will demand the good and not receive it, so they will kill and triumph. Then they will demand what they had been asking for. But they will not receive it, until they hand over power to a man from the family of my house who fill [the world?] with justice, just as it had been filled with injustice. Who among you understands this? You should go to them even if it requires crawling upon ice."[73] This text is glossed by Ibn Da'ud as having a weak isnad.

The Prophet said: "In my community the Mahdi will appear. His time will be limited to seven or nine [years?].[74] My community will prosper under him as it never has before. Food will be abundant, and no one will hoard anything. Wealth will be as abundant as grain. Any man will arise and say 'O Mahdi! Give to me!' And the Mahdi will reply 'Take!'"

The Prophet said: "Three [individuals?] will be killed at a place of your treasure, all of them sons of a caliph. So none of them will wind up with it [the treasure?]. Then the black banners will approach from the East and slaughter all of you violently, as no people has ever been slaughtered. . . . If you see him, swear loyalty to him, even if you must crawl upon ice—because he is the caliph of God, the Mahdi." This hadith is annotated by Abu Da'ud as sound, the highest level of historicity.

The Prophet said: "The Mahdi is from among us, the ahl al-bayt, blessed by God at night."[75]

The Messenger of God said: "The Mahdi is from the descendants of Fatimah."

The Messenger of God said: "We are all descendants of `Abd al-Muttalib,[76] head of the family of Paradise: myself and Hamzah[77] and `Ali and Ja`far[78] and al-Hasan[79] and al-Husayn and the Mahdi."

The Messenger of God said: "A people will come out of the East, and pave the way for the Mahdi."

IBN AL-TIRMIDHI, SECTION DEALING WITH THE MAHDI[80]

The Messenger of God said: "The world will not pass away until the Arabs possess a man from the family of my house whose name matches mine." Al-Tirmidhi glosses this as *hasan sahih*: very good.[81]

The Prophet said: "A man from my family will rule, whose name matches mine. The world would not continue except that God lengthen the day and postpone its dissolution." This one, too, is categorized as *hasan sahih*.

The Prophet said: "In my community the Mahdi will emerge, living five or seven or nine years. Men will come to him and say 'O Mahdi! Give to me!' And He will load such a one's cloak down unto his capacity to carry." This is a good tradition, according to al-Tirmidhi.

These traditions are the corpus of the raw data on the idea of the Mahdi, which has proved such a powerful religious and political force in Islam for over 14 centuries. Combining redundant statements and summarizing, what are the core beliefs about the Mahdi evident in these alleged sayings of the founder of Islam?

The Mahdi will definitely come, and if necessary God will lengthen or extend the span of historical time prior to the Judgment in order for this to take place. He will be from Muhammad's family, perhaps specifically from the offspring of Ali and Fatimah. His name will be the same as Muhammad's, and his father's name will be the same as that of the Prophet's father (Abd Allah). In terms of physical description, the Mahdi will have a distinct forehead (probably meaning a receding hairline) and a prominently curved nose. He will be extrememly generous and altruistic, personally, and will be a powerful enough leader to fill the earth with justice and economic equity, just as it had previously been saturated by oppression and inequity. More specifically, at one point before coming to power he will flee from Medina to Mecca and attempt to shirk his responsibilities.[82] However, he will be compelled by followers who swear loyalty to him in Mecca. Almost immediately an army from Syria will attack the Mahdi and his supporters but will be consumed by the desert at divine command. After triumphing the Mahdi will redistribute wealth and implement the Sunnah. He will reign for five, seven, or nine years.

Note that almost half of the traditions have the Prophet stating that the Mahdi will be from his family. It is difficult not to see pro-Shi`ah tendencies, if not outright propaganda, here. The hadiths that speak of black banners, a people coming from the East or Wara al-Nahr, and the defeat of an army from Syria are likely related to the Umayyad-Abbasid conflict. And the traditions that mention the Mahdi's role as the restorer of socio-economic justice for all are perhaps the most important. The term employed is `adl, "justice." It refers to equal treatment in a political or juridicial sense. Coupled with the predictions that the Mahdi will provide grain—and plenty of it—to anyone who asks, we can see that certain segments of the early Islamic empire were quite concerned with political and economic justice. Foremost among the groups agitating for such fair play were the Kharijis and early Shi`is, both of whom longed for a just imam or caliph to redress the inequalities that were perceived to have proliferated under the Umayyads.[83] Eventually this potentially damning critique of any Muslim ruler—that he was unfair, greedy, and unjust—"was increasingly postponed to the next world"[84] or subsumed in traditions about the Mahdi, who would balance society's scales before (if only just!) the end of time.[85] Consequently Mahdist claimants throughout history have made social, religious, political, or economic attacks on exploitative rulers part of their agenda. And modern works on, and expectations about, the Mahdi accentuate the same theme, as we shall see.

To understand Mahdism's historical irruptions as well as the hopes still swirling round the idea today, however, one must have some understanding of the other eschatological figures in Islam. The Mahdi, according to Islamic beliefs, will operate not in a vacuum but within a matrix that includes a number of other important End Time personages.

THE OTHER MAJOR ESCHATOLOGICAL FIGURES IN ISLAM

Besides the Mahdi, five other essential, penultimately eschatological actors are on the Muslim stage: (1) Jesus; (2) al-Dajjal, "the Deceiver" (the closest Islamic analog to the Christian Antichrist); (3) al-Dabbah, "the Beast"; (4) the collective entity Yajuj wa-Majuj, "Gog and Magog"; and (5) al-Sufyani, who is not generally included by Muslim commentators but is important nontheless. Together with the Mahdi, these beings will play out Allah's plan for the last phase of normal human history prior to the Last Trumpets that will sound to commence the Judgment. In addition to these, a number of events will mark the onset of the beginning of the end of history: the sun rising in the west; a wind that kills all believing Muslims; the erasing of the words from every text of the Qur'an; a great smoke from Yemen or South Arabia engulfing the entire planet; and a number of massive earthquakes, usually given as three in number.[86] Some Islamic commentators consider the Mahdi, Jesus, and the Dajjal the major signs, and all the others lumped together minor ones. But these beings and events are together tantamount to the "wars and rumors of wars," famines, earthquakes, false prophets, and lawlessness that for Christians will presage the eschaton—The End.[87]

Jesus is a crucial end-of-history figure in Islam—arguably of equal importance with the Mahdi—although his return and subsequent activities are found not in the Qur'an[88] but only in certain hadiths.[89] In general, the relevant Islamic traditions hold that the prophet Jesus will return by descending from heaven, likely onto a mosque in Damascus. This is the earthly Jesus returning, however, not the crucified and risen Christ of the Christian churches. In Islamic teachings Allah does not suffer his prophets to die an ignominious death such as crucifixion, and before his death on the cross—or perhaps even before he was actually nailed to it—Jesus was taken up bodily to heaven and someone made to resemble him (most likely Judas Iscariot, his betrayer) died on the cross in his place.[90]

Jesus will be of medium height, "ruddy" in coloration, with hair that flows down his head as if he had just bathed. He will proclaim the rightness of Islam and the wrongheadedness of his putative followers who blasphemously deified him, and then he will go on to smash all the world's crosses, kill all the pigs, and call all *Ahl al-Kitab*, or "People of the Book"—Jews and Christians, fellow monotheists—to join the one true religion, Islam. He and the Mahdi will lead the righteously monotheistic Islamic army that will battle the Dajjal and his forces, and Jesus will personally slay this Antichrist. Afterward Jesus will remain on earth for a considerable time, perhaps as long as 40 years, during which he will possibly marry, have children, and when he dies be buried next to the prophet Muhammad in Medina.

The Dajjal,[91] described not in the Qur'an but only in traditions, will appear before Jesus at about the same time the Mahdi emerges. He will be short and corpulent, with frizzy red hair, and he will be blind in one eye. *K-f-r*, the Arabic consonantal root for *kafir*, "unbeliever," will be written on his forehead. Some traditions say that he will be a Jew. This figure will perform miracles, enticing many to follow him and his false doctrines. He will be active for 40 days or 40 years and, ultimately, will be killed by Jesus.

The Dabbah, curiously enough considering his lesser importance than the Mahdi and the Dajjal, appears in the Qur'an[92] as well as in various hadiths. This "Beast" seems to be a more benign version of the Beast of Revelation.[93] In its Islamic form, this creature will remind humans of the coming Judgment and mock unbelievers, perhaps by placing *k-f-r* on their foreheads in emulation of the Dajjal. This is a far cry from the terrible and miraculous power of the dragonlike beast of Christian eschatology, however.

Yajuj wa-Majuj[94] seems to be the Islamic variant of the Gog and Magog of the Hebrew and Christian Scriptures.[95] In the Qur'an[96] and traditions they are the collective, berserker army that rides roughshod over believers in the Middle East. In Revelation they are "the nations in the four corners of the earth . . . the number of them [is] like the sand of the seashore,"[97] who gather to fight God's people. In the Qur'an and Hadith they are also an ungodly horde, but one penned up by Alexander the Great in the fourth century BCE somewhere in Central Asia in the course of his conquests. At the same time that the other end-of-history figures are active, Yajuj wa-Majuj will break loose and rampage across the Middle East. Jesus will pray to God for deliverance, however, and he will destroy them. Interestingly, the *Shah-namah*, or "Epic of the Kings [of Persia],"[98] recounts the story of Alexander imprisoning this huge ravening pack. Medieval Muslim cartographers sometimes labeled as "Yajuj wa-Majuj" unknown regions of what is now Siberia. This is likely an example of the refitting of this ancient belief to the geopolitical situation of medieval Islamic civilization, wary as it was of steppe nomads such as the Mongols and Turks.[99] A similar refashioning of all the eschatological traditions, especially those of the Mahdi, is underway in the modern Sunni Arab world, as we shall see.

The Sufyani is not usually listed as one of the major signs of the approach of the End Time, but a number of traditions about him abound. He will be a malicious leader who arises before the Mahdi in *al-Sham*, or greater Syria. The Sufyani seems to be the crystallization in Islamic tradition of resentment toward the branch of the Umayyad dynasty descended from Mu`awiyah b. Abi (or Abu) Sufyan.[100] In Sunni eschatological thinking the Sufyani plays the role of the Mahdi's opposite, much as the Dajjal is Jesus' evil "doppelganger."[101]

Summarizing and harmonizing all these major end-of-history figures with the related significant events, the Islamic sketch of the last century or so of human history on earth will look something like the following. Sin, in the form of fornication, drunkenness, great inequalities in wealth, women in positions of authority, everything just short of dogs and cats living openly together, will increase. False dajjals will appear[102] before the real one does. Colossal earthquakes will strike, and great smoke will issue from Yemen. The Sufyani will come to power and either be swallowed up by the deserts of Arabia or defeated by the Mahdi and his army. The Mahdi will confront the Dajjal but be unable to defeat him. But Jesus will return and kill the Dajjal, most likely (and appropriately) in Jerusalem. Thereupon the Mahdi, perhaps assisted by Jesus, will conquer "Constantinople" (Istanbul) and then Rome, defeating the forces of the Christian West and their allies.[103] The Mahdi and Jesus will then usher in a global Islamic state, and the Mahdi will rule a restored caliphate, albeit this time a planetary one. So for a time—some decades, perhaps a little over a century— justice will prevail upon the earth. Eventually the Mahdi and Jesus will both die natural deaths. Unbelief will again predominate such that one day people will awaken to find the sun rising in the west. Finally, Allah will wipe clean every copy of the Qur'an as punishment for ignoring it. A cold wind will sweep over the earth killing all believers (Muslims), after which the angel Israfil will blow his trumpet and all remaining men and

Sikandar Builds a *Barrier Against Yajuj* and *Majuj, from the Shahnama* of *Firdausi,* ca. 1460, ink, opaque watercolor, and gold leaf on paper, 26.7 cm × 17.8 cm (10½ in. × 7 in.) [Museum Purchase 1963/1.66. Courtesy of the University of Michigan Museum of Art.]

women will die. Then another trumpet will sound, resurrecting all who have ever lived for Judgment. This really will be the end of history.[104] But this second phase of Islamic eschatology, with its eternal consequences, is beyond the scope of this book. What the preceding has provided is a general eschatological framework, which is the necessary ground for any further discussion of historical Mahdist movements and any analysis of modern expectations of the Mahdi.

VIEW OF THE MAHDI IDEA THROUGHOUT ISLAMIC HISTORY

Although most Muslims, not just Shi`i but Sunni as well, have believed in the Mahdi as an article of Islamic doctrine, not all have. For a short time in the early Islamic movement, many believed that Jesus had been the one and only Mahdi.[105] But perhaps under the influence of the Zoroastrian dual messianic deliverers and out of a desire to differentiate the new religion of Islam from Christianity, the majority who accepted the problematic traditions about the Mahdi came to see him as a totally separate figure.

Some Muslims have, however, maintained that the Mahdi has three strikes against him: no mention in the Qur'an and an absence from both al-Bukhari and Muslim, the foremost authorities on traditions. Although this is a minority view in premodern and, I would argue, modern Islam, such a dismissal of the Mahdi idea and thus of any such manifestation in history has made its voice heard. In general Sunni Muslim views of the Mahdi can best be grasped by the following conceptual paradigm:

Mahdist Literalists	Mahdist Figurativists
1. Qur'anic literalists: no Mahdi in Qur'an, thus false (literally forbidden *bid`ah*, "innovation")	1. Pro-Mahdist: literally untrue but useful as model or guide for Muslims
2. Hadith literalists: a. Mahdi missing from al-Bukhari, Muslim, thus false b. Mahdi in other collections, thus true. i. Mahdi's coming indeterminable ii. Mahdi's coming determinable	2. Anti-Mahdist: Mahdi superstition at best and opiate of the masses at worst

One final general observation on the Mahdist traditions, before moving on to how they were utilized by Mahdist claimants over the years: the accounts of the future Mahdi—and, indeed, of most of the eschatological actors in Islam—are rather vague and open-ended. This fact has two ramifications: (1) many disparate interpretations of the world geopolitical, socioeconomic, religious, and military situation prior to the beginning of the end of history are possible; and (2) more important, any aspiring Mahdi can attempt to tailor these traditions into a Mahdist cloak for himself or, alternatively, alter his life and career so as to align with the traditions. Many have indeed tried to do.[106] And some would-be Mahdis have succeeded, at least for a season.

NOTES

1. Available at http://www.adherents.com/Religions_By_Adherents.html.

2. However, since the Muslim calendar is a lunar-based one, unlike the Western Christian solar-based system, the lengths of the months vary and so one cannot convert dates by simply subtracting 622 from the CE/AD date; rather, one must utilize a date conversion table or website.

3. "Koran," which is often used in Western articles and books, is an inaccurate transliteration of the Arabic; likewise for "Mohammed," and, for that matter, "Osama bin Laden," which should be rendered "Usamah bin Ladin" but which—as a concession to popular usage—will be retained herein.

4. See the following surahs: al-`Imran[3]:45; al-Nisa' [4]:157, 171; al-Ma'idah [5]:72; as well as G.C. Anawati, "`Isa," *The Encyclopedia of Islam, New Edition* [hereafter *EI2*], and Geoffrey Parrinder, *Jesus in the Qur'an* (London: Faber and Faber, 1965).

5. *A Hebrew and English Lexicon of the Old Testament*, s.v. "mashiakh."

6. One alternative school of thought holds that rather than having its provenance in the Hebrew or Greek terms, "al-Masih" stems from the Arabic verb *sayaha*, "to walk about, to be peripatetic"—certainly a characteristic of Jesus in the Gospels. See Riffat Hassan, "Messianism and Islam," *Journal of Ecumenical Studies*, 22:2 (spring 1985), pp. 261–91, and Sondra Campbell, "Millennial Messiah or Religious Restorer? Reflections on the Early Islamic Understanding of the Term *Mahdi*," *Jusur* 11 (1995), pp. 1–11.

7. On the Muslim debt to Christianity, see Richard Bell, *The Origin of Islam in Its Christian Environment* (London: Frank Cass & Co., 1968).

8. Two basic background sources on Mahdism, overall, are W. Madelung, "Al-Mahdi," *EI2*, and Robert S. Kramer, "Mahdi," *The Oxford Encyclopedia of the Modern Islamic World* [hereafter *OE*]. There is, of course, a much more extensive bibliography on various specific facets of Mahdism, and at relevant junctures I will mention many sources in the course of this book.

9. Over the course of Islamic history "al-Mahdi" or simply "Mahdi" has become a not-uncommon name for male Muslims as well.

10. On these alleged but actually non-Mahdist movements see Mervyn Hiskett, *The Sword of Truth: The Life and Times of Shehu Usuman don Fodio* (New York: Oxford University Press, 1973), and Peter Heine, "I Am Not the Mahdi, but . . . ," in Albert I. Baumgarten, ed., *Apocalyptic Time* (Leiden: Brill, 2002), pp. 70–78; A. Knysh, "Shamil," *EI2*; Jamil M. Abun-Nasr, *A History of the Maghrib in the Islamic Period* (Cambridge: Cambridge University Press, 1987), pp. 316ff; I.M. Lewis, "Muhammad b. `Abd Allah Hassan," *EI2*.

11. E. van Donzel, "Mudjaddid," *EI2*; and Aziz Batran, *Islam and Revolution in Africa* (Brattleboro, VT: Amana Books, 1984).

12. W. Cantwell Smith, "Ahmadiyya," *EI2*.

13. Yoginder Sikand, *Between Dialogue and Conflict: The Origins and Development of the Deendar Anjuman (1924–2000)*, available at http://www.truthindia.com/page58.html.

14. Abbas Amanat, *Resurrection and Renewal: The Making of the Babi Movement in Iran, 1844–1850* (Ithaca, NY: Cornell University Press, 1989); Peter Smith, *A Short History of the Baha'i Faith* (Oxford: OneWorld, 1996); and for a Muslim analysis of both the Ahmadis and Baha'is and their relationship to Mahdism, Mustafa Muhammad al-Hadid al-Tayr, *Al-Qawl al-Haqq fi al-Babiyah wa-al-Baha'iyah wa-al-Qadiyaniyah wa-al-Mahdiyah* (Cairo: Dar al-Misriyah al-Lubnaniyah, 1986).

15. For the linguistically minded careful reader, I should explain that the Arabic letter *ta marbuta* functions as an *h* in certain circumstances but changes to a *t* sound when it is the end of a word in construction with another; hence, "Shi`ah" when alone but "Shi`at `Ali."

16. *Imam* literally means "in front of" and refers generically to the leader of the Friday prayers in the mosque. The Shi`is invested it with a much more grandiose metaphysical and political cachet, however.

17. See W. Madelung, "Shi`a," and "Isma'iliyya," *EI2*; `Allamah Sayyid Muhammad Husayn Tabataba'i, *Shi`ite Islam* (Albany: State University of New York Press, 1975), translated by Sayyed Hossein Nasr, especially chapter 11, "Divisions within Shi`ism" (pp. 75–88); Fuad I. Khuri, *Imams and Emirs: State, Religion and Sects in Islam* (London: Saqi Books, 1990); and for a useful chart of all the Shi`I Imams, see Ira M. Lapidus, *A History of Islamic Societies* (Cambridge: Cambridge University Press, 1988), pp. 116–17.

18. Today the Shi`i, albeit a minority in worldwide Islam, constitute the majority in Iran, Iraq, and probably Lebanon (accurate demographic statistics for the latter are difficult to obtain). Twelvers predominate in Iran, Iraq, and Lebanon; Seveners or Isma'ilis are more scattered geographically, and Fivers or Zaydis are found mainly in Yemen. See Graham E. Fuller and Rend Rahim Francke, *The Arab Shi`a: The Forgotten Muslims* (London: MacMillan Press, 1999).

19. "Eschatology as Politics, Eschatology as Theory: Modern Sunni Arab Mahdism in Historical Perspective," (Ph.D. dissertation, The Ohio State University, 2001).

20. The best example is probably Farhad Daftary's masterful work *The Isma'ilis: Their History and Doctrines* (Cambridge: Cambridge University Press, 1990).

21. Douglas S. Crow, "Messianism: Islamic Messianism," *The Encyclopedia of Religion*, p. 48.

22. Prominent in this regard would be David Cook in works such as "Hadith Authority and the End of the World: Traditions in Modern Muslim Apocalyptic Literature," *Oriente Moderno* 21 (71) (2002), pp. 31–53, and *Studies in Muslim Apocalyptic: Studies in Late Antiquity and Early Islam* (Princeton, NJ: Darwin Press, 2002). Another is Sandra Campbell, "It Must Be the End of Time: Apocalyptic Ahadith as a Record of the Islamic Community's Reaction to the Turbulent First Centuries," *Medieval Encounters: Jewish, Christian and Muslim Culture in Confluence and Dialogue* 4, no. 3 (November 1998), pp. 178–87, as well as Barbara Freyer Stowasser, "The End Is Near: Minor and Major Signs of the Hour in Islamic Texts and Contexts," in Abbas Amanat and John J. Collins, eds., *Apocalypse and Violence* (New Haven, CT: Yale Center for International and Area Studies, 2004), pp. 45–67.

23. Here I am adapting the differentiation made by Fred Barnes, Fox News commentator and *The Weekly Standard* editor, between "September 10" American politicians who still think Islamic terrorism can be treated as a law enforcement issue, as does John Kerry, and "September 11" ones who see it as a war, as does President Bush. The point is not which of these approaches is correct, though I think it is the latter, but the quite different perspectives engendered by the September 11, 2001 attacks.

24. Notable in this regard are Thomas Scheffler, "Apocalypticism, Inner-worldly Eschatology, and Islamic Extremism," in R. Scott Appleby and A. Rashied Omar, eds., *In Multiple Voices: Islamic Peacebuilding after September 11* (Notre Dame: University of Notre Dame Press, 2004); Olivier Roy, "Bin Laden: An Apocalyptic Sect Severed from Political Islam," *East European Constitutional Review* 10, no. 4 (fall 2001), pp. 108–14; Daniel Benjamin and Steven Simon, *The Age of Sacred Terror: Radical Islam's War against America* (New York: Random House, 2003), especially pp. 91ff; Rohan Gunaratna, *Inside Al Qaeda: Global Network of Terror* (New York: Berkley, 2002), especially pp. 123ff; and Richard Landes, *Apocalyptic Islam and Bin Laden*, available at www.mille.org/people/ripages/Bin_Laden.html.

25. For example, in the *Encyclopedia of Islam* entry "al-Mahdi," Madelung stops with the eleventh century CE.

26. *Merriam-Webster's Collegiate Dictionary*, tenth ed. (1993), s.v. "apocalyptic."

27. Ibid., s.v. "apocalypticism."

28. Ibid., s.v. "eschatology."

29. Ibid., s.v. "utopian."

30. Ibid., s.v. "millenarianism." More scholarly sources than the dictionary actually change these definitions very little. For example, in Abbas Amanat and Magnus Bernhardsson, eds., *Imaging the End: Visions of Apocalypse from the Ancient Middle East to Modern America* (London: I.B. Tauris Publishers, 2002), Said Amir Arjomand defines terms in his essay "Messianism, Millennialism and Revolution in Early Islamic History" (pp. 106–24). He sees apocalpyticism as "denot[ing] the imminent expectation of the total transformation of the world," millennialism as "the expectation of a radical break with the present at the end of a 1,000-year age and . . . of the calculation of the time of the end." (p. 106). Robert R. Wilson, in the same work, prefers to use "apocalyptic" as an adjective, not a noun; see his "The Biblical Roots of Apocalyptic" (pp. 56–66).

31. Surahs: al-`Imran [3]:30, 55ff, 106ff, 161, 185; al-Nisa' [4]:87, 109, 159; al-Ma'idah [5]:36–37; al-An'am [6]:36, 74; al-A'raf [7]:32, 167; Ibrahim [14]:44ff; al-Nahl [16]:25ff; Bani Isra'il [17]:13ff; al-Kahf [18]:48ff, 106ff; Maryam [19]:85ff; Ta Ha [20]:100ff; an-Anbiya [21]:47, 103ff; al-Hajj [22]:1ff, 9ff; al-Furqan [25]:22ff; al-Qasas [28]:41–42, 61ff; al-`Ankabut [29]:25; al-Rum [30]:56–57; al-Saffat [37]:20ff; al-Zumar [39]:24ff, 47ff; al-Mu'min [40]:15ff; al-Jathiyah [45]:26ff; al-Mumthanah [60]:3; al-Qiyamah [75]:6ff; al-Naba' [78]:17ff; al-Takwir [81]:1ff; al-Infitar [82]:1ff; al-Inshiqaq [84]:1ff; al-Zalzalah [99]:1ff; al-Qari'ah [101]:1ff.

32. *Studies in Muslim Apocalyptic*, especially pp. 1ff and 301ff; also Cook, "The Apocalyptic Year 200/815–16 and the Events Surrounding It," in Albert I. Baumgarten, ed., *Apocalyptic Time* (Leiden: Brill, 2000), pp. 41–67.

33. See Marshall G.S. Hodgson, "A Note on the Millennium in Islam," in Sylvia L. Thrupp, ed., *Millennial Dreams in Action: Studies in Revolutionary Religious Movements* (New York: Schocken Books, 1970), p. 212.

34. The literature on Islamic fundamentalism is copious, but for a brief overview see my entry "Islamic Fundamentalism" in *The Encyclopedia of Fundamentalism* (2001), pp. 235–40.

35. Revelation 20.

36. See Hillel Schwartz, "Millenarianism," *The Encyclopedia of Religion*, Mircea Eliade, ed.-in-chief, vol. 9; George Shepperson, "The Comparative Study of Millenarian Movements," in Thrupp, *Millennial Dreams in Action*, pp. 45–52; Kenelm Burridge, *New Heaven, New Earth: A Study of Millenarian Activities* (Oxford: Basil Blackwell, 1969); Dale C. Allison, *Jesus of Nazareth: Millenarian Prophet* (Minneapolis: Fortress Press, 1998).

37. See Mary Boyce, *Zoroastrians: Their Relgious Beliefs and Practices* (London: Routledge, 1979); Mahnaz Moazami, "Millennialism, Eschatology, and Messianic Figures in Iranian Tradition," *Journal of Millennial Studies* 2 (winter 2000), pp. 1–16; Shaul Shaked, *From Zoroastrian Iran to Islam: Studies in Religious History and Inter-cultural Contacts* (London: Variorum, 1995), especially "Some Iranian Themes in Islamic Literature," pp. 143–58; and Monochehr Dorraj, *From Zarathustra to Khomeini: Populism and Dissent in Iran* (Boulder, CO: Lynne Rienner Publishers, 1990).

38. David Cook, "Zoroastrianism," *Encyclopedia of Millennialism and Millennial Movements*, pp. 460–63.

39. Some background sources are R.J. Zwi Werblowsky, "Messianism," in Arthur A. Cohen and Paul Mendes-Flohr, eds. *Contemporary Jewish Religious Thought: Original Essays on Critical Concepts, Movements and Beliefs* [hereafter *CJRT*] (New York: Charles Scribners' Sons, 1987), pp. 597–602; Arthur A. Cohen, "Eschatology," *CJRT*, pp. 183–88; *The Oxford Dictionary of the Jewish Religion*, s.v. "Messiah"; and Marc Saperstein, ed., *Essential Papers on Messianic Movements and Personalities in Jewish History* (New York and London: New York University Press, 1992).

40. Arthur A. Cohen, "Eschatology," *CJRT*, p. 184.

41. On this transformation of Jewish messianic expectations, see Allison, *Jesus of Nazareth: Millenarian Prophet*, especially "Detached Note: Some Common Features of Millenarianism," pp. 78–94.

42. See Revelation in general, but particularly 19:11–22:21.

43. I Thessalonians 4:16–5:3.

44. Matthew 24:36ff; Mark 13:32ff.

45. Specifically, Daniel 9:25–26, but also Isaiah 9:2–7 and Jeremiah 23:3–8.

46. For just the Gospel references, see Matthew 1:16, 16:13ff; Mark 8:27ff; Luke 9:18ff; John 1:41, 4:25, 26.

47. General works on hadiths are H.A.R. Gibb, *Mohammedanism: An Historical Survey* (London: Oxford University Press, 1970 [1949]), especially chapter 5, "The Tradition of the Prophet," pp. 49–59; R. Marston Speight, "The Function of Hadith as Commentary on the Qur'an, as Seen in the Six Authoritative Collections," in Andrew Rippin, ed. *Approaches to the History and Interpretation of the Qur'an* (Oxford: Oxford University Press, 1988), pp. 63–81; R. Marston Speight, "Hadith," *OE*; and J. Robson, "Hadith," *EI2*.

48. See Ira Lapidus, *A History of Islamic Societies* (Cambridge: Cambridge University Press, 1988), p. 104; and Marshall G.S. Hodgson, *The Venture of Islam: Conscience and History in a World Civilization* (Chicago: University of Chicago Press, 1974), pp. 327–29.

49. On the Shi`i hadith collections and their formation, see Heinz Halm, *Shi`a Islam: From Religion to Revolution* (Princeton, NJ: Markus Wiener Publishers, 1997),

translated by Allison Brown, particularly pp. 97–100; William C. Chittick, `Allamah Sayyid Muhammad Husayn Tabataba'i, and Seyyed Hossein Nasr, eds., *A Shi`ite Anthology* (Albany: State University of New York Press, 1981), pp. 5–13.

50. Cook, *Studies in Muslim Apocalyptic*, pp. 188–228 in particular, analyzes these two views of the Mahdi.

51. These Kharijis, "those who departed," abandoned Caliph Ali in 657 CE because he was negotiating with the rebellious governor of Syria, Mu`wiyah (who eventually established the Umayyad dynasty). It was a Khariji who killed Ali in 661. The Kharijis would flee Umayyad territories for the margins of the Islamic world, particulary North Africa west of Egypt, where several Khariji states would be established. See Abun-Nasr, *A History of the Maghrib in the Islamic Period*, pp. 37 ff; and G. Levi della Vida, "Kharidjites," *EI2*.

52. On this exploitation of Shi`a hopes, see Jacob Lassner, *The Shaping of `Abbasid Rule* (Princeton, NJ: Princeton University Press, 1980), especially pp. 1–16, and his *Islamic Revolution and Historical Memory: An Inquiry into the Art of `Abbasid Apologetics* (New Haven, CT: American Oriental Society, 1986).

53. On the Abbasid revolution, see Moshe Sharon, *Black Banners from the East: The Establishment of the `Abbasid State—Incubation of a Revolt* (Jerusalem: Magnes Press, 1983); Elton Daniel, "Arabs, Persians and the Advent of the `Abbasids Reconsidered," *Journal of the American Oriental Society* 117, no. 3 (July–Sep. 1997), pp. 542–48.

54. In *Muhammadenische Studien* (1890), published in English as *Muslim Studies*, translated by C.R. Barber and S.M. Stern (London: George Allen & Unwin, 1971).

55. See his *The Origins of Muhammadan Jurisprudence* (Oxford: Clarendon Press, 1950).

56. In *Muslim Tradition: Studies in Chronology, Provenance and Authorship of Early Hadith* (Cambridge: Cambridge University Press, 1983) and, more recently, *Studies on the Origins and Uses of Islamic Hadith* (Brookfield, VT: Variorum, 1996), particularly "Early Islamic Society as Reflected in Its Use of *Isnads*," pp. 151–94.

57. *Islamic Revolution and Historical Memory: An Inquiry into the Art of `Abbasid Apologetics*.

58. This is the gist of his *An Introduction to Hadith* (Edinburgh: Edinburgh University Press, 1994).

59. *Rethinking Tradition in Modern Islamic Thought* (Cambridge: Cambridge University Press, 1996).

60. Ibid., pp. 106–7.

61. For basic information on these three, see the respective *EI2* entries J. Robson, "Abu Da'ud al-Sidjistani"; J.W. Fück, "Ibn Madja"; and the one from the *Shorter Encyclopedia of Islam* [hereafter *SEI*], "al-Tirmidhi."

62. For those who wonder, such a chain goes like this: "`Uthman v. Abi Shaybah reported to us that Mu`awiyah b. Hisham reported that `Ali b. Salih reported from Yazid b. Abi Ziyad, from Ibrahim, from `Alqamah, from `Abd Allah, who said the Prophet said. . . ." One can see why I have chosen just to provide the actual alleged text, rather than the chain.

63. Dar al-Ihya' al-Sunnah al-Nabawiyah, vol. 4 (no date, no location), pp. 106–9.

64. Or "if only one day of this age remained, God would raise up a man from my family."

65. Fatimah was the daughter of Muhammad who married `Ali.

66. In Arabic, between *al-rukn wa-al-maqam*. *Rukn* refers to the corner of the Ka`bah, the shrine in Mecca housing the Black Stone and the center of circumambulation during the Hajj, or pilgrimage; *maqam* is the nearby spot which is said to have still on it the footprints of Abraham, now housed in a small building.

67. Kalb was the Arab tribe of the mother of Yazid (d. 683), the second Umayyad caliph after his father Mu`awiyah. They were from southern Arabia and major rivals of Qays, the tribe leading the northern Arab tribes in the Islamic empire. This hadith would seem to reflect these tribal rivalries. See Patricia Crone, "Were the Qays and Yemen of the Umayyad Period Political Parties?" *Der Islam* 71, no. 1 (1994), pp. 1–57.

68. Muhammad appears to be speaking of himself in the third person here, not exactly a ringing endorsement of the legitimacy of this hadith.

69. The ancient Arab geographical term for the area on the eastern fringe of their empire between the Amu Darya and Syr Darya rivers, in modern Uzbekistan and southwestern Kazakhstan. This is according to *Transoxiana*, http://www.fact-index.com/t/tr/transoxania.html.

70. The tribe of Muhammad.

71. Dar Ihya' al-Turath al-`Arabi, vol. 2 (no location, 1395/1975), pp. 1326–28.

72. This Arabic phrase is usually rendered "the Prophet's family," but that seems problematic here, for why would Muhammad say, "I am of the Prophet's family"?

73. The Arabic term *thalj* can also refer to snow.

74. Eschatological hadiths are not consistent in always providing the actual units of time to accompany the numerical lengths. "Years" is probably meant here and has been understood as the intention by most Muslim interpreters over the years.

75. This may be a reference to the *laylat al-qadr*, "night of power" described in the Qur'an (Surah al-Qadr [97]), which briefly speaks of the night Muhammad first received his revelation.

76. Muhammad's grandfather.

77. Uncle of Muhammad, killed in the battle of Uhud against the Meccans in 625 CE.

78. Probably a reference to Ja`far al-Sadiq (d. 765), the fifth imam for the Isma`ili Shi`ah, the sixth for the Twelvers of Iran.

79. Hasan and Husayn were Ali's sons.

80. Matba'at al-Madinah al-Munawwarah, vol. 3 (Cairo, 1964), pp. 342–44.

81. As noted previously, traditions were ranked as *sahih, hasan or da`if*—"sound," "good," or "weak." Al-Tirmidhi seems to have his own special way of combining these terms when ranking the hadiths he accepted. But, as J. Robson points out in "Hadith," *EI2*, "he has unfortunately not explained what he means by all the terms he uses."

82. The rendering of Aragorn in the recent wildly successful *Lord of the Rings* movies comes to mind here, especially as regards his reluctance to seek or take the reins of power. Tolkien enthusiasts are well aware, however, that Viggo Mortensen's character was quite different in the original book version of the trilogy, however: there Aragorn was much less reluctant to claim the throne of Gondor.

83. See Louise Marlow, *Hierarchy and Egalitarianism in Early Islamic Thought* (Cambridge: Cambridge University Press, 1997), especially pp. 13–41, 93–116 and

174–77. See also Majid Khadduri, *The Islamic Conception of Justice* (Baltimore: Johns Hoplins University Press, 1984), pp. 1–12, 20–21 and 174–91.

84. Marlow, p. 174.

85. For this element of Hadith, see Mahmoud Ayyoub, "The Islamic Concept of Justice," in Nimat Hafez Barazangi, M. Raquibuz Zaman, and Omar Atal, eds., *Islamic Identity and the Struggle for Justice* (Gainesville: University Press of Florida, 1996), pp. 19–26.

86. On Muslim eschatology posthistory see Yvonne Haddad and Jane Smith, *The Islamic Understanding of Death and Resurrection* (Albany: State University of New York Press, 1981); for a general overview of these figures, consult Ibn Kathir, *The Signs before the Day of Judgement*, translated by Huda Khattab (London: Dar al-Taqwa, 1991), and A. Hijazi, *But, Some of Its Signs Have Already Come! Major Signs of the Last Hour* (Arlington, TX: Al-Fustaat [*sic*] Magazine, 1995).

87. Jesus speaks of these in Matthew 24 and Mark 13.

88. Jesus, in one capacity or another, is mentioned in the following Qur'anic surahs: Maryam [19], al-Zukhruf [43], al-Shura [42], al-An`am [6], al-Baqarah [2], al-`Imran [3], al-Saff [61], al-Hadid [57], al-Nisa' [4], al-Ahzab [33], and, most extensively, al-Ma'idah [5].

89. For a summary of these see Ibn Kathir, *The Signs before the Day of Judgement*, and Emmanuel Sudhir Isaiah, "Muslim Eschatology and Its Missiological Implications: A Thematic Study" (Ph.D. dissertation, Fuller Theological Seminary, 1988).

90. See Surah al-Nisa' [4]:157–58 and its explication by Anglican Bishop Kenneth Cragg in the "Introduction" to Muhammad Kamel Hussein, *City of Wrong: A Friday in Jerusalem*, translated by Kenneth Cragg (Oxford: OneWorld, 1994), pp. 11–25. For a fascinating look at this topic in light of the recent film *The Passion of the Christ*, see Aluma Dankowitz, "Reactions in the Arab Media to 'The Passion of the Christ,'" April 20, 2004, available at http://www.memri.org/bin/latestnews.cgi?ID–IA17104.

91. A basic history of this figure is given by A. Abel, "Dadjdjal," *EI2*.

92. Surah al-Naml [27]:82.

93. Revelation 13:11ff.

94. A.J. Wensinck, "Yadjudj wa-Madjudj," *EI2*.

95. Ezekiel 38 and 39; Revelation 20:7–9.

96. Surah al-Kahf [18]:95ff, al-Anbiya' [21]:96.

97. Revelation 20:8ff.

98. Firdowsi, *Shah-Namah*, translated by Reuben Levy (Chicago: University of Chicago Press, 1967), pp. 246–48.

99. See Hodgson, *The Venture of Islam*, pp. 39–42, 157–59.

100. Cook, *Studies in Muslim Apocalyptic*, pp. 122ff. An alternative view—that the Sufyani actually predates the Umayyads—is that of Wilferd Madelung, "The Sufyani between Tradition and History," in *Religious and Ethnic Movements in Medieval Islam* (Hampshire, UK: Variorum 1992), pp. 5–48.

101. Cook, *Studies in Muslim Apocalyptic*, pp. 80–134. He uses "doppelganger" on pages 101 and 122. He also points out, on page 134, that for the Shi`ah the Sufyani is actually the more powerful evil figure than the Dajjal, which is understandable considering Shi`ah history.

102. This is an interesting Islamic parallel to what Jesus says in Matthew 24:24: "For false Christs and false prophets will arise and will show great signs and wonders so

as to mislead, if possible, even the elect" (New American Standard Bible [NASB]). This is also in Mark 13:22.

103. This has to be seen as a hope, which became a prediction, in the early Islamic community about the taking of the Byzantine Empire's capital, which was finally accomplished by the Ottoman Turks in 1453 under Mehmet II. For this to make sense in the modern world, the Muslim eschatologist must posit, as many Muslim fundamentalists like Osama bin Laden do, that the current government of Turkey is un-Islamic and deserves defeat, and that its major city Istanbul should be called by its former Christian name. See J. Mortdmann, "Al-Kunstantiniyya," *EI2*, on Muslim Arab attempts to conquer the city in pre-Ottoman times.

104. See Ibn Kathir, *The Signs before the Day of Judgment*, pp. 79–96; Emmanuel Sudhir Isaiah, passim; Rudolph Peters, "Resurrection, Revelation and Reason: Husayn al-Jisr (d. 1908) and Islamic Eschatology," in J.M. Brenner, Th.P.J. van den Hout, and R. Peters, eds. *Hidden Futures: Death and Immortality in Ancient Egypt, Anatolia, the Classical, Biblical and Arabic-Islamic World* (Amsterdam: Amsterdam University Press, 1994), pp. 220–31.

105. Al-Hasan al-Basri (d. 728 CE), a prominent early theologian, believed this. See Madelung, "Al-Mahdi," *EI2*.

106. David Cook maintains that there have been "upwards of 5,000" aspiring mahdis in the last 1,400 years. I am not sure how he arrives at that high a figure. See David Cook, "Alternative Apocalypses," inteview by Rachael Kohn, April 18, 1999, available at www.abc.net.au/rn/relig/spirit/stories/s22196.htm.

CHAPTER 2

Mahdist Movements throughout History

INTRODUCTION

Mahdism has not always been limited to the future. Numerous times over the last 14 centuries of Islamic history self-professed mahdis have tried to fulfill the traditions by fomenting rebellion against allegedly illegitimate governments (usually, but not always, Muslim) in the name of installing more Islamic and egalitarian Mahdist regimes. Most aspiring mahdis soon found that such an impudent claim amounted to signing their own death warrants. However, a number of particularly politically and militarily adroit individuals have, with a little luck, succceded over the years not only in inciting religious revolution but in taking power as Mahdis for at least a time.

Most such Mahdist insurrections have been Sunni. But some have been Shi`i. The three most prominent were the Fatimids, who ruled Egypt and parts of the Levant and Arabia from 969 CE to 1171 CE; the Buwayhids, dominant in Iraq between 945 CE and 1012 CE;[1] and the Safavids, who during their reign in Iran from 1501 to 1723 converted the country from Sunnism to Shi'ism.[2] In fact, arguably the single most successful Mahdi-based movement in history was that of the Fatimids.[3] Despite this book's focus on Sunni Mahdism some background on this Isma'ili Shi`i group is necessary because of its importance as an influence upon later Sunni Mahdist movements in North Africa. The Fatimids began in the Maghrib (northwestern Africa: modern Morocco, Algeria, and Tunisia) in the early tenth century CE and by 969 had conquered Egypt. Whether the movement's leader Ubayd Allah considered himself or his successor al-Qa'im to be the Mahdi is unclear, but at least one of them was billed as such to the populace. At their height the Fatimids ruled from Morocco to Mecca, and they were responsible for building the city of Cairo as their new capital. Fatimid theology was a melange of several elements that included Shi`i Islam, Gnosticism,[4] and Neoplatonism.[5] This theology powered an expansionst ideology that led the Fatimids to try to conquer the entire Muslim world. Inveterate enemies of the other major Islamic state, that of the Abbasids, the Fatimids undermined the Baghdad caliphs by sending out *da`is*, or "religious propagandists." These operatives attempted to convert Muslims in Abbasid territories to Fatimism with the ultimate aim of overthrowing that rival Sunni state and its caliph. Unlike a number of other medieval

Muslim states, the Fatimid state was normally quite tolerant of Christians and Jews and was in many ways a sophisticated society that encouraged the life of the mind, exemplified by the founding of al-Azhar Mosque, now a university that is the oldest and most respected seat of learning in the Sunni Muslim world. Despite its many positive aspects, however, the Fatimid dynasty was eventually overthrown in 1171 CE by the great Sunni Kurdish leader Salah al-Din, better known as Saladin, famous for retaking Jerusalem from the Crusaders in 1187 and for his subsequent bloody friendship with Richard the Lion Heart during the Third Crusade.

Several aspects of the Fatimid legacy would influence later, especially North African, Mahdist movements. First, there is of course the overt claim to having the living, breathing Mahdi in their midst—no longer occulted or deferred—running the government. Second, the Fatimids made respectable the critique of, and attack upon, the Islamic world's center by those on the peripheries, especially Mahdists. Every subsequent Mahdist movement, with one possible exception, would originate on the Muslim geographic and sociopolitical margins in opposition to the regime(s) at the core. Third, in a subset of the center-versus-periphery paradigm, the pattern was set of a conquered people who had converted to Islam (in the Fatimid case, certain Berber groups) chafing under the yoke of the conquerors, usually Arabs or other Berber tribes. Fourth, the Fatimids sprang from a strongly mystical Islamic base, a characteristic that would prove the rule to one degree or another in most of the later Mahdist currents. Fifth, the Fatimid utilization of trained religious propagandists as a fifth column undermining their enemies would be emulated by later, Sunni Mahdist movements. Sixth, and perhaps most important, the Fatimids demonstrated that a Mahdist movement—albeit, from a Sunni perspective, a heretical Shi`i one—could not only critique and contest but also conquer.

IBN TUMART AND THE MUWAHHIDS, TWELFTH-THIRTEENTH CENTURIES CE

The earliest Sunni Mahdist movement and one of the two most successful in history was that founded by Abu Abd Allah Muhammad b. Tumart al-Susi, better known as Ibn Tumart (d. 1130 CE).[6] The movement predicated on belief in him as the Mahdi was called that of the al-Muwahhids,[7] better known to Western history as the Almohads. A muwahhid was a person who signed onto Ibn Tumart's doctrine of the overwhelming importance of tawhid, or "divine unity,"[8] an idea he promulgated to counter the regime then ruling Morocco and Spain, the al-Murabits or, as they came to be known in Europe, the Almoravids.

Ibn Tumart was a fascinating man, as is every individual who claims to be the Mahdi, and in many ways paradigmatic of the many self-appointed Mahdis who followed in his wake. He was probably born in 1081 under

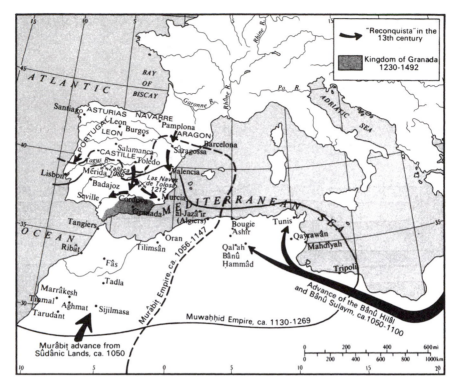

The Murabits and Muwahhids [Marshall G.S. Hodgson, *The Expansion of Islam
in the Middle Periods* vol. 2 of *The Venture of Islam: Conscience and History in a
World Civilization* [(University of Chicago Press, 1974), p. 271. © 1974 by The
University of Chicago. All rights reserved. Reprinted with permission.]

the rule of the Murabits, who had taken over that part of the Islamic
world some three decades earlier. Very little is known of his early life
except that he was a very pious youth and something of a loner. "He took
no part in games . . . [and] lived in a world of his own. He loved to light
the lamps in the mosques and by their pale light he would study deep
into the night."[9] Evidence suggests that when he was in his twenties he
journeyed to the *Mashriq*, the Muslim "East"—Arabia, Egypt, Iraq, and
Syria. Legend has it that Ibn Tumart met the great Islamic scholar and
saint Abu Hamid Muhammad al-Ghazali (d. 1111 CE) in Baghdad, who is
said to have told Ibn Tumart he would be Allah's instrument for destroying the Murabits. Al-Ghazali was an establishment religious scholar who
had gone off on a decade-long quest for a more complete Islamic faith. He
studied philosophy, Islamic metaphysics, and Sufi mysticism and, once he
resumed his regular career, made Sufism palatable to mainstream Islam
through his writings.[10]

Whether the meeting with al-Ghazali actually happened or not, by the time Ibn Tumart made his way back west to his native Morocco some years later, somehow he had become convinced that Allah had ordained him to critique, if not yet to overthrow, the Murabit regime. Ibn Tumart was now at the point, reached eventually by all who manifest Mahdist tendencies, where he "judge[d] Islam, at least the formal side of the faith, to be a failure and for this reason ha[d] harsh words to say about the religious leaders of his time, as well as the political ones."[11] These were the Murabits, who by the mid-eleventh century CE had emerged from their monastic fortresses, called *ribats* (hence Murabits, "those from the ribat") in what is now Mauritania and Western Sahara; in rather short order they conquered most of what is now modern Morocco and much of the Iberian Peninsula. They were primarily of the Lamtuna and Sanhaja tribes of the Berbers, and their ideological founder was Abd Allah b. Yasin (d. 1059), who had formulated a strict, almost fundamentalist view of Islam and Islamic law.

Several aspects of Murabit doctrine and practice upset Ibn Tumart. The most galling was their almost modern fundamentalistic emphasis on a strictly literal reading of the Qur'an regarding the characteristics of Allah.[12] In Ibn Tumart's view, this limited and compromised the divinity and was tantamount to *kufr*, "idolatry." However, Ibn Tumart also despised Murabit practice, not just their theory. Men and women mixing in public; the playing of music; men wearing *litham* or veils, as was the Berber practice of the Murabits—all were objects of Ibn Tumart's ire. And not just rhetorical ire, either: he is said to have taken a stick to those engaged in such practices. He had made himself into an early type of religious policeman, who publicly enforces Islamic morality.[13] Supporters, some with sticks also, soon joined him.

By 1120 or 1121 Ibn Tumart had made his way to Marrakesh, where under the Murabits' reign "he was shocked to see women unveiled, wine shops frequented and pigs roaming in its streets."[14] A short time later at Friday prayer in the central mosque he actually publicly confronted the Murabit ruler, Ali b. Yusuf, and criticized him for allowing such practices. To his credit the amir took the criticism well. Later Ibn Tumart debated, and in so doing rhetorically vanquished, some Murabit religious scholars.[15] At this point these experts in the Murabit establishment realized the potential danger Ibn Tumart represented, but opinion was divided as to how to deal with him. Eventually he was exiled, which took place in two stages, both of which Ibn Tumart turned to his advantage. The first was when he and his followers—foremost of whom was one Abd al-Mu'min (d. 1163), later to become Ibn Tumart's right-hand man and the Muwahhid leader after his death—fled to Ibn Tumart's birthplace, the town of Igilliz, whence they sent out missionaries to win over anyone opposed to the Murabits. The second was when, probably in 1124, he and his supporters trekked to Tinmallal in the Moroccan Atlas Mountains. Ibn Tumart exploited this second phase, in particular, by transforming it into a replication of the hijrah, the flight of Muhammad and the first Muslims from Mecca to Medina in 622 CE in order to escape persecution. Ibn Tumart also used this self-imposed exile to spread his Mahdist word by sending missionaries throughout the Murabit domains, much as the prophet had done from his Medinan base between 622 and 630, when the early Muslims finally returned to Mecca and conquered it. Thus, from a prospective Mahdist point of view, this repeat of the hijrah not only solidified Ibn Tumart's credentials and resonated with the populace but also provided a haven from which to convert and win over the masses.

At some point, perhaps at the beginning of this period of banishment from the centers of Murabit power, Ibn Tumart's followers declared allegiance to him as the Mahdi. Whether he openly claimed this role or manipulated his followers into proclaiming it for him by, for example, reading traditions about the Mahdi and implying he fulfilled them, is unclear. But by the early 1120s the Murabit amirs were facing not simply a stick-wielding fundamentalist but a messianic dissenter, and one with a growing multitude of followers. Many came from the Masmuda and Zanata Berber tribal confederations and thus had their own ancestral reasons for opposing the Murabits' official enfranchisement of other tribes. But belief in Ibn Tumart as the Mahdi was the primary factor in uniting the opposition to the Murabits.

The new Mahdi also established a hierarchical chain of authority that rivaled if not totally superseded any tribal affiliations. Ibn Tumart as Allah's rightly guided one was, of course, at the pinnacle. Buttressing his self-confidence and authority were his *hadrahs*, mystical "presences," in which he received supernatural, divine revelation.[16] Below the Mahdi were four primary administrative bodies: (1) the "people of the house," his inner council; (2) the "people of ten"; (3) the council of 50; and (4) below that, one of 70.[17] The Mahdi's aide-de-camp, who would become the Muwahhid ruler upon Ibn Tumart's death in 1130, was Abd al-Mu'min.[18]

A new hierarchy was not the only method by which Ibn Tumart as the Mahdi attempted to create community out of otherwise balkanized tribes, unity out of disunity. He employed more brutal methods as well. Twice during his lifetime Ibn Tumart ordered great purges of opposition. The first was when the Muwahhids decamped to Tinmallal. Not much information has survived, but indications are that the Mahdi had the original residents of the town exterminated, whether to make way for his own people or because they put up resistance no one knows for certain. The second horrific example of sacred cleansing took place in 1129–30. This is euphemistically referred to in the Muwahhid chronicles as a *tamyiz*, or "sifting out." This amounted to the murder of all those deemed insufficiently fervent in their Mahdist loyalties. Long before the Committee on Public Safety was killing the revolutionary lukewarm during the French Revolution, Ibn Tumart had perfected the concept. Mahdis, by their very nature, cannot countenance opposition or even cooperative apathy. Joining forces with a mahdi requires total dedication—or else.

One impetus for Mahdi Ibn Tumart's insistence on utter devotion was probably his belief in his own infallibility, or `ismah`. This is historically a much more powerful belief in Shi`i than in Sunni Mahdism. But the Fatimids and their North African propagandists of years past seem to have imbued the Sunni Magrib's Mahdist expectations with something of a Shi`ite cast, foremost among which was this atypical belief that the Mahdi was infallible.[19] (In fact, Ibn Tumart went so far as to fashion a geneaology linking himself back to Ali and Fatimah.)[20] To Ibn Tumart and his Mahdist devotees, in practice this meant that he alone could reliably interpet the Qur'an and Hadith; recourse to what any intermediate Islamic interpreters had said over the preceding 500 years was henceforth unnecessary. Thus, the Muwahhid Mahdi was rejecting a pillar of Islamic religio-legal interpretation: ijma`, or "consensus" of the scholars. The source of Islamic law was to be the Qur'an, the traditions, and Ibn Tumart; and not always necessarily in that order. "The Mahdi was third in place after Allah and His Messenger."[21]

His view of public morality rivaled that of the recent Taliban regime of Afghanistan:

Public morality demanded a strict application of the canonic law. Both sexes were to be rigidly segregated and the veiling of women was compulsory. There was to be no music, no wine-drinking, and prayer should be in public. As the hour of the Lord was at hand all attention was to be fixed on the world to come which was now imminent. . . . Among the eighteen faults which were chosen as the gravest, lying and hypocrisy were capital offences. Every ten persons formed a group. Their conduct was to be closely watched and their lives governed by a leader.[22]

Once he had outlined his domestic policies—manifesting a degree of control over personal morality that Jean Calvin's Protestant Geneva could later only hope for[23]—the infallible Mahdi was free to turn his attention to foreign policy, as it were: how best to eliminate those false Muslims ruling North Africa and al-Andalus (Spain), the Murabits.

Ibn Tumart's first stage was a propaganda war against the Murabits much like the criticism he had levied in person against the amir Ali b. Yusuf. The Muwahhid Mahdi composed and disseminated antiestablishment leaflets in Berber and Arabic, savaging the Murabits for their un-Islamic veiling of men; the untoward public lives the women; the allegedly poor interpretations of Islamic law, stemming from their wooden literalism regarding the Qur'an, put forth by the official religious scholars; and their ruling classes' avarice and hypocrisy.[24] Even worse, they were mere "shepherds turned kings," who levied unjust taxes and, most egregious, ignored the true commandments of Allah.[25] To spearhead his rhetorical attacks Ibn Tumart personally trained talabah, "petitioners,"[26] and huffaz, "memorizers," who were inculcated with his Madhist teachings and then sent out into the general populace like Muwahhid wolves among Murabit sheep.

The Maghribi Mahdi also lived long enough to see military confrontations between his followers and the Murabits, who attacked the Muwahhids but were unable to wipe them out. In 1130 his supporters launched an abortive attack on Marrakesh, the primary Murabit city, but were defeated at the battle of al-Buhayra. Later that year, in August 1130, the Mahdi Ibn Tumart died. Chosen as leader, Abd al-Mu'min made the decision to keep the Mahdi's death a secret—which the leadership did for several more years. This, perhaps more than anything, demonstrates the importance to the movement of Ibn Tumart's Mahdihood. Just how the Muwahhid supreme council and Abd al-Mu'min managed to hold their embryonic state together and fight the Murabits while plausibly maintaining the fiction that the Mahdi was still issuing orders is a mystery. However, it can be done. In recent American history the Woodrow Wilson administration hid the president's incapacitation following a stroke in his second term and allowed his wife, Eleanor, to serve as virtual chief executive.[27] Were Wilson to have died, though, the subterfuge might have been more problematic. Finally, in 1132 or 1133, Abd al-Mu'min was officially made the ruler and it was admitted that the Mahdi had shaken loose the mortal coil. He would rule for the next 30 years and would lead the Muwahhids to final victory over the Murabits in the name of the Mahdi.

Abd al-Mu'min was no religious fanatic. He was, however, an able commander and administrator. He held fast to belief in Ibn Tumart as the Mahdi and in fact ordered that Mahdist rulings be taught along with the Qur'an and Hadith. Of course, only those educated religious scholars who had accepted that the Mahdi had come could be trusted to interpret the Qur'an and Hadiths, so there grew up a de facto two-tiered socioreligious system: Mahdist religious leaders, enfranchised and less heavily taxed, lorded it over the former population and their religous experts who had not yet professed Ibn Tumart as the Mahdi.[28] Thus, during Abd al-Mu'min's three decades in power Mahdism was still an operative ideology, which would not prove the case under later Muwahhid rulers. Abd al-Mu'min took the titles of *khalifah*, or "caliph"—"successor" to the prophet Muhammad as ruler—and also *amir al-mu'minin*, "commander of the faithful." As a Berber, Abd al-Mu'min was the first non-Arab bold enough to describe himself as the latter.[29]

Most important, he led the military campaign against the tottering Murabit regime in North Africa, Iberia, and the Balearic Islands. In 1147 the Muwahhids finally took Marrakesh; shortly thereafter, when some tribes revolted, Abd al-Mu'min ordered another purge, which may have killed as many as 33,000. By 1150 the Murabit empire had been whittled down to Granada and Valencia in Iberia. In 1160 the Muwahhids, in a great jihad, took what is now Tunisia from the Norman French and in the process gave Christians there a choice between conversion or death.[30] Franciscan friars were not so fortunate: they were simply put to death. Jews, too, were persecuted by the Mahdi's caliph. Told to convert or die, many were killed by the Muwahhids in Sijilmasa, Marrakesh, and Fez. Many fled for Christian Spain, Sicily, Italy, and Salah al-Din's domains in Egypt and Syria.[31] Brutal though he was, by the time Abd al-Mu'min died in 1163, the Muwahhid Mahdist state stretched from modern Libya to Portugal—and it would survive him by more than a century.

Although still officially Mahdist, the Muwahhid empire had begun to change even toward the end of Abd al-Mu'min's life. By appointing his sons as regional governors, the sucessor to the Mahdi had made a fateful decision that undermined Mahdist ideology by instituting a dynastic principle.[32] In such a situation the myth of extant Mahdism could not long be sustained. Before the end of the twelfth century CE the Muwahhid caliph Abu Yusuf Ya`qub al-Mansur (d. 1199) formally anathematized the doctrine of Ibn Tumart's Mahdist infallibility—not, it seems, out of any deep religious conviction but because of political considerations. Rather than rallying round the now-deceased Mahdi, the state was to be imperially centered on its caliph. Eventually the Muwahhid leaders would openly repudiate belief in Ibn Tumart as the Mahdi, beginning in 1129 with Idris b. Ya`qub, who also had hundreds of Muwahhid shaykhs executed.[33] Military decline followed on the heels of the ideological. In 1212 the Muwahhids were dealt a devastating defeat by the armies of the Christian Iberian states at Las Navas de Tolosa. By 1228 Muwahhid power in Spain was over.[34] Although they managed to hold onto their North African dominions a while longer, the Muwahhid empire had disintegrated by 1269, marking the end of one of the most influential Mahdist movements in history, and one of the few to actually form a ruling government.

What assessment can be made of this first example of a successful Sunni Mahdi and the state he established? As for Ibn Tumart himself, there are a number of observations. First, in terms of his personal characteristics, he was austere bordering on ascetic, supremely pious, intolerant of those who did not take Islam as seriously as he did, and—perhaps the flip side of such religiosity—humorless. Second, his sense of divine election was purchased with a double-sided coin of validation: on one side, his subjective mystical experiences no one could deny; and on the other and probably more important side, his military and political successes against the target regime, the Murabits. Third, he realized the importance of recapitulating the life of the prophet Muhammad and the history of the early Islamic community, especially the hijrah, in terms of the religious resonance a successful emulation would produce among the populace. Fourth, he brooked neither opposition nor lukewarm support, punishing both with brutal, deadly purges. Fifth, he rejected a mainstay of orthodox Islam: the consensus of all the preceding scholars, a policy that gave him wide latitude in formulating his doctrines and approach to political power. Sixth, he saw Sunni Islam as under assault from non-Sunnis—from Shi`ites, especially, in the form of the Fatimids but also from Crusaders[35]—and took it upon himself to save it. Seventh, he was the progenitor in stressing the doctrine of tawhid, which, *mutatis mutandis,* still motivates Islamists and jihadists today.[36]

As for the post-Mahdi Muwahhid state, it is not inaccurate to say that its "government was much worse than that of the the Almoravids."[37] The modern mind finds this counterintuitive because it was, after all, the Murabits who were the literalist fundamentalists, not their successors. Wouldn't the "Qur'an-thumpers" be the more intolerant? No, the allegorical mystics were. But under the Muwahhids not only were coreligionist Muslim opponents executed *en masse* but fellow monotheist Jews had their synagogues destroyed and then were given a choice between conversion and death. As for the Christians, many were compulsorily converted to Islam or simply massacred, especially if they were members of Catholic religious orders. Muwahhid treatment of Jews and Christians, if nothing else, demonstrates the vacuity of the myth that medieval Islamic societies were always more religiously tolerant than were Christian ones.[38] While Salah al-Din in Syria and some of the rulers of smaller Islamic states in Spain were broadminded regarding their non-Muslim subjects, the same cannot be said of all medieval Islamic regimes, and most certainly not of the Muwahhids.

In the end Ibn Tumart's Mahdism proved a powerful oppositional ideology, but an impotent governing one. Once he was dead, the force of the Mahdi eventually waned and more prosaic political considerations eclipsed the quasi-messianic quest. So for the first time, but certainly not the last, we see the power of Mahdism as an adversarial tool, as a means of at least weaponizing religious discontent.

SAYYID MUHAMMAD JAWNPURI'S INDIAN MAHDISTS, FIFTEENTH AND SIXTEENTH CENTURIES

The next major Sunni Mahdist movement occurred on the other end of the Islamic world, on its eastern periphery in India, in the late fifteenth and early sixteenth centuries CE. Sayyid Muhammad Jawnpuri of Gujarat, in western India, declared himself the Mahdi in 1495 CE. The Muslim year 900 had dawned in 1494, so this movement was most likely motivated by expectations of the centennial Muslim mujaddid or renewer.

India is, of course, home to Hinduism, the world's third largest religion.[39] But for much of the last millennium, the throngs of Indian Hindus were ruled by Muslim conquerors, the largest of which was the Mughal Empire, which controlled most of the Indian subcontinent from the sixteenth century until the British conquest in the early eighteenth.[40] Before Mughal ascendancy, however, there were a number of smaller, regional Islamic states such as the Gujarat Sultanate, which lasted from 1407 until its incorporation into the Mughal state in 1572.[41]

Sayyid Muhammad[42] was born in Jawnpur (or Jaunpur) in 1443. In adulthood he joined a mystical Sufi order popular in India, the Chishtiyah.[43] Little more is known of his life until, when in his early fifties and living in Gujarat, Jawnpuri declared himself the Mahdi, informing the sultan of that state that it was incumbent upon all Gujarati government officials to accept him as such. Jawnpuri called for the establishment of a Muslim community modeled on that of Muhammad and his followers in Medina and a hijrah to prepare for the coming millennium, since the year 1591 would be the year 1000 of the Muslim calendar.[44] He rejected the corpus of settled opinions of Islamic scholars and advocated using only the Qur'an and Hadiths as sources of Islamic law—presumably, of course, as interpreted by himself as the Mahdi. Opponents, like the Gujarati sultans, were accused of *takfir*, "unbelief" (a variant of kufr that means the same thing). Jawnpuri promoted asceticism not just for himself but for his followers as well, who came to be called the Mahdawis or Mahdavis. They were to live in communities, share their possessions, devote themselves to prayer and piety, and avoid contamination from the outside world.[45] Jawnpuri seems to have viewed his followers as "sort of [a] vigilante body, prepared to intervene wherever justice was miscarrying . . . [Mahdavism] was perhaps the most thoroughgoing attempt, since the Khariji movement . . . to place Islamic social responsibility squarely on the shoulders of Muslim believers and to strike down all the social distortions introduced by wealth and descent."[46] Jawnpuri's Mahdist movement, then, was powerfully oriented toward social justice, not just lax Islamic practices.

Although Sunni, Jawnpuri's Mahdavi movement could appeal to Shi`is in India because he claimed descent from Musa al-Kazim, the seventh imam in Twelver Shi`ism.[47] So it was something of an ecumenical Mahdism. Also, it was elitist because the Arabo-Persian discourse employed by Jawnpuri and his supporters was the language of the Muslim privileged in India, not of the masses.[48]

The Mahdavi movement went through two phases: first an activist, militaristic one that kicked off with Sayyid Muhammad's death in 1505 CE and continued through the first five Mahdavi caliphs, as the successors to Mahdi Jawnpuri were known, and then a quietist one that began under Mughal rule and lasted till the movement largely died out in the eighteenth century.[49] In the first phase the Gujarati Sultan Muzaffar II (r. 1511–1526) forced many of the Mahdavis into exile. The second Mahdavi caliph, Sayyid Khundmir, tried to turn this persecution to political advantage by likening it to the mistreatment of the early Muslims in Mecca. Khundmir then led an armed struggle against Gujarat, until he was killed in 1523 and his head put on public display as an example. Mahdavis in northern India and Afghanistan met similar fates, some being ripped in half by elephants as a lesson to the populace.[50]

Eventually the Mahdavis tired of gruesome martyrdoms and deemed them counterproductive, moving into a quietist phase and ceasing to recruit new members. Then with the failure of Jesus to appear in the year 1000 AH (1591 CE), the Mahdavi movement lost its conviction and fervor, descending into a religious lassitude that would pose no threat to the Mughal sultanate, as it had to that of the Gujaratis.[51] Eventually the movement died out, neither tranforming into a separate religion, as did the Ahmadiyah later, nor being reabsorbed into mainstream Islam, as were the Muwahhids.

What are the charactertistics of this first major Indian Mahdist movement? First, it was rather ecumenically Muslim in that Sayyid Muhammad Jawnpuri was overtly Sunni, as was his Mahdism, yet he adduced a Shi`i lineage. Perhaps the minority status of Muslims in predominantly Hindu India made such an approach necessary, as would not be the case in a majority Sunni Muslim society. Second, Jawnpuri seems to have exploited not just the centennial renewal of Islam paradigm but, unusually so for a Muslim leader, even a self-styled Mahdi, also the approaching Muslim millennium. Third, Jawnpuri's Mahdism went out with a whimper rather than a bang as it tranformed itself from a militant, rebellious religio-political movement into an ultimately disappointed End Time sect within Islam. Fourth, to a great extent the Mahdavis extolled social justice and decried the socioeconomic inequalities in Indian society, or at least those between Muslims. In all four of these aspects Sayyid Muhammad's movement was unlike that of its predecessor, Ibn Tumart Muwahhid.

In five other ways, however, Mahdavism and Muwahhidism were alike. Both excoriated the extant ruling Islamic regimes as unbelieving and unworthy of loyalty. Both founders were pious ascetics, although Jawnpuri imbued his followers with an ascetic streak to a greater extent than did Ibn Tumart. Both movements formed separatist communities, though this tendency lessened among the Muwahhids once they seized power, which the Mahdavis never did. The Mahdavi and the Muwahhid movements both rejected what even the greatest of Muslim interpreters had had to say and went straight back to the Hadiths and, ultimately, to the Qur'an as building blocks of Islamic law (glossed, of course, by each Mahdi himself). And finally, both the Mahdism of Western Sahara and this Mahdism of the Indian subcontinent were elitist movements that never really caught on among the general population.

Ultimately, which should be judged the more successful Mahdist movement: the Muwahhid, which actually took power but only for a century, or the Mahdavi, which never seized the reins of government but survived as an ideology for over twice as long? The answer depends on how we define success. Jan-Olaf Blichfeldt distilled three stages of Mahdist

movements: (1) dissemination of revivalist propaganda aimed at undermining a regime; (2) formation of a renegade "military theocracy" and
attempts to seize power; and (3) the conquest or formation of a territorial
state that eventually wanes in ideological fervor.[52] Ibn Tumart's Muwahhid
movement encompassed all three stages. Sayyid Muhammad Jawnpuri's
Mahdavis only reached stage 2. But Mahdavism again demonstrates the
allure, and potential power, of Mahdism.

IBN ABU MAHALLAH'S MAHDISM VERSUS THE SA`DIYANS OF MOROCCO, EARLY SEVENTEENTH CENTURY

The third major Sunni Mahdist movement erupted in the early seven-
teenth century CE, again in northwestern Africa. In fact, this movement,
led by one Ibn Abu Mahallah who claimed he was the Mahdi, may have
been a conscious emulation of Ibn Tumart's uprising.[53] The Abu Mahallah
uprising marks the first time that Mahdism would crop up in a context of
European incursion and influence, in this case the Portuguese and Spanish,
if not yet full-blown imperialism.

The Sa`diyan dynasty ruled all of Morocco for a little over a century,
1549–1659.[54] At one point their influence extended all the way south to
Timbuktu, in modern Mali, as they sought to control the trans-Saharan
gold trade. Their progenitors, the Banu Sa`d tribe, claimed to have come
from Arabia and to be of the Prophet's lineage; thus the Sa`idyan fancied
themselves *sharifs*,[55] or descendants of Muhammad, and their leaders took
the title of *mawlay*, "lord." The Sa`diyans were often involved in political
machinations, as well as sometimes military struggles with the Portuguese
and Spanish advancing from the northwest and, on their other flank, with
the Ottoman Turks advancing from the east. On more than one occasion
the Sa`diyans found themselves forced into *de facto* alliances with, and even
territorial concessions to, the Christian powers of the Iberian Peninsula as a
means of fending off Ottoman conquest.

It seems to have been one of these land-for-support deals with the
Europeans that sparked a Mahdist movement in 1610. When the Sa`diyan
regime conceded the city of al-`Ara'ish (Larache) to the Spanish, one Ahmad
b. Abd Allah Muhammad b. al-Qadi, or Ibn Abu Mahallah, led a rebellion
against the ruling dynasty, claiming at some point that he was the Mahdi. He
and his followers took over the city of Sijilmasa, Ibn Abu Mahallah's home,
and attacked Marrakesh, driving out Mawlay Zaydan in 1612.[56] Eventually
Zaydan and his allies returned and expelled Abu Mahallah and his
Mahdists, most likely killing him in the process, since he died in 1613.

Not much is known about the Mahdist rebellion of Ibn Abu Mahallah, but
some conclusions can be drawn despite the sketchy information available.
First, he was a member of the Qutbaniyah mystical order and, ironically, a
member of the *ulama* (singular *alim*)—the religious establishment—as well.[57]

So Abu Mahallah was not totally a marginalized outsider vis-à-vis the regime, as were both Ibn Tumart and Sayyid Muhammad Jawnpuri. Second, he seems to have been aware of, and realized the power of, the predecessor Mahdism of Ibn Tumart and very likely drew inspiration, if not a revolutionary blueprint, from the example of the Muwahhids.[58] Third, much like Jawnpuri a continent away, Abu Mahallah conflated the recently passed Muslim millennium with the encroaching Christianity of the Spanish and Portuguese into an eschatological threat that only the Mahdi could counter.[59] Fourth, and again reminiscent of both Ibn Tumart and Jawnpuri, Abu Mahallah declared jihad[60] against what he considered an apostate and thus illegitimate Muslim regime, primarily because of the Saʿdiyan failure to protect Muslim lands from Christians.[61]

Ibn Abu Mahallah's short-lived Mahdist movement did attain level 3 on the Blichfeldt scale, however briefly (three years, maximum) and however microcosmic (ruling one or at the most two cities). Interestingly, the movement seems to have largely skipped phase 1, in which Islamic propaganda aimed at delegitimitizing the extant government is formulated. Indeed, Abu Mahallah's Mahdist jihad seems to have been fueled largely by visceral Islamic rage against an ostensibly Muslim ruling class that appeared impotent against Christian powers, rather than by any sophisticated or even rudimentary doctrinal rationale articulating his Mahdiyah. Nonetheless, we see once again the negative clout of Mahdism and its great potential to undermine and supplant an existing Islamic power structue, even if only temporarily.

SAYYID AHMAD BARELWI OF INDIA, EARLY NINETEENTH CENTURY

In the early nineteenth century a Mahdist movement erupted in northwestern India in the name of one Sayyid Ahmad Barelwi.[62] Born in 1786, Barelwi became a soldier and a Naqshabandiyah Sufi who, after making the hajj in 1821, returned to the subcontinent and proclaimed himself Imam. He aimed to renew Islam by purifying it of unacceptable practices such as Shiʿism and devotion to shrines[63] and by removing un-Islamic rulers, whether British or Sikh.[64]

While fighting jihad against the Sikhs in 1831, Barelwi went missing-in-action (MIA) on the battlefield, and his body was never recovered.[65] Afterward his supporters transformed this seeming tragedy into a victory by claiming it was merely an occultation and that Sayyid Ahmad would eventually return as the Mahdi. Some of his followers probably saw him as the Mahdi even before his MIA status, however, though there is debate about whether he openly claimed the status for himself.[66] Later Indian Muslim scholars like Muhammad Thanesari (d. 1905) wrote that Sayyid Ahmad Barelwi was not the Mahdi but a mahdi, the "mahdi of his time," and thus more akin to a caliph or mujaddid.[67] One theory suggests that the idea of Barelwi as the Mahdi originated with William Hunter, the editor of the British Christian publication the *Church Missionary Intelligencer*, as anti-Wahhabi propaganda.[68] But evidence points more conclusively to a belief among Sayyid Ahmad's flock that he was the Mahdi, at least posthumously.

A number of observations about the Barelwi Mahdist movement can be made. First, it too sprang from a Sufi context, in this case the Naqshabandiyah order. Second, it was to some extent anti-imperialist. The nineteenth century saw the British tightening their grip on India, and Sayyid Ahmad no more wanted Muslims in the subcontinent to be ruled by European Christians than he did by infidel Sikhs. Third, there is this interesting matter, unique in the annals of Sunni Mahdism, of occultation. Occultation is the state of "hiddenness" normally reserved for, and applied only to, the Shi`i imams. That such a condition became attached to belief in a Sunni Mahdi is fascinating and may have ramifications for our own time. Fourth, there is little doubt that Sayyid Ahmad was influenced by the Wahhabi doctrine of Islam during his pilgrimage to Mecca. Wahhabism, the official brand of Sunni Islam in the Kingdom of Saudi Arabia today, was formulated by Shaykh Muhammad b. Abd al-Wahhab (d. 1792) and empha-sized tawhid, a literal interpretation of the Qur'an, criticism (and eventual prohibition) of the veneration of Sufi saints and shrines, and intolerance for lax Islamic piety and practice. The latter was primarily aimed at the allegedly un-Islamic practices of the Ottoman Turks, the imperial power of the time in Arabia.[69] Although the Wahhabis had not been officially installed in power yet—since their political ally, the house of Sa`ud, would not gain power till the 1920s—their ideas were prevalent in the Arabian peninsula at the time that Sayyid Ahmad made the hajj. Thus, an interest-ing phenomenon developed: a Muslim mystic became imbued with the ideology of a virulently antimystical strain of Islam and incorporated it into his jihadist strategy, whereupon his followers attributed the Shi`i char-acteristic of occultation to him.

Barelwi's Mahdism was much closer to Sunni mujaddid-led Islamic reform than it was to full-blown Mahdism, his followers' claims after his disappearance notwithstanding. As such, this movement never moved beyond stage 2 of Mahdist development. Nonetheless, it is yet another demonstration of Mahdism's power to inspire jihad and rebellion, as well as reform, though to a lesser extent. And its incorporation of a major Shi`i element might have ramifications for modern Mahdism.

THE "MAHDISTS" OF NINETEENTH-CENTURY ALGERIA

In the third quarter of the nineteenth century a number of near-Mahdist movements erupted in Algeria.[70] These were sparked mainly by the French occupation that had begun in 1830 and the resulting onerous taxation, as well as by the perception that the local Muslim authorities were either complicit with, or impotent before, the dictates of Paris. The culmination of this Mahdism *manque* sequence was that someone did finally openly claim to be the Mahdi, however. The background to these movements was the "patriotic revolt" led by Abd al-Qadir between the early 1830s and 1847, when he was captured by the French and exiled rather than killed,[71] perhaps out of a political consideration that killing him would have created a Maghribi martyr. Although similar, the "apocalyptic revolts" that followed were different in that they were sparked by and railed against a perceived Muslim-French conspiracy of oppression[72]—and, of course, by Mahdism.

The first of these was that of Bou Zian/Abu Ziyan[73] in 1849, who led the people in the oasis town of Za`atsha in a jihad against the French.[74] Sources disagree as to whether Abu Ziyan proclaimed himself the Mahdi or simply the "deputy" or caliph of the Mahdi.[75] In either event, after a series of dreams in which the prophet Muhammad appeared to him and that left parts of his body tinted green, Abu Ziyan and his followers took over Za`atsha for about six months. In November 1849, however, French forces surrounded the town and razed it, killing Abu Ziyan and most of his followers. In 1858–59 Si Sadok Ben al-Hadj, who had fought with Abu Ziyan, declared a jihad against the French occupation forces but never attracted more than 100 followers, and the movement went quietly into the desert night in early 1859.[76] There is little indication that al-Hadj's abortive uprising contained much Mahdist element beyond that which had survived from Abu Ziyan's borderline Mahdism. A little over a decade later Si Mohammed Ben Bou Khentach proclaimed himself "caliph" of the Mahdi following dreams and visions. After being vetted and approved by a council of his tribal and religious elders, Bou Khentach started a jihad that attracted several thousand followers but was quickly crushed by the French in March 1860.[77] Finally, after these movements that never quite crossed the actual Mahdist threshold, one did: Mohammed Amzian pronounced himself the Mahdi in 1879, after which he killed several Muslim officials in the French-run government and led several hundred Mahdists into a jihad. The French military obiterated the movement in June 1879.[78] There are no indications that Paris sought the approval of the international community before annihilating these religious rebellions.

Before the nineteenth century, Mahdism in the Maghrib does seem to have developed a belief in precursors to the Mahdi who would prepare the way for him. Such "Lords of the Hour" would come forward in times of crisis to save the Muslims, albeit temporarily, and prepare the way for the actual Mahdi.[79] This might explain the proliferation of almost-Mahdis during the initial period of French conquest and rule in Algeria. Such a figure would be akin to a mujaddid, and claiming that status would, of course, be much easier than taking on the role of the Mahdi. Mahdis, mujaddids, or just plain early jihadists—during the colonial period in

North Africa and other parts of the Muslim world, all utilized, extant Sufi organizations as ready-made resistance mechanisms. All these Algerian near-Mahdist rebellions, as well as the actual one of Amzian, sprang from a Sufi context, in this case the Rahmaniyah order.[80] This was also true of the Mahdist movements of Jawnpuri and Barelwi in India as well as with Abu Mahallah in Morocco. Mahdism in the past was often, but not always, associated with Sufism. Usually this is for the most practical of reasons: at certain times, in certain contexts, the Sufi orders present the only alternative mode of organized Islamic resistance and one that is generally predisposed to at least giving an aspiring Mahdi a fair hearing, if not guaranteed acceptance, since the traditions about him are generally accepted by Sufis and since he is, after all, a rather mystical figure.

These examples of Algerian near and actual Mahdism amount, in the final analysis, to little more than antiestablishment jihads coated with a thin veneer of green Mahdist paint—especially, and literally, it seems, in the case of Abu Ziyan. None of them came anywhere close to the third stage of Mahdist development and in fact they all seem to have skipped the important first stage of formulating effective anti-regime propaganda and tried to move directly into the second stage of attempting to seize power—with predictable results, especially in the face of French resolve and artillery.

MUHAMMAD AHMAD, THE MAHDI OF THE SUDAN

With the possible exception of Ibn Tumart's movement, the Mahdist movement of Muhammad Ahmad bin Abd Allah of Sudan in the late nineteenth century has been the most successful Sunni one so far in history.[81] The story of the Sudanese Mahdists fighting against the British has even made it into popular culture through movies such as 1966's *Khartoum*, starring Charlton Heston and Laurence Olivier, and more recently, if less impressive cinematically, *The Four Feathers* (2002). Of course, since this movement happened fairly recently in historical terms and affected two great empires, the British and the Ottoman, a great deal more is known about Sudanese Mahdism and its founder than any its predecessors. Also, because Muhammad Ahmad succeeded in creating not only an opposition movement predicated on Mahdism but also a viable state that survived for almost two decades, the Mahdiyah of Sudan has been studied probably more than any other in history. Yet, some commentators make the mistake of writing about this movement as if it were the sole example of Mahdism in history.

Muhammad Ahmad b. Abd Allah was born in northwestern Sudan in 1844 CE/1260 AH.[82] Sudan—today the largest state, territorially, in Africa—was then a remote province of the Turkish Ottoman Empire, administered as a subprovince of Egypt. Muhammad Ali, an Ottoman general, had become the ruler, or *khedive*,[83] of Egypt by the early 1820s. His ultimately futile effort to replace the Ottoman dynasty with his own included conquering south, into Sudan, as a means of eliminating potential political troublemakers,[84] as well as exploiting the natural resources of Sudan and central Africa. The goal was to enrich Egypt and fund the military buildup requisite for his imperial dreams in northeastern Africa and perhaps even across the Red Sea into Arabia.[85]

Muhammad Ali's son Isma'il began the Egyptian conquest of Sudan, and by the time the future Mahdi was born in the 1840s much of what is now Sudan had been recognized as de facto Egyptian territory by the Ottoman sultans in something of a *fait accompli*,[86] since there was little they could have done otherwise. Egyptian territorial ambitions in Sudan quieted for a few decades after Muhammad Ali's death in 1848 but were roused again with the opening of the Suez Canal in 1869. Another Isma'il, this one Muhammad Ali's grandson, sent an army with British officers farther into Sudan and incorporated even more of it into Egypt's ambit.

Modern ideas of pan-African brotherhood notwithstanding, as far as the inhabitants of the Sudan were concerned, they had been conquered by foreigners: not by the British; rather, by Ottoman Turks, and Egyptians. Albeit fellow Muslims, the Egyptians and Turks were seen primarily as exploiters, profiting from onerous taxation, *samgh* (gum Arabic), cotton, and slaves. Although legal under nineteenth-century Sudanese Islamic law, the slave trade had been criminalized in 1857 by the Ottomans in most of their empire following intense British pressure.[87] In 1880 interdiction of the African slave trade was elevated to an even higher status with the Anglo-Ottoman Convention for Suppression of the African Slave Trade.[88] In Sudan, however, unlike in Istanbul or Cairo, attempting to wipe out the slave trade was considered not only a contravention of Islamic law but a heavy-handed, imperial infringement on a lucrative means of living for many. Sudanese traders bought or captured slaves, theoretically non-Muslim, from farther south in Africa—a practice that in some fashion continues even today. Opposition to this slaving ban would prove a key plank in Muhammad Ahmad's Mahdist platform.

When Egypt tottered on the edge of defaulting on its debt owed to European banks for the funding of the Suez Canal, the British and French took over the Caisse de la Dette Publique in order to supervise payments. Part of this political maneuver included the installation of a British general, the famous Charles George Gordon, as governor of Sudan in 1879.[89] Gordon had fought in the Taiping Rebellion in China in the 1860s and had previously worked in Sudan for the Ottoman Egyptian regime in a number of capacities, including as a staff officer supervising former American army officers (both Confederate and Union) serving in the Egyptian army.[90] Gordon lasted in the job as governor of Sudan until 1880.

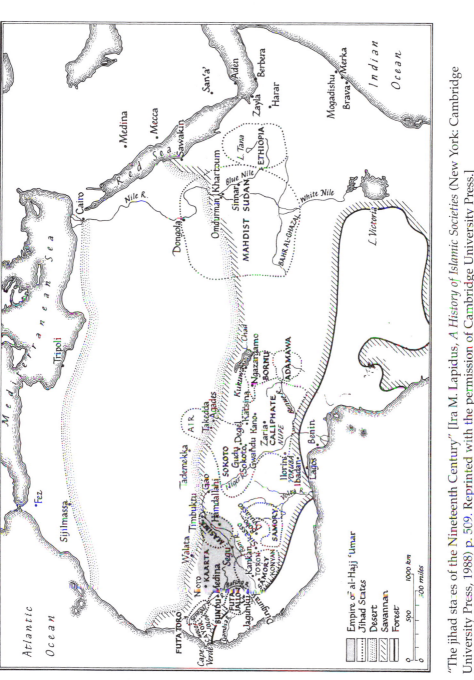

"The jihad states of the Nineteenth Century" [Ira M. Lapidus, *A History of Islamic Societies* (New York: Cambridge University Press, 1988) p. 509. Reprinted with the permission of Cambridge University Press.]

In 1881–82 the British gave up stage-managing events behind the scenes and simply moved onto the stage by taking over Egypt. The alleged proximate cause was the attempted coup against the government by Urabi Pasha, a disaffected Arab Egyptian army officer chafing under the Turkish yoke. The British, in order to secure their Suez Canal route to India as well as maintain the territorial integrity of the Ottoman Empire—their main ally against the Russians—occupied Egypt.[91] Preoccupation with managing this occupation would distract both the British and the Ottomans from the Mahdist movement to the south in Sudan when it erupted in 1881.

Sudan's incorporation, between 1820 and 1881, into the Ottoman sphere of influence had profound religious, political, and economic repercussions and set the stage for Muhammad Ahmad's Mahdist revolt. The Ottomans tightened their hold not just economically, as mentioned, but religiously by appointment of politically sympathetic ulama and *qadis*.[92] In fact, only religious scholars who had the Ottoman seal of approval could deliver formal religio-legal opinions, or *fatwas*. The Turks even sent some of these *muftis*, or "renderers of fatwas," to study at al-Azhar in Cairo. Certain Sufi orders were officially sanctioned, too, while others were disregarded. Muhammad Ahmad's order, the Sammaniyah, was one of the latter and competed intensely with another one, the Khatmiyah (also known as the Mirghaniyah), which allied with the Ottoman regime.[93] In sum, the Ottomans also practiced a divide-and-rule administration in which tribe was set against tribe, Sufi order against Sufi order, and trader against trader. Some tribes were forcibly relocated in order to weaken them. Others were socially marginalized, and many of their members became dependent on the charitable Sufis for food. The Ottoman Egyptian regime thus had six decades to sow resentment among the peoples of Sudan, and as Mahdi, Muhammad Ahmad would not hesitate to exploit this—and he did so quite successfully.

Muhammad Ahmad, the future Mahdi, was raised in a family of Nile boat-builders on the outskirts of Khartoum, modern Sudan's capital.[94] This meant they were probably a notch above poverty level for the time. His parents died before his eighth birthday, about the time he entered a *khalwah*,[95] or Qur'anic school. Muhammad Ahmad's brothers wanted him at home helping build boats, however, so they forced him to leave the khalwah, whereupon he fled back. When his brothers kidnapped him again, he went on a hunger strike until they relented and let him resume his theological studies. "Such stubbornness, allied with his intelligence and aptitude, would have led him to become an alim had not his path been redirected"[96]—into that of the Mahdi.

When he was about 17 Muhammad Ahmad went to Katranj, south of Khartoum, to study with Sufi scholars there. He left sometime in 1863–64, seemingly with the intention of making the long trek north to Cairo in order to matriculate at al-Azhar. However, in one of those twists of fate that prove decisive in history, he was convinced to stop in Birbir, north of Khartoum, and study with Shaykh Muhammad al-Khayyir Abd Allah Khujali (d. 1888). The servant would later become the master, as Mahdi, and appoint his old teacher the governor of that region of Sudan.[97] He would never travel any farther down the Nile. While studying at Khujali's school, Muhammad Ahmad at first refused any of the food provided there because it was provided as part of a stipend from the Turco-Egyptian government; but he was eventually persuaded otherwise by his shaykh and by hunger. It was at this time that Muhammad Ahmad read and was profoundly influenced by al-Ghazali's book *Revival of the Religious Sciences*. Thus, al-Ghazali greatly affected two Sunni Mahdis: Ibn Tumart and Muhammad Ahmad.

Around this time Muhammad Ahmad was married for the first time, to his cousin, Fatimah bint[98] Hajj. There is an account that when she tried to hide his religious books and persuade him to get a real job, he divorced her. Then for a number of years and at the behest of Muhammad Sharif, another Sufi shaykh under whom he was studying, Muhammad Ahmad became a peripatetic pupil, traveling throughout Sudan and learning from various Sufi masters. One prosaic byproduct of this lifestyle would have been gaining familiarity with the condition of the Sudanese people throughout the land under the Ottoman Egyptian regime. He sometimes gathered and sold firewood in order to support himself, but he refused to do business with anyone who sold wine, thereby gaining a reputation for piety. He also seems to have totally broken with his brothers and sister at this point, substituting the Sammaniyah mystical order as his surrogate family. Finally he settled near Khartoum, built a small mosque and khalwah, and took up teaching. He married again, to one Fatimah bint Ahmad Sharfi, and then moved with her to her home, Aba Island in the White Nile.[99]

There Muhammad Ahmad's public ministry as Mahdi can be said to have begun. At a wedding celebration for one of the daughters of Muhammad Sharif, Muhammad Ahmad openly criticized the music and dancing. This resulted in a break between the two Muhammads, in which the future Mahdi's intolerance of frivolity may have been only one symptom of the disease of generational rift in Sudanese society[100] between the old guard that endured foreign rule and the younger one that eventually could not or would not.

Muhammad Ahmad joined the retinue of another Sufi teacher, al-Qurashi Wad` al-Zayn, in 1878 and took as his second wife this shaykh's daughter. Back on his Aba Island retreat he became increasingly disenchanted with mere world-renouncing Sufism and began to attract his own band of disciples who thought likewise. In this period of transition to intense religious activism he is said to have collapsed while reading a Qur'anic verse that says that "on the Day of Judgement, the people will be scattered like moths."[101]

In 1879, at about the same time his latest mentor, al-Qurashi, died, Muhammad Ahmad met Abd Allah b. Muhammad (or later, to the Brits, "Abdullahi") who would become eventually his Mahdist caliph. This fellow seems to have been scouring Sudan for someone to whom to swear fealty as the Mahdi. In 1873 he had written a letter to al-Zubayr Pasha Rahman Mansur (d. 1913), a slave trader and strong man who had gained a position in the Turco-Egyptian administration, hailing him as the Mahdi. Al-Zubayr, no doubt realizing the danger of such a claim, rebuffed Abd Allah b. Muhammad.[102] Little did Abd Allah know that he would before too long get his wish in the person of Muhammad Ahmad.

All these years of travel and trial look as if they convinced Muhammad Ahmad that he met all the requirements for the role of Mahdi. If not now, when? If not him, who else? In 1879–80 he embarked on phase 1, as it were, of his transition by secretly informing his disciples that he was the Mahdi. Doing this surreptitiously tranformed Muhammad Ahmad from a mere Sufi propagandist on the periphery of the extant system to a harsh— indeed, revolutionary—critic from the outside. He was reinforced in this fateful decision by disembodied voices that addressed him as "O Mahdi of God." Eventually these voices gave way to the hadrahs so characteristic of mystical rebels in which the Prophet of Islam and deceased Sufi shaykhs appear, validating the claim to Mahdihood. Of course, much like Christian leaders or even rank-and-file who claim the authority of the Holy Spirit as sanction for their teachings and actions, a Muslim leader who adduces such subjective validation is difficult to refute: who, after all, is to say the prophet Muhammad is not appearing to such a one as Muhammad Ahmad?

Phase 2 was a trip in 1880 to southwestern Sudan, the Kurdufan region—the same area of that country so riven with strife today. Clad in a traditional white Sufi *jubbah*, a long outer garment open in front and having wide sleeves, he carried only a clay jug, a staff, and prayer beads. Followers flocked to him as he walked. Eventually he issued a formal *da`wah*, or "summons," to support him as the Mahdi. The resonance of a call to da`wah in Islamic history cannot be overstated. It is "the invitation to adopt the cause of some individual . . . claiming the right to the imamate over the Muslims; that is to say civil and spiritual authority, vindicating a politico-religious principle which, in the final analysis, aims at founding or restoring an ideal theocratic state" and which often is "one of the means of founding a new empire. . . ."[103] At this point the da`wah seems to have been extended only to the people of Kurdufan. Finally, however, in October 1880 (Rajab 1298) Muhammad Ahmad openly proclaimed himself the Mahdi and broadened the Mahdist da`wah to include all of Sudan and, eventually, the entire Islamic world.

Muhammad Ahmad returned to his home base of Aba Island, and almost immediately delegations from all over Sudan began making the pilgrimage there. He had drawn up *mawathiq*, "contracts," avowing that he was the Mahdi for these representatives to sign. Although some were skeptical that the Mahdi should be only 36 years of age, most inked their acceptance and returned home to await marching orders.

Some of the Mahdi's writings fell into government hands about this time, but the Ottoman Egyptian leadership saw him as merely a "deluded Sufi" and ignored the warnings of Shaykh Muhammad Sharif—Muhammad Ahmad's former teacher—that this man and his movement should be taken seriously. The sixteenth-century Vatican dismissal of Martin Luther, the founder of Protestantism, as merely a "drunken German" comes to mind here. The governor of Sudan, Ra`uf, did write a letter of inquiry to Muhammad Ahmad, who replied that he was indeed the Mahdi. The governor then asked for the assistance of the ulama, who decided to send an official religious delegation to Aba Island in order to interrogate this pretentious shaykh and bring him back to Khartoum for re-education. The religious establishment foolishly believed Muhammad Ahmad would yield. The governor's assistant, Muhammad b. Abi Saud, headed up this delegation, which consisted of relatives[104] and erstwhile students of Muhammad Ahmad, accompanied by 25 soldiers. Plan A was to religiously intimidate Muhammad Ahmad into abandoning his Mahdist fantasy; should that fail, Plan B was to seize him by force and take him back to Khartoum, short-circuiting his movement.

In August 1881 the anti-Mahdi mission reached Muhammad Ahmad's headquarters. Rebuffed when he requested that Muhammad Ahmad return with them to Khartoum, Ibn Abi al-Sa`ud quoted the Quran: "O Believers! Obey God and His Messenger and those entrusted with authority among you."[105] Muhammad Ahmad riposted with an audacious restatement of his claim: "I am the one entrusted with authority among you and you owe obedience to me, as does the entire community of Muhammad; so heed what I bring you from God." The governor's representative then warned him that this would mean war with the government, whereupon the Mahdi pointed to his followers and scoffed, "I will kill you with such as these." Then he asked his band, "Are you ready to die for the path of God?" And they shouted as one, "Yes!" After a last-ditch failed attempt to bribe away some of the Mahdi's followers, the government taskforce returned to to Khartoum and recommended armed intervention.

A battalion-sized unit of about 800 men was then dispatched, again under al-Saud's command, in August 1881. The Mahdists in Muhammad Ahmad's retinue at that time numbered at most 300, most armed with swords, lances, and staffs—none with firearms. Yet somehow they repulsed the Turco-Egyptian troops, losing only 12 men and gaining a cache of rifles in the process. Thus the first armed clash between the troops of the Ottoman sultan and those of the Mahdi ended in the latter's victory.

But Muhammad Ahmad was not yet prepared to follow up this win with a full-blown Mahdist uprising. Instead, he decided on the time-honored mode of continuing the struggle while consolidating Mahdist power: hijrah. Like Ibn Tumart, who similarly faced a powerful and hostile establishment regime, Muhammad Ahmad took his followers out of the government's purview, much as Ibn Tumart had done with his supporters and in similar imitation of the prophet Muhammad and the early Muslims. In the nineteenth century African Islam, in particular, saw a number of such hijrahs led by powerful, charismatic religio-political figures, albeit none who claimed to be the Mahdi. The most important of these include the aforementioned (1) Usman don Fodio, founder of the Sokoto caliphate; (2) Abd al-Qadir of Algeria; (3) Muhammad Abd Allah Hasan of Somalia; and (4) al-Hajj Umar al-Futi (d. 1864), in what is now Mali and Burkina Fasso (western Africa), who claimed to be a mujaddid as well as "minister"[106] of the Mahdi.[107] Why did the hijrah work so well, and resonate so strongly, with African Muslims? Perhaps one reason relates to the peripherality of Islam on that continent. For unlike the core Islamic lands (Arabia, Egypt, Syria, Iraq, and Iran), in Africa it was possible for a renegade religious leader and his retinue to flee to an area not ruled by a Muslim state, where purification of the community could take place free from the taint of the apostate official brand of Islam—an area where the government's troops were loathe to go. Also, nothing bonds people together more tightly and quickly than sharing hardship, and so perhaps the hijrah enabled followers of a new Islamic dispensation, who hailed from disparate tribal and societal backgrounds, to forge for themselves a new group solidarity.

When Muhammad Ahmad, now surnamed "al-Mahdi," decided to repeat the hijrah paradigm, he was probably doing so not only to buy time and muster his forces but, perhaps just as important, to fix in his followers' minds the legitimacy of the jihad he was about to launch against the most powerful Islamic state of the time, the Ottoman Empire. Hard times lay ahead, but—led by the Mahdi—they would ultimately prevail. Muhammad Ahmad also reminded his supporters of the prophetic community by calling his followers Ansar, the term for the first Muslims who follow Muhammad, and his subcommanders "caliphs," in imitation of the successors to the prophet as rulers of the early Islamic state. "The Mahdi's use of [such] prophetic parallels was not a blind antiquarianism. He and his followers were deliberately re-enacting in their own persons the sufferings and triumphs of the early days of Islam and the consciousness of playing a part in this great drama was an inspiration to them."[108]

Thus, on August 15, 1881, the Mahdists embarked on their hijrah, their "Medina" being Qadir in southwestern Sudan. Their ranks swelled along the way as many Sudanese joined. The government launched several attacks on the fleeing Mahdists, only to be defeated each time. On October 24, 1881, the fourth of the Islamic month of Dhu al-Hijjah, 1298, they arrived. Now they would gather their strength, send the Mahdist summons to other parts of Sudan by means of *khalayah*, revolutionary Mahdist cells whose job was to convert local notables, like tribal and Sufi leaders. All the Mahdist faithful would then await the year 1300 so they could conquer the apostate regime in Khartoum.

In summer 1881 the Mahdi began his offensive. His forces attacked al-Ubayd, the capital of Kurdufan Province, and finally took it in January 1883. The Mahdists plundered the city while their leader prayed in the main city mosque. Muhammad Ahmad now controlled Kurdufan, which meant that the more southwesterly provinces of Darfur and Bahr al-Ghazal were lost to Khartoum's control as well. Furthermore, Mahdist forces captured even larger caches of modern weapons, including artillery as well as rifles, and began to deploy them. Meanwhile, the Madhist lieutenant Uthman Diqna was recruiting followers in the mountains of the Red Sea coast, thus opening another front against the Ottoman Egyptian regime in Sudan.

Diqna's broadening of the rebellion into the Ottoman Red Sea littoral prompted Ottoman Sultan Abdülhamid II to take the Mahdists seriously, if not religiously, then geopolitically:

Abdülhamid was far less interested in the Mahdi's ideology than in his opportunities. Mahdism was a hostile force on a map; what worried the Sultan most was the presence of revolt in the eastern Sudan, from where it might easily spread across the Red Sea into Arabia. The Red Sea was a conduit, not a barrier; its African and Arabian shores were bound by numerous trading links; Osman Digna himself was a slave trader who originated from Jeddah, and enjoyed numerous connections in the Hijaz. Consequently the Ottoman government's first concern was to prevent the insurrection from spreading into neighboring regions, and above all into Arabia.[109]

The Ottoman sultan was quite concerned about rebel contagion in his Arab domains for two reasons. First, the Hijaz, the western coastal strip of Arabia bordering the Red Sea directly across from Sudan and Egypt, contains the two holy cities of Mecca and Medina and so is of paramount importance to any Muslim ruler in terms of both religious legitimacy and income derived from pilgrims making the hajj.[110] With forays into the Red Sea coastal region of Sudan, the Mahdi threatened the Hijaz. Furthermore, the Ottomans had already had to put down the Wahhabi revolts in Arabia earlier in the nineteenth century.[111] Nonetheless, the Sultan eventually decided against sending troops from Istanbul to deal with the Mahdi because he secretly suspected that the British were manipulating the Mahdists for their own ends and he refused to play into London's dirty imperial hands.[112] Thus, the Egyptians and the British, fresh from their occupation, were left to deal with Muhammad Ahmad and his Mahdist multitudes.

In 1883 the British sent several thousand Egyptian and British troops under General Willam Hicks up the Nile. They were routed by a Mahdist force of some 20,000. With this stunning victory over the world's foremost imperial power Muhammad Ahmad al-Mahdi gained legitimacy throughout the Islamic world. Delegations came to him from Tunis, Morocco, and India, and even from the semi-autonomous ruler of the Hijaz, all of which could only have infuriated the Ottomans even more.

The British made one last effort to salvage Sudan by sending General Charles Gordon, the former governor, to Khartoum in January 1884. Gordon enlisted the establishment ulama to renew their propaganda fusillades against the Mahdi, but to no avail. Interestingly, one twist in this regard was Gordon's order that in the mosques the imams read from al-Bukhari's anthology of traditions—the most authoritative collection and one that contains no mention of the Mahdi.

However, the time for a successful ideological and rhetorical refutation of Muhammad Ahmad as the Mahdi was long past. The issue had become a military one. The Mahdists besieged Khartoum in August 1884 with, it was said, 200,000 men. The Mahdi offered clemency to those in the city if they would surrender, and he is said to have personally written to Gordon at least eight times imploring him to do so.[113] The general, perhaps mindful of the role he would need to establish for Charlton Heston to follow, steadfastly refused. On January 26, 1885, the final assault began and the Mahdist army soon entered the city in triumph, killing and beheading Gordon in the process—against the Mahdi's express orders. Muhammad Ahmad himself waited until Friday to enter the city so that he could go directly to the main mosque for prayers. The long road from boat-building youth to Sufi novice and master to Mahdi and ruler of Sudan was now complete.

Within five months, however, the Mahdi would be bedridden, most likely with malaria exacerbated by the pace of his writings (seven volumes, collected) and, of course, conquests. The modern world's only successful Mahdi to date died on June 22, 1885.

The Sudanese Mahdi possessed a personality charismatic enough to weld together quite different strains of his society—disenfranchised mystics, slave traders, forcibly relocated tribes, and even some nomadic herders—and sufficient military and political acumen to exploit the lack of legitimate control from Istanbul, through Cairo, in the last decades of the nineteenth century. Muhammad Ahmad's Mahdist polity would survive him by some 13 years, when it would fall victim to colonial European rivalries in northeastern Africa.

What administrative form did the Mahdist state take?[114] Before his death the Sudanese Mahdi had appointed caliphs, a conscious reimaging of the early Islamic community's polity, like so much of his Mahdist career.

Muhammad Ahmad's right-hand man, Abd Allah, was first among equals and commanded the army: he received the title "righteous caliph," equating him with Abu Bakr, the first caliph. Two other caliphal posts were given to, respectively, Ali b. Muhammad Hilu and Muhammad Sharif b. Hamid. The fourth slot was offered by the Mahdi to Muhammad al-Mahdi al-Sanusi, the son of the famous founder of the Libyan Sanusiyah Sufi order, but he declined.

Under the caliphs were *umara*, "commanders"; *umalan*, "viceregents"; *nuwwab*, "deputies"; and *umana*, "proxies." Commanders were military officials, whereas viceregents headed areas without military garrisons. Deputies were charged with administering Islamic law in tandem with *qadis*, "judges." The proxies were organized into a *majlis*, or "assembly," and given responsibility for temporal affairs. He also appointed a supreme *qadi* or judge, who was to base his legal decisions on the Qur'an and Hadith and the Mahdi's writings.

Muhammad Ahmad also repudiated the Ottoman sultanate and caliphate, declaring both roles of the empire's leader illegitimate. For most of Ottoman history the rulers had used the title "sultan" for their supreme political and military leader. With the conquest of Egypt and the Hijaz in the sixteenth century, the Ottoman sultans had laid claim to the greater title of "caliph," but had not actually applied and trumpeted this role until the nineteenth century when Sultan Abdülhamid II needed a means of uniting Sunni Islam against outside threats, in particular European imperialism.[115] Muhammad Ahmad's rejection of the Ottoman caliph-sultan was tantamount to political treason and religious apostasy rolled into one.

The Sudanese Mahdi also dissolved all Sufi orders—an ironic move, given the crucial support he received from a number of them. The primary reason seems to have been to ensure that loyalty to one's Sufi shaykh would not undermine loyalty to the Mahdi. He also tried to abolish the four Sunni schools of law (*madhahib*) on the grounds that they had not existed in the early Islamic community.[116] Islamic law, as defined by Muhammad Ahmad's own esoteric exegesis and ascetic proclivities, was strictly enforced. This law was to be found in the Qur'an and Traditions, filtered through his own Mahdist *ilham*, or "direct revelation"; this, of course, meant a total rejection of previous Islamic religious verdicts. Muhammad Ahmad's Mahdist jurisprudence thus resembles modern Islamic fundamentalism in its rejection of what Islamic scholars have had to say over the centuries and its ostensible dependence on only Qur'an and Hadith. However, the Mahdi's direct divine or prophetic revelation made him, if anything, even less prone to doubts than a modern fundamentalist Muslim leader.[117]

The apostasy of falling away from belief in Muhammad Ahmad as the Mahdi was punishable by death, at least while the Mahdi still lived. This was tantamount to making belief in the extant Mahdi a sixth pillar of Islam, to go along with the historical five: profession of faith in one god,

Allah, and in Muhammad his messenger; prayer five times daily; the pilgrimage to Mecca; fasting from sunup to sundown during the month of Ramadan; and charity for the poor.

Even day-to-day moral behavior was constrained in a draconian fashion.[118] Drinking wine or smoking earned the perpetrator 80 lashes and prison time. Libel and swearing in public were also whippable offenses, as were insults like calling someone "son of a dog." The latter could also result in 80 lashes and incarceration. Games like backgammon were outlawed as frivolous. Women were banned from the marketplace and main roads and when they did appear in public had to wear the hijab—the head and partial face covering—and avoid nonrelative males. Mahdist women were also to avoid "imitating masculine manners," except when fighting unbelievers. Divorce was mandated for anyone married to a Turk or a spouse who doubted Muhammad Ahmad's Mahdiyah.

On a number of points, though, Muhammad Ahmad al-Mahdi changed Islamic law, which was his right to do as the Mahdi. He asserted, for example, that as Mahdi he could take more than the traditional four wives. In a perhaps less self-serving interpretation, Muhammad Ahmad changed Islamic inheritance law such that a widow whose husband had been "martyred" fighting against the Turks was entitled to his entire estate, not just a portion (the dead man's brothers getting the lion's share) as the Qur'an mandates.[119] Thus, whereas the Mahdi was quite austere in most of his renderings of Islamic law, his treatment of women's inheritance is perhaps a kinder, gentler exception.

On the fiscal and economic front a central public treasury, the *bayt al-mal*, was established based on a common storehouse for booty that had been set up before the Mahdists took Khartoum. Much land belonging to the former Ottoman Egyptian regime was put under the aegis of the bayt al-mal. The Mahdi and then the Caliph Abdullah utilized this as a means of controlling commerical activity as much as possible, in something of a Mahdist command economy. Enormous amounts of gold, silver, livestock, and slaves, as well as munitions and arms, were handed over to the treasury and then redistributed as the Mahdi saw fit. As for taxes, the Mahdist government imposed them under the euphemism of *zakat*, or Islamic charitable contributions. The Sudanese Mahdiyah dedicated most of its revenues to the military, salaries, and pensions.

On the foreign policy front, before his death Muhammad Ahmad engaged in perhaps the first instance of Pan-Islamic activity. He tried to ally with both the Sokoto Caliphate of West Africa (now Nigeria) and with the Sanusiyah Sufi order in North-Central Africa (now Libya). Both attempts were rebuffed. In 1888–89 Abd Allah sent an army to invade Egypt, but it was thrown back by British and Egyptian troops. The Mahdi was gone, but the Mahdist state was still expansionist.

By the 1890s, however, European imperial designs in Africa could no longer tolerate the Mahdist state. In the last quarter of the nineteenth century the "Scramble for Africa" resulted in almost every square mile of the continent's territory coming under European rule—that is, what had not already in the preceding centuries. Eventually only Liberia, Ethiopia, and Sudan's Mahdiyah were left independent: the first because it had been founded by freed American slaves, the second because of European respect for its ancient allegiance to Christianity. In 1896 Britain, construing French and Italian encroachments into east and central Africa as potential threats to Her Majesty's Suez Canal and India access, sent a large army (18,000 Egyptians, 7,000 Brits) under General Horatio Herbert Kitchener (d. 1916)[120] into Sudan. The Mahdist army was totally defeated, most tellingly at the battle of Omdurman on September 1, 1898. The Caliph Abd Allah was killed not long after and Sudan was reincorporated into imperial rule, albeit British rather than Ottoman. Thus ended the most recent example in world history of Mahdism as a conquering and state-building movement, not merely an oppositional, revolutionary one.

Muhammad Ahmad's Sudanese Mahdism proved not only a huge influence on Sudan proper but, more important for the world at large, a case study in how Mahdist movements arise and can come to power. As such, it is the Mahdist movement par excellence for understanding that important mode of Islamic resistance. In Sudan Mahdism became the cornerstone of that country's nationalism, especially vis-à-vis Egypt. Eventually Mahdist ideology was sublimated into Sudan's Ummah Party, which for much of modern history constituted the opposition party in that country.[121]

With all due respect to the Sudanese people, however, the import of Mahdism is in how it compares to other Mahdist movements and in what it tells us about the form successful Mahdism might take. Obviously Muhammad Ahmad's Mahdism made it to stage 3 of the Blichfeldt paradigm. Geographically, this Mahdist revolt did flame up on the southeastern African periphery of the Islamic world and, politically, on the southernmost battlements of the far-flung Ottoman realms. Muhammad Ahmad himself bears an amazing resemblance to Ibn Tumart in a number of respects: ascetic, intolerant, prone to mystical trancelike states, fond of al-Ghazali, somber and lacking a sense of humour, convinced that he was the one to right the wrongs of society. Also like Ibn Tumart's Muwahhidism, his Mahdism first served as a means of excoriating, then later delegitimizing, an extant Muslim regime. Once in power as Mahdi, Muhammad Ahmad, as had Ibn Tumart and Sayyid Muhammad Jawnpuri, claimed the right to his own interpretations of Islamic law, unbound by previous, accepted legal precedent. Like all previous Mahdist claimants except Ibn Tumart, Muhammad Ahmad was a Sufi and used that to great advantage for his movement. Sudanese Mahdism was centennial in that it exploited the year 1300 of the Islamic calendar, which turned in 1882 CE; in this it resembled the previous Mahdisms of Jawnpuri and Sayyid Ahmad Barelwi. Like all Mahdist uprisings before it as well as after, that of Sudan was directed at a ruling regime that was deemed insufficiently Muslim in practice; like all except those of Ibn Tumart and Jawnpuri—which erupted before European world expansion began in 1492—Muhammad Ahmad's Mahdism was also anti-European and anti-Christian. It is important to note, too, that the most successful Mahdist movements, the ones that manage to take power, at least for some length of time, manifest a power-sharing arrangment in which a Mahdi creates the revolutionary fervor and fans the flames thereof, then hands off the reins of power to a chosen right-hand man as caliph: this was the case with Ibn Tumart and Abd al-Mu'min, as well as with Muhammad Ahmad and Abd Allah.

But the relevance of Sudan's successful Mahdist movement should not be pressed too far. Some of the conditions that allowed it to arise are no longer extant in much of the Muslim world today. For instance, although the rumors of Sufism's demise may have been greatly exaggerated, Sufism has nowhere near the mystical or institutional power today that it had in previous centuries. And Sufism was crucial to five of the eight Mahdist movements canvassed herein. Nonetheless, Muhammad Ahmad's Sudanese Mahdism was probably the closest history has come to a paradigmatic Mahdist movement.

THE SHORT-LIVED TURKISH MAHDISM OF MEHMET (D. 1930)

After World War I (1914–1918) the Sudanese Mahdi got his wish and the Ottoman Empire came crashing down, largely through the efforts of its erstwhile ally Britain, which along with France had imperial designs on Ottoman Arab territories. The Turkish Republic rose phoenixlike from the smoldering ashes of the empire, the Muslim world's first attempt, and to date the only relatively successful one, at a Western-style secular democracy. But less than a decade after the proclamation of the Turkish Republic on October 29, 1923,[122] the new state faced a Mahdist uprising. Influential in this movment was, no doubt, not only the abolition of the sultanate in 1922 but, more important, the obliteration of the caliphate in 1924[123]—both integral parts of Kemal Atatürk's plan to replace the Islamic state that was the empire with a secular Turkish republic modeled on Western lines.

In Manisa, in west-central Turkey, one Mehmet (the Turkish variant of the Arabic "Muhammad" and possibly not his real name) declared himself the Mahdi in 1930.[124] He may have been a Sufi, of the Naqshabandiyah order prominent in the Ottoman Empire and then Turkey. He and six followers who had been engaging in Sufi *zhikrs*, or group meditiative prayers, took the names of the "Seven Sleepers"—in the Qur'an,[125] seven Christian youths persecuted in the pre-Christian Roman Empire for refusing to participate in pagan religion and so went to sleep in a cave in western Anatolia, only to be protected by God and awaken several centuries later.[126] Mehmet is said to have announced to them his intention of overthrowing the Turkish government. From Manisa the small Mahdist troupe trekked to Menemen and arrived in that town on December 23. According to the records of the military tribunal set up afterward, Mehmet went to the town mosque and, after Friday prayers, proclaimed himself "Mahdi of the Messenger of God" and called for the reestablishment of Islamic law—presumably that of the Ottomans, officially abandoned by the Turkish nationalists. A military officer came to see what all the commotion was about and found a crowd of perhaps 1,000 led by a man who called himself the Mahdi. The local garrison sent troops, but the crowd fought them and its commmander was killed and decapitated, his head placed on a flag pole and paraded around the town. Reinforcements were called for and sent. President Mustafa Kemal Atatürk, the founder of Turkey, and Prime Minister Isma'il Pasha showed up because this religious threat to the legitimacy of the Turkish state was taken very seriously at the highest levels. The Turkish army put down the Menemenite Mahdists, and of those arrested 37 were eventually sentenced to death, presumably for treason.

Not much more is known about the course of this, one of only two examples of twentieth-century Mahdism in the central Islamic lands.[127] This Turkish Mahdist movement has been interpreted as the socioeconomic frustration of marginalized folks on the periphery—in this case, many probably descended from Cretan immigrants and were thus virtual second-class citizens—taking eschatological form insofar as they averred that not just the Mahdi but the Dajjal, in the person of Mustafa Kemal, was present.[128] The Turkish government responded with overwhelming, one might say disproportionate, force because the last sort of challenge the new, secular administration could countenance was a religious one.[129] This might not only erode the shaky legitimacy of the new government but spark calls for the resurrection of the Ottoman caliphate. Hence, any religious revivalism, and thus all the more so a Mahdist one, had to be terminated with extreme prejudice.

From the sparse information available on the momentary Mahdi Mehmet of Menemen, what conclusions can be drawn about that outbreak of Turkish Mahdism? Mehmet seems to have been a Sufi, who declared a jihad de facto if not de jure against an illegitimate, albeit non-Muslim, regime. Although he did not imitate the prophet Muhammad's hijrah openly, he and his followers did try to recapitulate Qur'anic symbolism through their assumption of the roles of the Seven Sleepers. Like Muhammad Ahmad, too, Mehmet's Mahdists seemed rather fond of decapitating opponents—a theme that has resurfaced here in the twenty-first century with Islamic militants beheading Americans like Daniel Pearl, Nicholas Berg, Paul Johnson, and Jack Hensley, as well as a number of Turks, Bulgarians, Brits, Egyptians, Koreans, and

Nepalese.[130] However, given that Turkey never saw another such open Mahdist challenge, the shock and awe employed by the Turks against this Mahdi and his followers must have proved effective.

JUHAYMAN AL-UTAYBI AND MUHMAMMAD AL-QAHTANI: MODERN ARAB MAHDISM

The most recent irruption of Mahdism took place in modern times. In 1979 in Saudi Arabia a militant dissident named Juhayman al-Utaybi led an ultimately failed attempt to overthrow the House of Sa`ud in the name of the Mahdi, whom he claimed was present in the person of his brother-in-law Muhammad b. Abd Allah al-Qahtani.[131] On 1 Muharram 1400 AH—November 20, 1970, CE—at dawn the imam in the great mosque of Mecca, Islam's holiest city, was shoved aside as al-Utaybi strode to the microphone and, backed up by hundreds of followers,[132] proclaimed over the public address system that al-Qahtani was the Mahdi and he would lead the destruction of the apostate Saudi regime.

Once the great mosque was secured for the Mahdists and after a dozen worshippers had been killed, a five-point agenda of demands was broadcast:

1. Sever relations with the West in order to protect Islamic values.
2. Expel all foreigners from Saudi Arabia.
3. Stop all oil exports to the West, particularly the United States.
4. Overthrow the illegitimate Saudi royal family's regime, including its apostate ulama.[133]
5. Redistribution of Saudi wealth.

Two primary elements seem to have characterized al-`Utaybi's movement. One was, of course, the religious. The Mahdists were trying to hoist the Saudi government by their own Wahhabist petard, savaging them for their hypocritical transgressions of the austere brand of Islam they themselves professed. The second element was more sociopolitical and has its origins in the tribal history of Saudi Arabia. The Utaybah tribe had at one time been the second most powerful tribe of the Arabian peninsula,[134] and like the others, it had been relegated to secondary status by the Saud tribe in the 1920s and 1930s. Thus this movement may have been an ideological Trojan Horse, transporting within its Mahdism more mundane complaints and resentments.[135]

Earlier in life al-Utaybi, born in 1936, had belonged to the Saudi National Guard, which despite its name was more akin to an interior paramilitary force than to the "weekend warriors" of American society. He attended the Islamic University in Medina and at some point began writing and disseminating letters criticizing the government and, supposedly, reiterating Islamic beliefs about the Mahdi. In this period he seems to have gained a core group of followers, many of whom would assist him in this 1979 revolt.

This Arabian Peninsular Mahdism managed to hold out in the mosque and environs for a little over two weeks, fending off several attempts by the government to snuff out their movement. Finally, on December 5, 1979, following intense fighting and suffering heavy losses, Saudi troops killed or captured al-Utaybi, al-Qahtani, and all their followers.[136] The failed Mahdi, al-Qahtani, was killed in the fighting. His mouthpiece, al-Utaybi, was captured alive and after a perfunctory trial beheaded along with 62 others on January 9, 1980, in a number of different Saudi cities, presumably to impress upon the populace the wages of such a religious and political sin as Mahdism. Two-thirds of those put to death were Saudis, and the next largest grouping Egyptian,[137] in what amounts to an eerie foreshadowing of the September 11, 2001, terrorists' national mixture. Thus ended the world's most recent Mahdist movement—a scant quarter-century ago.

After his death the writings of this Mahdist movement's leader and spokesman, al-Utaybi, were collected and published.[138] One of the letters is entitled *al-Fitan wa-Akhbar al-Mahdi wa-Nuzul `Isa (alayhi al-salam) wa-Ashrat al-Sa`ah*, that is, "The Clashes as well as the Accounts of the Mahdi, the Descent of Jesus and the Signs of the [Last] Hour." This section, despite its grandiloquent title, does not specify who the Mahdi is. Rather, it simply recapitulates many of the traditions about the coming of the Mahdi and the attendant signs (Jesus' return, the Dajjal, the status— broadly speaking—of the Muslims, etc.). Perhaps it was intended more as a means to legitimize the idea of the Mahdi among non-Arab Sunni Muslims[139] than to identify who the Mahdi might be. It merely pointed out that in al-Utaybi's eyes, the Muslim world was embroiled in the *fitnat al-dahimah*, the "clash of the masses," and that the Mahdi was thus nigh.[140]

The geopolitical context of the 1979 Mahdist movement is relevant. It was the dawn of the Islamic year 1400, so expectations of at least a mujaddid were high. Closer to home, the Shah of Iran had just been replaced earlier the same year by a religious regime headed by the Ayatollah Ruhollah Khomeini. From a Sunni point of view, and all the more a Wahhabi Sunni one, the Shi`is of Iran had the wrong view of the Mahdi, but some of the shi`is of eastern Saudi Arabia had wondered whether Khomeini might be the un-Hidden Imam. Also, eastern Saudi Arabia, on the Persian Gulf between Kuwait and Qatar, the main oil-producing region, has a sizable Shi`i minority that has sometimes clashed with the Saudi rulers.[141] In fact, several weeks before the al-Utaybi uprising there had been riots in the Kingdom's Eastern Province and the Kingdom's officials tried to link the clashes with Iranian instigation.[142] In fact, al-Utaybi seems to have expressed at least some measure of sympathy with the repressed Saudi

Shi`is, which no doubt caused the government to detest him more, if that were possible.

How does the al-Utaybi and al-Qahtani Mahdism stack up against previous examples? Since little is known of the lives of either progenitor, analysis is primarily limited to the movement itself. Jihad was, of course, an intrinsic part, and one directed against an illicit Islamic establishment. Al-Utaybi made social justice a plank of his Mahdi's platform by calling for the redistribution of Saudi oil wealth. Unlike some previous Mahdist movements, this one was at least somewhat sympathetic to the Shi`a, if only in an attempt to garner more political support. The Arabian Mahdists were centennial, capitalizing on the turnover of the fifteenth Islamic century. And the paradigm of a Mahdi being assisted—in this case, in fact, overshadowed—by his able second-in-command is present as well. The 1979 movement in Saudi Arabia thus reached the second stage of Mahdism with its fleeting occupation of the sacred mosque of Mecca, but it was forcefully and rhetorically prevented from metastasizing into the third stage of actually taking power.

CONCLUSION

A number of conclusions can be drawn from this admittedly rather lengthy survey of eight prominent Sunni Mahdist movements over the last millennium. First, and most obvious, they serve as proof that non-Shi`i Mahdism is alive and well and an ever-present threat in the Muslim world. The outbreaks of these movements spanned almost the entire geographical length of the African and Asian landmasses, from the Atlantic coast of Morocco to the Bay of Bengal.[143] Most were peripheral, if not in actual geographic origins, then in terms of their sociocultural or sociopolitical genesis (Mehmet, al-Utaybi). The four characteristics in common among almost all of these historical irruptions of Mahdism were a declared jihad, some degree of Sufi adherence, and grievances against an extant Muslim government and its European Christian allies. Mahdism with its holy wars directed against allegedly illegitimate Islamic regimes and against Western imperialists seems at first glance to have much in common with modern Islamic fundamentalism. Yet Muslim fundamentalism, while necessary, is ultimately insufficient to explain Mahdism as a compelling force—a topic to fully explored in this work's conclusion. Finally, the examples of these historical Mahdist movements, all of which predate the modern period of American unrivaled global supremacy, should help lay to rest the assertion by some Bush administration critics today that "apocalyptic holy warriors come into being primarily because of specific American actions."[144] "Apocalyptic" holy wars were around long before George Bush or, for that matter, any Western king, prime minister, or president sent troops into the Middle East. Mahdi movements and their religion-based insurrections often—indeed, usually—have more to do with the internal dynamics of the Islamic world than with Western foreign policy.

NOTES

1. For background see John J. Donohue, *The Buwayhid Dynasty in Iraq: 334 H./945 to 403 H./1012. Shaping Institutions for the Future* (Leiden: Brill, 2003), especially chapter 6, "The Caliphate" (pp. 262–87) and chapter 7, "Religio-Political Institutions" (pp. 288–314). The Buwayhids seem to have been politically Shi`i, but religiously they retained the Abbasid Sunni caliphs.

2. See Roger Savory, *Iran under the Safavids* (Cambridge: Cambridge University Press, 1980).

3. General sources on the Fatimids include M. Canard, "Fatimids," *EI2*; Hugh Kennedy, *The Prophet and the Age of the Caliphates: The Islamic Near East from the Sixth to the Eleventh Century* (London: Longman, 1986), especially pp. 309–45; Farhad Daftary, *The Isma'ilis: Their History and Doctrines* (Cambridge: Cambridge University Press, 1990); Yaacov Lev, *State and Society in Fatimid Egypt* (New York: E.J. Brill, 1991); and Heinz Halm, *The Empire of the Mahdi: The Rise of the Fatimids* (Leiden: Brill 1996).

4. Defined by *Merriam-Webster's Dictionary* (tenth edition) as "the thought and practice esp. of various cults of late pre-Christian and early Christian centuries distinguished by the conviction that matter is evil and that emancipation comes through gnosis." *Gnosis* is the Greek word for "knowledge."

5. Again, according to *Merriam-Webster's*, "Platonism modified . . . to accord with Aristotelian . . . and oriental conceptions that conceives of the world as an emanation from an ultimate indivisible being with whom the soul is capable of being reunited in trance or ecstasy."

6. General sources on Ibn Tumart and his movement include J.F.P. Hopkins, "Ibn Tumart," *EI2*; Roger LeTourneau, *The Almohad Movement in North Africa in the Twelfth and Thirteenth Centuries* (Princeton, NJ: Princeton University Press, 1969); Abdallah Laroui, "Sur le Mahdisme d'Ibn Tumart" in Abdelmajid Kaddouri, ed., *Mahdisme: Crise et Changement dan l'Histoire du Maroc. Actes de lat table ronde organisee a Marrakech par la Faculte des Lettres et des Sciences Humaines de Rabat du 11 au 14 Fevrier 1993* (Rabat: Royaume du Maroc Universite Mohammed V, 1994), pp. 9–13; Mohamed Zniber, "L'Itineraire Psycho-Intellectuel d'Ibn Toumert," in Kaddouri, pp. 15–29; Jamil M. Abun-Nasr, *A History of the Maghrib in the Islamic Period* (Cambridge: Cambridge University Press, 1987), especially pp. 77–101; M. Shatzmiller, "al-Muwahhidun," *EI2*; H.T. Norris, *The Berbers in Arabic Literature* (London and New York: Longman, 1982), especially "Ibn Tumart: The Mahdi of the Moroccan Masmuda," pp. 157–83; Richard Fletcher, *Moorish Spain* (Berkeley: University of California Press, 1992), especially chapter 6, "The Moroccan Fundamentalist," pp. 105ff; Abdallah Laroui, *The History of the Maghrib: An Interpretive Essay* (Princeton: Princeton University Press, 1977), translated by Ralph Mannheim; `Ali Muhammad al-Sallabi, *Dawlat al-Muwahhidin* (Amman, Jordan: Dar al-Biyaraq, 1998); Ahmad `Azawi, *Risa'il Muwahhidiyah* (Qunaytra: Ibn Tufayl University, 1995).

7. The Arabic definite article *al* should not strictly speaking, be used in tandem with the English *the*. However, it sounds less awkward to do so.

8. The Arabic root is *wahada*, "to be alone, unique, singular." *Wahhada* means "to declare God to be one"; that is, to be an uncompromising monotheist. See Hans Wehr, *A Dictionary of Modern Written Arabic*, s.v. *"wahada."*

9. Norris, pl. 159.

10. See Mustansir Mir, "Abu Hamid al-Ghazali," *OE*.

11. Cook, *Studies in Muslim Apocalyptic*, pp. 312–13.

12. For example, Surah II [al-Baqarah]:255, in which Allah has a literal throne or III [`Imran]:26, in which the divinity has a hand.

13. Ibn Tumart was what was then called a *muhtasib*, or "one who keeps accounts with God," according to Norris, p. 160. Compare this to the modern morals police in Saudi Arabia.

14. Ibid., p. 165.

15. See Norris, Hopkins, and LeTourneau. The official Murabit "school" of Islamic law was that of the Malikis. This is in many ways a more conservative interpretive school than the other three: the Hanafis, Hanbalis, and Shafi`is.

16. Laroui, "Sure le Mahdisme d'Ibn Tumart," p. 12.

17. The terminology employed for these different levels of the Muwahhid hierarchy varies. See Hopkins and Shatzmiller.

18. On this individual, who was perhaps as important as Ibn Tumart in creating the Muwahhid Mahdist state, see E. Levi-Provencal, "`Abd al-Mu'min," *EI2*; Abun-Nasr; Shatzmiller.

19. See Hopkins and Zniber, especially.

20. Laroui, *The History of the Maghrib*, p. 177.

21. Norris, p. 169.

22. Ibid., pp. 168–69.

23. This was a sixteenth-century Reformed Protestant attempt at establishing a community in which personal conduct and morals were publicly enforced. See Williston Walker et al., *A History of the Christian Church* (New York: Charles Scribners' Sons, 1985), pp. 477–79.

24. See Nevill Barbour, "La Guerra Psicológica de los Almohades contra Las Almoravides," *Boletín de la Asociación Española de Orientalista*, vol. 2 (1996), pp. 117–30.

25. Norris, pp. 172–73.

26. The Arabic root is *talaba*, which means a myriad of things, including "to study, seek, call for, entreat, demand." It is the source of the term *Taliban*, the former rulers of Afghantistan. Journalists used to translate their name literally as "students," which was quite ridiculous. Laroui, *The History of the Maghrib*, p. 179, renders it as *talabah*, "ideologist," but I think that too divorced from the word's root.

27. See Esmond Wright, *The American Dream: From Reconstruction to Reagan*, vol. 3 (Cambridge, MA: Blackwell, 1996), pp. 186–87.

28. Abun-Nasr, pp. 94ff.

29. On the importance of this title see Bernard Lewis, *The Political Language of Islam* (Chicago: University of Chicago Press, 1988), pp. 50–51.

30. LeTourneau, *The Almohad Movement*, pp. 49ff.

31. Shatzmiller.

32. Ibid., p. 60, and Laroui, *History of the Maghrib*, p. 182.

33. See Laroui, *History of the Maghrib*, pp. 185ff; LeTourneau, pp. 77ff; Abun-Nasr, pp. 97ff.

34. Fletcher, chapter 6, "The Moroccan Fundamentalist," especially pp. 125ff.

35. See Laroui, *The History of the Maghrib*, pp. 159–60.

36. For the evolution of *tawhid* as an ideological weapon, see Tamara Sonn, "Tawhid," *The Oxford Encyclopedia of the Modern Islamic World*.

37. Ibid., pp. 191–92.

38. As a world history teacher I encounter this idea often. Perhaps the best example of it is in the video series *The Crusades* (A&E/History Channel, 1995), wherein Terry Jones, the former Monty Python member, repeatedly mentions the tolerance and open-mindedness of medieval Islam and contrasts it unfavorably with the alleged close-mindedness and fanaticism of medieval Christian Europe.

39. Christianity is the largest, with 2 billion adherents, Islam second with 1.2 billion, and Hinduism third with 800 million (and, for the sake of completeness, Buddhism is fourth with about 350 million).

40. Ira Lapidus, *A History of Islamic Societies* (Cambridge: Cambridge University Press, 1988), pp. 452ff; Marshall G.S. Hodgson, *The Venture of Islam: Conscience and History in a World Civilization. Volume 3: The Gunpowder Empires and Modern Times* (Chicago: University of Chicago Press, 1974), pp. 59ff.

41. Lapidus, pp. 438ff. Some data indicate that the Gujarat state actually began a bit earlier (1396) and lasted a bit longer, however (1583): see the list of Gujarat sultans according to coin minting, available at www.215.pair.com/sacoins/public_html/gujarat/gujarat_main.htm.

42. Sources on this man and his movement are sparse. The best, albeit brief—and the one upon which this section primarily relies—is Derryl N. MacLean, "La sociologie de l'engagement politique: Le Mahdawiya indien et l'Etat," in Mercedes Garcia-Arenal, ed., *Mahdisme et millenarisme en Islam. Revue de mondes Musulmans et de la Medieterranee* (Aix-en-Provence: Edisud, 2000), pp. 239–56. Lapidus also has a brief section, pp. 449–50, as does Hodgson, vol. 3, pp. 70–80.

43. Sufi *turuq* or *tariqat*, "orders," (singular *tariqah*), rather like Roman Catholic ones, are usually named after their founder. Sufism is dedicated to a direct experience of God, with different orders emphasizing different aspects of Islam (prayer, devotion to Islamic law, and metaphysical enlightenment, for example) as a means of doing so. The literature on Sufism is vast, but for some general background see Lapidus, pp. 254ff; Hodsgon, vol. 3, pp. 201ff; Julian Baldick, *Mystical Islam: An Introduction to Sufism* (New York: New York University Press, 1989); Anne Marie Schimmel, *The Mystical Dimensions of Islam* (Chapel Hill: University of North Carolina Press, 1975).

44. As explained in chapter 1, millennial expectations are a Christian, not a Muslim, characteristic. Thus, it is interesting that MacLean describes Jawnpuri, p. 241, as telling his followers to prepare for the imminent millennium. This may simply be a reference to his having come as Mahdi, rather than to the approaching year 1000 of the Muslim calendar, and MacLean may be using the adjective "millenial" to describe this state of affairs (erroneously, as I pointed out in chapter 1).

45. Lapidus, p. 450.

46. Hodgson, vol. 3, pp. 70–71.

47. Lapidus, p. 449.

48. Maclean, p. 245.

49. Ibid., pp. 241ff.

50. Ibid., pp. 246–50.

51. Ibid., pp. 250–52.

52. Jan Olaf-Blichfeldt, *Early Mahdism, Politics and Religion in the Formative Period of Islam* (Leiden: E.J. Brill, 1985).

53. This is the view of Abdelmajid Kaddouri, "Ibn Abi Mahalli: A Propos de L'Itineraire Psycho-Social d'Un Mahdi," in Kaddouri, ed., *Crise et Changement dans l'Histoire du Maroc*, pp. 119–25. Other sources on this movement include Mercedes Garcia-Arenal, "Imam et Mahdi: Ibn Abi Mahallah," in Garcia-Arenal, ed., *Mahdisem et Millenarisme en Islam*, pp. 157–79; Abun-Nasr, chapter 5, "Morocco Consolidates Her National Identity, 1510–1822," especially pp. 206–19, "The Sa`diyans, 1510–1603"; and Chantal de La Veronne, "Sa`dids," *EI2 Extract*, p. 4.

54. On this state see De La Veronne; Abun-Nasr, chapter 5; Lapidus, pp. 403–5.

55. De La Veronne, p. 1.

56 .Whether these Mahdists actually conquered Marrakesh seems unclear. De La Veronne says that Abu Mahallah's forces "succeeded in entering Marrakush" (p. 4), but Abun-Nasr has it that the Mahdists "succeeded in taking Marrakish from Zaydan" (p. 220). Garcia-Arenal simply says that Abu Mahallah took power for three years in Sijilmasa only. The term and location of his actual Mahdist reign seems about as clear as the proper transliteration of Marrakesh.

57. Garcia-Arenal, pp. 166ff.

58. Kaddouri, "Ibn Abi Mahallah," pp. 119–20.

59. Ibid., pp. 163ff.

60. Ibid., p. 161.

61. Kaddouri, "Ibn Abi Mahalli," p. 121.

62. The primary source here is Marc Garborieau, "Le mahdi oublie de l'Indie britannique: Sayyid Ahmad Barelwi (1786–1831)," in Garcia-Arenal, ed., *Mahdisme et millenarisme en Islam*, pp. 257–73; Lapidus at least mentions him and his movement, p. 721.

63. Lapidus, p. 721.

64. Sikhism has about 19 million members worldwide today. It began in the fifteenth century CE when a Punjabi named Nanak (d. 1539?) began trying to assimilate some aspects of Hinduism to Islam. For that reason it is considered a virtual Islamic heresy by fundamentalist Muslims. *Time Almanac, 2003*, pp. 431, 436.

65. This is what Garborieau says, p. 259. Lapidus, p. 721, says he was killed. On this issue, I put more stock in Garborieau because he is an expert on Indian Islam.

66. Garborieau, pp. 267ff.

67. Ibid., pp. 266ff.

68. Ibid., pp. 263, 267.

69. Sources on Wahhabism include George S. Rentz, "Muhammad ibn Abd al-Wahhab and the Beginnings of Unitarian Empire in Arabia" (Ph.D. dissertation, University of California–Berkeley, 1948); Arvind Sharma, "The Wahhabi and Sufi Approaches to the Qur'an in Relation to the Modern World," *Bulletin of Christian Institutes of Islamic Studies* 5, no. 3–4 (July–Dec. 1982), pp. 62–65; Elizabeth Sirriyeh, "Wahhabis, Unbelievers and the Problems of Exclusivism," *Bulletin of the British Society for Middle Eastern Studies* 16, no. 2 (1989), pp. 123–32; John O. Voll, "Wahhabism and Mahdism: Alternative Styles of Islamic Renewals," *Arab Studies Quarterly* 4,

no. 1–2 (1982), pp. 110–26; M.S. Zaharaddin, "Wahhabism and Its Influence out-side Arabia," *Islamic Quarterly* 23 (1979), pp. 146–57.

70. Sources here include Julia Clancy-Smith, "La revolte de Bu Ziyan en Algerie, 1849," in *Mahdisme et millenarisme en Islam*, pp. 181–208; Peter Von Sivers, "The Realm of Justice: Apocalyptic Revolts in Algeria (1849–1879)," in *Humaniora Islamica* 1 (1973), pp. 47–60; Lapidus, pp. 682–83.

71. See Abun-Nasr, pp. 253ff.

72. Sivers, p. 52.

73. North African Arabic dialects are quite different from their Middle Eastern counterparts, being heavily influenced by the Berber language. In this section the transliteration from the Algerian Arabic for the proper names will be provided first.

74. Von Sivers, pp. 50–52; Clancy-Smith.

75. Clancy-Smith says he claimed Mahdihood; Von Sivers says he did not.

76. Von Sivers, pp. 52–54.

77. Ibid., pp. 54–57.

78. Ibid., pp. 57–59.

79. Ibid., p. 49.

80. Lapidus, p. 682.

81. Sources on the Sudanese Mahdiyah and Muhammad Ahmad are numerous, but some of the most important general ones are Muhammad Sa`id al-Qaddal, *al-Imam al-Mahdi: Muhammad Ahmad ibn `Abd Allah, 1844–1885* (Beirut: Dar al-Jil, 1992), upon which this chapter draws heavily; P.M. Holt and M.W. Daly, *The History of the Sudan from the Coming of Islam to the Present Day* (London: Weidenfeld and Nicholson, 1979); P.M. Holt, *The Mahdist State in the Sudan, 1881–1898* (London: Oxford University Press, 1970) and "Al-Mahdiyya," *EI2*; Richard Hill, *Egypt in the Sudan, 1820–1881* (London: Oxford University Press, 1959); Gabriel Warburg, *Historical Discord in the Nile Valley* (Evanston, IL: Northwestern University Press, 1992) and *Egypt and the Sudan: Studies in History and Politics* (London: Frank Cass, 1985); Richard Dekmejian and Margaret Wyszomirski, "Charismatic Leadership in Islam: The Mahdi of the Sudan," *Comparative Studies in Society and History* 14, no. 2 (March 1972), pp. 193–214; John Voll, "The Sudanese Mahdi: Frontier Fundamentalist," *International Journal of Middle East Studies* 10 (1979), pp. 145–66. The Sudanese Mahdi's writings have been collected and edited in seven volumes by Muhammad Ibrahim Abu Salim, *Al-Athar al-Kamilah lil-Imam al-Mahdi* (Khartoum: Dar Jami`at al-Khartum lil-Nashr, 1990).

82. The best biographical information on him is found in al-Qaddal and in Holt, *The Mahdist State*.

83. Ottoman Turkish contained a number of loan words from Persian, such as the one whence *khedive* came: *khidiw*, "lord" or "monarch." Under Muhammad Ali it replaced the Ottoman *misir beylerbeyi*, "governor-general of Egypt." See Hill, p. 116, note 2.

84. Primarily the members of the former Ottoman administration in Egypt, the Mamluks, who had fled south up the Nile after Napoleon's conquest of Egypt in 1798.

85. See Afaf Lutfi al-Sayyid Marsot, *Egypt in the Reign of Muhammad Ali* (Cambridge: Cambridge Univerity Press, 1984), especially pp. 196–264.

86. On this process in the 1840s but especially later in the century, see F.A.K. Yasamee, "The Ottoman Empire, the Sudan and the Red Sea Coast, 1883–1889,"

in Selim Deringil and Sinan Kuneralp, eds., *Studies on Ottoman Diplomatic History*, vol. 5 (Istanbul: Isis Press, 1990), pp. 87–102.

87. This was a dilatory aspect of the famous Ottoman *tanzimat* reforms, begun in 1839, which were aimed at modernizing the empire. See M.E. Yapp, *The Making of the Modern Near East, 1792–1923* (London and New York: Longman, 1987), pp. 108–14; F. Robert Hunter, *Egypt under the Khedives, 1805–1879: From Household Government to Modern Bureaucracy* (Pittsburgh: University of Pittsburgh Press, 1984).

88. On slavery and the slave trade in the Ottoman Empire see Ehud Toledano, *The Ottoman Slave Trade and Its Suppression: 1840–1890* (Princeton, NJ: Princeton University Press, 1982) and *Slavery and Abolition in the Ottoman Middle East* (Seattle: University of Washington Press, 1998); Y. Hakan Erdem, *Slavery in the Ottoman Empire and Its Demise, 1800–1909* (New York: St. Martin's Press, 1996); Reda Mowafi, *Slavery, Slave Trade and Abolition Attempts in Egypt and the Sudan, 1820–1882* (Malmo: Scandinavian University Press, 1981).

89. See Richard Hill, *A Biographical Dictionary of the Sudan* (London: Frank Cass & Co., 1951); John H. Waller, *Gordon of Khartoum: The Saga of a Victorian Hero* (New York: Athenaeum, 1988); Holt, *The Mahdist State*.

90. Pierre Crabites, *Americans in the Egyptian Army* (London: George Routledge & Sons, 1938).

91. See Yapp, pp. 221–28; Robert T. Harrison, *Gladstone's Imperialism in Egypt: Techniques of Domination* (Westport, CT: Greenwood Press, 1995), especially chapter 3, "Egypt before the Invasion," pp. 31–66.

92. The best source on this topic, and one used extensively in the next chapter, is Abd Allah Ali Ibrahim, *Al-Sira` bayna al-Mahdi wa-al-`Ulama'* (Khartoum: Dar Nubar, 1994 [1966]).

93. For a study of all the mystical orders in Sudan, see Ali Salih Karrar, *The Sufi Brotherhoods in the Sudan* (Evanston, IL: Northwestern University Press, 1992); and for a look at them in the total context of African Islam, see B.G. Martin, *Muslim Brotherhoods in Nineteenth-century Africa* (Cambridge: Cambridge University Press, 1976).

94. The bulk of this biographical information, not surprisingly, comes from al-Qaddal.

95. *Khalwah* in most Islamic contexts refers to Sufi "retreat" but in nineteenth-century Sudan it also meant a religious school. See Holt, *The Mahdist State*, pp. 18ff.

96. Al-Qaddal, p. 45.

97. Richard Hill, s.v. "Muhammad al-Khayyir Abd Allah Khujali."

98. *Bint* means "daughter of."

99. The White Nile and the Blue Nile are the two rivers that flow north out of East-Central Africa to meet at Khartoum and form the Nile proper before it flows on to Egypt. Aba Island in the White Nile is thus southwest of Khartoum.

100. R. Sean O'Fahey, "Sufism in Suspense," in DeJong and Radtke, eds., *Islamic Mysticism Contested*, pp. 267–82.

101. Surah al-Qar`iah [101]:3.

102. See Holt, *The Mahdist State*, p. 53: "The incident with al-Zubayr had shown that `Abdullahi was seeking a Sudanese Mahdi." Also Hill, pp. 390–91.

103. M. Canard, "Da`wa," *EI2*.

104. One is reminded of Jesus' "mother and brothers and sisters" coming to find him and take him home at the onset of hic public ministry (Matthew 12:46ff; Mark 3:33) and John 7:5: "For even his own brothers did not believe in him."

105. Surah al-Nisa' [4]:59.

106. This is "minister" in the European governmental official sense, not in the normal American understanding of "Protestant religious figure." The Arabic term is *wazir*.

107. See Martin, pp. 33ff; Batran, infra.

108. Holt, *The Mahdist State*, p. 54.

109. Yasamee, pp. 90–91.

110. See Joshua Teitelbaum, *The Rise and Fall of the Hashemite Kingdom of Arabia* (New York: New York University Press, 2001), especially chapter 2, "The Social and Political Legacy of Ottoman Rule in the Hijaz, 1840–1916."

111. See Yapp, *The Making of the Modern Near East, 1792–1923*, pp. 173ff; and John Sabini, *Armies in the Sand: The Struggle for Mecca and Medina* (London: Thames and Hudson, 1981).

112. Yasamee, pp. 91–92.

113. It may have been that Gordon's well-known reputation for Christian piety led the Mahdi to treat the general with such solicitude.

114. On this topic see Holt, *The Mahdist State* and *EI2*; Holt and Daly, *A History of the Sudan*; al-Qaddal; and Aharon Layish, "The Mahdi's Legal Methodology as a Mechanism for Adapting the Shari`a in the Sudan to Political and Social Purposes," in Garcia-Arenal, ed., *Mahdisme et millenarisme en Islam*, pp. 221–37.

115. See Lewis, *The Political Language of Islam*, pp. 35, 48ff; D. Sourdel, A.K.S. Lambton, F. DeJong, P.M. Holt, "Khalifa," *EI2*; Selim Deringil, *The Well-Protected Domains: Ideology and the Legitimation of Power in the Ottoman Empire, 1879–1909* (London: I.B. Tauris, 1998).

116. See O'Fahey, "Sufism in Suspense," in DeJong and Radtke, eds., *Islamic Mysticism Contested*, pp. 267–82.

117. Layish, pp. 223–24.

118. Ibid., pp. 232ff.

119. Surah al-Nisa' [4]:11ff. Layish, pp. 232, 235–37.

120. See Philip Warner, *Kitchener: The Man behind the Legend* (London: Hamish Hamilton, 1985), as well as Hill's relevant entry.

121. On Mahdism's influence after 1898 see Warburg, *Historical Discord*, pp. 42–61 and 186–91; O'Fahey, "Sufism in Suspense," pp. 277ff; M.W. Daly, *Empire on the Nile: The Anglo-Egyptian Sudan, 1898–1934* (Cambridge: Cambridge University Press, 1986); Heather Sharkey-Balasubramanian, "The Egyptian Colonial Presence in the Anglo-Egyptian Sudan, 1898–1932," in Jay Spaulding and Stephanie Beswick, eds. *White Nile, Black Blood: War, Leadership and Ethnicity from Khartoum to Kampala* (Lawrenceville, NJ: Red Sea Press, 2000), pp. 279–314; and Muddathir `Abdel Rahman, *Imperialism & Nationalism in the Sudan: A Study in Constitutional and Political Development, 1899–1956* (London: Oxford University Press, 1969).

122. See M.E. Yapp, *The Near East since the First World War* (London: Longman, 1991), pp. 147ff; and for background on the transition from Ottoman Empire to Turkish Republic, see his *The Making of the Modern Near East, 1792–1923* (London: Longman, 1987), pp. 301ff.

123. Yapp, *The Near East since the First World War*, p. 157; as well as "Caliphate," available at http://www.almanach.be/search/i/caliph.htm; and in greater detail, Bernard Lewis, *The Emergence of Modern Turkey* (London: Oxford University Press, 1968 [second edition]), especially chapters 8, "The Kemalist Republic" (pp. 239–93) and 11, "State and Government" (pp. 362–400).

124. Hamit Bozarslan, "Le mahdisme en Turquie: L' incident de Menemen' en 1930," in Garcia-Arenal, *Mahdisme et millenarisme en Islam*, pp. 237–319; Ayse Kadioglu, "The Paradox of Turkish Nationalism and the Construction of Official Identity," *Middle Eastern Studies*, 32, 2 (April 1996), pp. 177–93. See also Lewis, *The Emergence of Modern Turkey*, pp. 266–68, 416–17.

125. Surah al-Kahf [18]. See the explanatory note 2337 by Abdullah Yusuf Ali in his *The Meaning of the Glorious Qur'an* (Cairo: Dar al-Kitab al-Masri, 1934), pp. 730ff, as well as R. Paret, "Ashab al-Kahf," *EI2*.

126. It in interesting that the Qur'an holds up these Christians as examples of unyielding monotheism. Perhaps there is a lesson here for modern Muslim fundamentalists (as well as, for that matter, Christian ones).

127. Strictly speaking, only Arab areas like Arabia, Egypt, and Syria are "core" Muslim territories, but Anatolia (modern Turkey) had been Islamic for so many centuries that it certainly can be deemed closer to core status than peripheries such as Sudan or India.

128. Bozarslan, p. 305.

129. Ibid., pp. 305ff.

130. The genesis of decapitation in Islamic militant thought requires its own dissertation, but it is noteworthy that the practice is validated—and, indeed, recommended—in the Qur'an: Surah Muhammad [XLVII]:4ff. See my article "Sticking Your Neck Out for Islam: Decapitation in the Islamic World," *Middle East Quarterly*, 12, 2 (spring 2005), pp.

131. Sources on this movement include Rif'at Sayyid Ahmad, *Rasa'il Juhayman al-ʿUtaybi, Qa'id al-Muqtahmin lil-Masjid al-Haram bi-Makkah* (Cairo: Matbaʿah Atlas, 1988); Joseph A. Kechichian, "Islamic Revivalism and Change in Saʿudi Arabia: Juhayman al-ʿUtaybi's 'Letters to the Saʿudi People,'" *The Muslim World* 80, no. 1 (January 1990), pp. 1–17; Nazih N. Ayubi, *Political Islam: Religion and Politics in the Arab World* (London: Routledge, 1991), especially pp. 99–104, "The Islamic Movement in Saʿudi Arabia"; ʿAbd al-Azim Ibrahim Matʿani, *Jarimat al-Asr: Qissah Ihtilal al-Masjid al-Haram. Ruwayah Shahid ʿAyan* (Cairo: Dar al-Ansar, 1980); R.B. Winder, "Makka" [Subsection on "Seizure of the Haram"], *EI2*; H. Kindermann and C.E. Bosworth, "ʿUtayba," *EI2*; Ayman al-Yassini, *Religion and State in the Kingdom of Saudi Arabia* (Boulder, CO: Westview Press, 1985), especially pp. 124ff.

132. The exact numbers of Mahdists—as well as other important facets of this episode—are in dispute. Kechichian and Winder maintain the number was in the several hundreds, Ahmad puts it closer to 500, and Ayubi says there may have been 2,000 of them.

133. Kechichian, pl. 12.

134. Kindermann/Bosworth, "ʿUtayba," *EI2*.

135. See Ayubi and Kechichian.

136. There are conflicting accounts about who rendered military assistance to the Saudis. Kechichian in his article says it was the French Groupe d'Intervention de la Gendarmerie. Professor R.S. O'Fahey of the University of Bergen has informed me that according to his contacts in the British government, it was the British SAS (Special Air Services, their equivalent of American Special Forces). Quite interestingly, Kechichian also states that French forces used "nerve gas" against the Mahdists (p. 7).

137. Winder, "Makka," *EI2*.

138. Ahmad, *Rasa'il Juhayman al-`Utaybi*.

139. Kechichian, p. 15.

140. Ahmad, p. 18.

141. See Graham E. Fuller and Rend Rahim Francke, *The Arab Shi`a. The Forgotten Muslims* (London: MacMillan Press, 1999), pp. 180ff.

142. Marvin Zonis and Daniel Brumberg, *Khomeini, The Islamic Republic of Iran, and the Arab World*, Harvard Middle Eastern Papers Modern Series, no. 5 (Cambridge, MA: Harvard University Press, 1987), pp. 50–54.

143. A particularly fruitful field of study would be Islam in Indonesia (the world's most populous Muslim country) and Southeast Asia in general and the degree to which Mahdism has occurred there. Very few have the linguistic and historical training for such an endeavor, however.

144. Reuel Marc Gerecht, "Not a Diversion: The war in Iraq had advanced the campaign against bin Ladenism," *The Weekly Standard*, April 12/April 19, 2004.

CHAPTER 3

Counter-Mahdist Rationales and Policies

INTRODUCTION

Despite its frequency and power throughout Islamic history, Mahdism is not accepted by all Muslims. Opposition to the idea of the Mahdi has often taken the form of polemical works denigrating its true believers. Foremost among such propagandists in Islamic history was Ibn Khaldun, the great Muslim historian in the late fourteenth century, early fifteenth century CE. But obviously antagonism toward Mahdism has not always been limited merely to religious rhetoric. Any Muslim establishment bearing the brunt of Mahdist ire would have had to respond on several fronts: ideological, religious, rhetorical, political, and of course military. This is what the Murabit Empire, Gujarat sultanate, Sa`diyan state, Ottoman Empire, Turkish Republic, and Saudi Kingdom did to varying degrees. (The anti-Mahdist programs of the French in Algeria and the British in India and Sudan were a bit different, however, in good imperialist fashion relying more on the military dimension and less on ideological ripostes.) However, most modern Muslim confutations of Mahdism have contained as a key part of their agenda some aspects of the anti-Mahdist rationale spelled out by Ibn Khaldun six centuries ago. When Mahdism appears again, Ibn Khaldun will probably also be in the ammo train of those attacking it.

IBN KHALDUN ON THE MAHDI

Ibn Khaldun[1] was born in what is now Tunisia in 1332 CE and died in Cairo, probably in 1406. After a classical Muslim education in North Africa and al-Andalus, which essentially amounted to cross-training in Islamic jurisprudence and philosophy, he held a number of administrative posts in the post-Muwahhid states. Following his hajj in 1382, however, Ibn Khaldun took a job in Egypt, when the Mamluk rulers appointed him a qadi and teacher. By 1389 he rose to become head of the most important Sufi monastic institution in Egypt.[2] In his writings, especially his *Muqaddimah* or "Introduction" to history, Ibn Khaldun sought to identify patterns and cycles in world history and subject them to critical analysis. In this he was far ahead of his time and is sometimes considered to be the first modern historian, and not just of the Arab or Muslim world. He was "the greatest historical thinker of the time, and perhaps the greatest mind in any field."[3] As such, Ibn Khaldun's negative assessment of Mahdis and Mahdism is an invaluable weapon in any anti-Mahdist's armory.

Ibn Khaldun had two self-styled Mahdist movements to look back upon: the Fatimids and the Muwahhids. Also, as he was ruminating on the ebb and flow of history from his fourteenth-century CE perspective, Ibn Khaldun would have been quite aware of the military and political vise that the Muslim world had been caught in just before his time: the Mongols hammering from the East, conquering all the way to the borders of Egypt; the Christians of the Iberian Peninsula setting up the anvil of the Reconquista, which would by 1492 eliminate Muslim rule there; and in between more European Christians plunging the tongs of the Crusades into the Muslim heartland of Palestine and Syria. Ibn Khaldun chalked such Muslim defeats to the loss of *asabiyah*, or "group solidarity," by Islamic dynasties. But other Muslims would blame their own societies and leaders for failing to live up to the true religion and so would take refuge in the idea of the Mahdi who would set religious matters aright and go on to conquer the impudent pagans and Christians.

History having proved that the Muwahhid Mahdi, Ibn Tumart, was in reality an impostor, by Ibn Khaldun's time shrines thought to be potential materialization points for the real Mahdi were maintained throughout the Maghrib.[4] So, Ibn Khaldun would have been well acquainted with extant Mahdist expectations through several venues: the populist shrines; of course the intellectual traditions of the Mahdi; and probably Sufi predictions about, and yearnings for, the Mahdi. Although there is no clear proof that Ibn Khaldun was himself heavily involved in any Sufi orders, strong circumstantial evidence suggests that he was at least on the fringes thereof. It seems unlikely that a non-Sufi, or at least a non-Sufi opposed to mysticism, would have been appointed to the leadership of Egypt's most prestigious *khanaqah*, or Sufi "lodge," by Sultan al-Malik Zahir al-Barquq (r. 1382–1399), the same ruler who also made Ibn Khaldun Grand Qadi of the Maliki school of law in Egypt.[5] Furthermore, upon his death Ibn Khaldun was buried in the Sufi cemetery outside Cairo. Even if he were not an active member of a Sufi order, Ibn Khaldun was very likely intellectually and experientially acquainted with the Sufi brief for the Mahdi, which may differ from order to order but nonetheless contains many of the same common themes.

In chapter 3 of the *Muqaddimah*, Ibn Khaldun deals with royal authority and types of governments in Islamic history. In the midst of this discussion he swerves into a disquisition on Mahdism in which he makes five major points.[6] Ibn Khaldun begins with an introduction in which he provides a terse recapitulation of extant Muslim traditions concerning the Mahdi, his mission, and his role in assisting Jesus in the destruction of the Dajjal. It is important to note that Ibn Khaldun uses "Mahdi" and

"Fatimi" interchangeably, no doubt because of the abiding influence of the Fatimid Dynasty. Then his first actual observation is that the doctrine of Mahdism became so widespread in Sufism because of the belief's infiltration from Shi`ism,[7] a process Ibn Khaldun clearly disapproves. Next he links Mahdism to his core historical thesis: the centrality of *asabiyah*, "solidarity" or "group feeling":

> If the appearance of this Mahdi is true, his propaganda will have no validity unless he is from the ranks [of the people] and God unites their hearts in following him until he achieves sufficient power and solidarity to secure the ascendancy of his influence and convert the people to him. Any way other than this, such as . . . summoning the people from distant regions of the Earth to this authority without solidarity and power, adducing only his relationship to the ahl al-bayt, will not succeed.

For Ibn Khaldun, then, even Mahdis are bound by historical and sociological reality, for unless they engender communal cohesion, they are bound to fail. Third, the author of the *Muqaddimah* notes that it is the "gullible masses of the common people, who do not depend in this [matter] on guiding intelligence or beneficial knowledge" who are prone to fall for claims of Mahdism. Ibn Khaldun then adds that the flip side of this coin of ignorance is that those who await the Mahdi live "in the nether regions of the kingdoms and the fringes of civilization." Finally, in a section that prophetically presages the rise of modern Islamic fundamentalism, Ibn Khaldun excoriates the Mahdists:

> "Arab tribal renegades who propagandized for the truth and the establishment of the Sunnah, yet not embracing therein the propaganda of the Fatimi or any other. . . . However, their religious character is not deep-rooted. . . . And thus the follower of this is dedicated to the call for establishing the Sunnah, as they term it, but lacks depth in following it. . . . Those who wrapped themselves in the Sunnah, but were not really of it (except for a very small number)—neither they nor those who came after them succeeded."

Although the greatest Muslim historian of all time does not overtly condemn the doctrine of the Mahdi, clearly he has a rather low opinion of it. It is striking, however, that his scorn is directed almost entirely at Fatimid-style Shi`i Mahdism, and he has nothing explicit to say about earlier Mahdism of Ibn Tumart and the Muwahhids, a movement he would have undoubtedly known very well and whose empire had crumbled a little more than a century earlier. Although Ibn Khaldun was undoubtedly a pious Muslim,[8] he was at best a skeptic regarding the Mahdi. He seems to have viewed Mahdism as just another means of producing group feeling, that crucial building block of Islamic states. In fact, he put group cohesiveness ahead of the religious aspect, even of Mahdism: "The requisite truth that should be settled in everyone's mind is that religious or political propaganda does not succeed unless the impetus of some group feeling exists to produce victory (or until God's purpose comes to pass regarding it)." At best, Ibn Khaldun viewed Mahdism as an opiate of the masses; at worst, he saw it as a dangerous Shi`i heresy. Both of these views are echoed in modern anti-Mahdist polemic. But how Islamic establishments throughout history dealt with Mahdist irruptions must be examined first.

MURABIT COUNTER-MAHDIST POLICIES

Counter-Mahdism has been little documented and studied, compared to Mahdism itself. The Murabits' struggle with Ibn Tumart is a case in point. Some rudiments of the Murabit policy in attempting to stave off the Mahdist Muwahhids' burgeoning movement can be discerned from eight centuries away, however.[9]

The Murabit regime had its chance to put out the Mahdist fire of Ibn Tumart when it was but a spark, but its leaders failed to do so. When Ibn Tumart was still at the stick-wielding morals policeman stage, one faction of the Murabit religious establishment recommended clapping him in irons, warning that Ibn Tumart "if allowed to preach in freedom would in the end make the *Amir* hear the sound of the war drum."[10] Another clique saw him as simply a "misguided zealot" who should be tolerated.[11] The Murabit leader hesitated, thereby ultimately costing his successors the entire kingdom.

Ibn Tumart fled on his hijrah and began his rhetorical religious assault on the Murabits. They responded at first by labeling him a "Khariji," which was tantamount to branding him a heretic, and a rebellious one at that. Mere *tu quoque* argumentation was not going to win the day for the regime at this point, however. They ratcheted up the counter-revolutionary torque by formulating plans to seize Ibn Tumart; but none succeeded. Ultimately, of course, the Murabits had to play the military card, but to no avail.

We should not be too hard on the Murabits, perhaps. They were, after all, fighting a two-front war to defend a state that spanned two continents, Africa and Europe. In the same timeframe that Ibn Tumart was challenging their legitimacy and Abd al-Mu'min their battlefield acumen, the Murabits were fighting against the resurgent Christian states of the northern Iberian Peninsula. Caught between the hammer of the Messiah and the anvil of the Mahdi, the Murabits really had little chance once Ibn Tumart's Mahdism was out of its mystical bottle. The most instructive lesson that the Murabits hold for modern anti-Mahdists might be, simply, don't hesitate. Terminate Mahdists with extreme prejudice at their first manifestation. Kinder and gentler is no way to survive against ruthless Mahdist certitude.

GUJARATI, SA`DIYAN, FRENCH, BRITISH INDIAN, AND TURKISH POLICIES TOWARD MAHDISM

The comprehensive record of these five establishments' responses to their respective Mahdist threats has yet to be written. But some idea of the general shape of their programs is discernible. Gujarati Sultan Muzaffar II (d. 1526) tried exiling Sayyid Muhammad Jawnpuri's Mahdavis, escalating that to the threat of execution and finally resorting to military suppression. The Gujarati Sultanate made rather gruesome examples of some of the Mahdavis. Jawnpuri's successor Sayyid Khundmir, for example, was killed in 1523 and his head put on public display.[12] Other Mahdavis were tied between elephants and ripped apart in public spectacles as an example not just to rebels but to any other would-be Mahdis and their supporters.[13] The Gujarati state seems to have simply crushed the movement, not deigning to bother with mere rhetorical or ideological confutation, at least insofar as current scholarship indicates. The sultans of Gujarat were lucky, however, in that Jawnpuri's Mahdism drew a great deal of its inspiration from the centennialism of 900 AH (1494 CE) and the millennialism of 1000 AH (1591 CE), for when the latter date came and went without earthshaking, supernatural events occurring—most notably Jesus' return—the movement lost its bellicose urgency and degenerated into a quietist sect. The Gujarati anti-Mahdist program does reinforce the idea that in the final analysis, forceful—indeed, bloody—containment of Mahdism is crucial.

The Sa`diyan dynasty of Morocco, as far as is known, fought much as did the Gujaratis (sans the elephants) vis-à-vis the Mahdist uprising of Ibn Abu Mahallah, 1610–1613. No records of any propaganda war being waged have come to light. What is perhaps most illuminating about Abu Mahallah's movement is that it demonstrates that Muslim governments cannot always depend on Ibn Khaldun being right about Mahdism erupting only on the fringes of society either geographically or socio-politically, because although he was a Sufi, Abu Mahallah was also one of the establishment ulama before starting his revolt.[14] Also ominous for Muslim rulers today and in the years to come is that one of this Mahdi's main grievances and raisons d'être was that the ruling Islamic regime was working with Christian powers at the same time that it was too feeble to fend them off.

Fortunately, the British in India and their Sikh allies did not have to wage a long campaign against the Mahdism of Sayyid Ahmad Barelwi in the early nineteenth century, for he disappeared in battle rather early on in his career. But two lessons can be drawn from the example of his posthumous Mahdism. First, in certain contexts a Sunni Mahdist claimant may be accorded the status of occultation, normally reserved strictly to Shi`i Imams. For the modern world this might have ramifications vis-à-vis an Osama bin Laden or another out-of-sight Muslim leader. Furthermore,

Barelwi saw the first manifestation of the marriage of Mahdism to Wahhabism. This occurred once more in 1979 and may be coalescing again in today's troubled Kingdom of Saudi Arabia.

Since mere ideological warfare was not their forte, the French used force to crush the several quasi-Mahdist movements of the mid-nineteenth century in Algeria, culminating in the full-blown Mahdism of Mohammed Amzian in 1879. This really only tells us two things. First, the line between a nationalistic revolt and a religious Mahdist one might be thinner than presumed, especially in that a lapdog Muslim regime fronting for an imperialistic Christian overlord seems to engender more hatred than a merely illegitimate Muslim government. (The House of Saud might well hearken to this.) Perhaps more important, the French treatment of the Algerian Mahdist movements makes it clear that superior firepower is always a good thing to have when confronting Mahdists—propaganda be damned.

The Turkish Republic's answer to the ill-timed Mahdism of Mehmet and his followers demonstrates, much as the French one in North Africa did, that shock and awe sometimes solves the problem quite effectively. Of course, the Mahdists' labeling of Mustafa Kemal Atatürk as the Dajjal, or Antichrist, probably sealed their fate, if the beheading of the police officer hadn't already. One might conclude that the abortive 1930 Mahdism in Turkey demonstrates that a secular government in the Muslim world has more to fear from a Mahdist uprising than would a state that officially enshrines at least some elements of Islamic law. But though Turkey has had its share of political unrest in the almost three-quarters of a century since Mehmet, it has never faced another Mahdist movement. The same was not true, however, of the Turkish Republic's predecessor state, the Ottoman Empire.

THE OTTOMAN EGYPTIAN BATTLE
AGAINST SUDANESE MAHDISM

Sudanese Mahdism was perceived as a very real threat to the Ottoman Empire even if, in retrospect, it really was not a serious danger to the imperial center. Muhammad Ahmad's movement did succeed in detaching the province of Sudan from imperial control, however, threatening Egypt (arguably the empire's most important province, undoubtedly its most important Arab one), and alarming Istanbul because as Sultan Abdülhamid II fully realized, it had for its stated aim the destruction of the Ottoman government:

The sole and single cause of the Sudanese revolution is the seditious political notion of establishing an independent Arab government in opposition to the Empire, the Caliphate and the Sultanate, and of transferring the Islamic Caliphate there. Both the rebels and those who encourage them—secretly or openly, by word or deed—have taken this notion as their goal, and they have many servants and supporters in Egypt, in Istanbul and in other parts of the Ottoman Empire.[15]

Accordingly, the Ottoman Empire responded to the Sudanese Mahdist uprising on two fronts: military and ideological, the latter mainly, but not entirely, religious. The former was greatly hobbled, however, by real as well as perceived concerns regarding international diplomacy and politics, especially vis-à-vis the British. Egypt was de jure if not de facto part of the Ottoman Empire and Sudan was administered, then, twice removed: orders from Istanbul had to pass through the government of Muhammad Ali and then his successor sons before being applied on the ground in Khartoum and environs by the *hukumdar* there.

The military dimension of the Ottoman sultan's anti-Mahdist response, as we have seen, was a disaster. Perhaps if the sultan had been more willing to commit substantial numbers of his own troops instead of relying upon whatever the khedive in Cairo could be ordered to scrounge together, reinforced by relatively small detachments of British soldiers, the Mahdism of Muhammad Ahmad might have been nipped in the bud. The Ottoman military may have been no match for those of the British or the French, but it could probably have defeated the fervent but ill-equipped hordes following Muhammad Ahmad. But Abdülhamid II's paranoia regarding the British prevented him from doing so.

Diplomatically, the sultan refused to deal with Mahdist Sudan as a separate issue from Egypt. By 1882 he feared that sending Turkish troops directly to fight the Mahdi's forces would legitimize the British occupation of Egypt and permanently detach Sudan from its northern neighbor, thereby granting the khedives the de jure independence they had been seeking, as well as the de facto kind they already possessed (in relation to Istanbul, if not London).[16] After the Mahdi died in 1885, the Ottomans and British jointly attempted to open a diplomatic channel to the Mahdist caliph, Abd Allah, but to no avail.[17] The Mahdiyah in Sudan remained as a military and ideological threat to the sultan's theoretical dominions in Egypt and his still real ones across the Red Sea in the Hijaz until the British finally ended the matter in 1898.

While Muhammad Ahmad was still alive, the most active front upon which the Ottomans engaged him was that of ideology, and more specifically that of religious principles. Ottoman newspapers were ordered to describe the Sudanese Mahdi as a *sakı*, or "rebel."[18] More important, the religious establishment in Egypt and pre-Mahdist Sudan was enlisted in an Islamic propaganda war with Muhammad Ahmad.[19]

As soon as Muhammad Ahmad showed up on the radar screen of the governor in Khartoum, religious officials, including ulama, muftis, and qadis, were summoned to rebut the alleged Mahdi's *manshurat*, or "proclamations." This was the second of the double-barreled attack on him, the other being military. Before long the center of Sunni orthodoxy, al-Azhar in Cairo, was being prompted to issue deprecating fatwas about the pretender in Sudan. Three prominent Ottoman-appointed religious officials in Sudan itself composed letters opposing Muhammad Ahmad's da`wah, which were then circulated throughout the country. Sayyid Ahmad al-Azhari b. al-Shaykh Isma'il al-Wali al-Kurdufani, the Shaykh al-Islam for western Sudan, wrote "General Advice to the People of Islam about the Attack on the Obedience to the Ummah." Shaykh al-Amin al-Darir, Shaykh al-Islam for the eastern part of the province,[20] composed "Guidance for the Seekers of Direction regarding the Mahdi and the False Mahdi." And Mufti Shakir, head of the Appeals Court of Sudan, wrote his own untitled refutation of Muhammad Ahmad. When General Gordon was reinstalled as governor in Khartoum, he had even more ulama issue anti-Madist fatwas and even went so far as to convince the religious establishment to allow the Muslim soldiers under him to break the fast during Ramadan, citing as precedent that the prophet Muhammad's troops had done so while besieging Mecca. Gordon also convinced the imams to read from the hadith collection of al-Buhkari in the mosques, presumbly because it contains no references to the Mahdi.

In September 1884 yet another fatwa was issued, at Gordon's request, under the names of Shaykh al-Amin Muhammad, chief of the ulama of Sudan; the aforementioned Mufti Shakir; Shaykh Husayn al-Majdi, Professor of Religious Sciences at the University of Khartoum; Muhammad Khawjali, Supreme Qadi of Sudan; and Muhammad Musa, Mufti of the Sudanese Majlis. Far from dissuading Muhammad Ahmad and his followers, however, these establishment fusillades simply reinforced their conviction that he was the Mahdi.

In all these fulminations against the Sudanese Mahdi, 13 major points stand out. First, appeal was made to Hadith that the Mahdi would come from Arabia, and more specifically from the Hijaz, most likely from Medina. Muhammad Ahmad, to the contrary, was from Dongola in Sudan. Then, it was observed that the traditions clearly stated the Mahdi would be of the family of the prophet Muhammad and thus an Arab, or *ahmar* (literally "red"). Muhammad Ahmad, in contrast, was not Arab and was in fact *aswad*, "black." Third, the traditions made no allowance for the Mahdi to emerge in Sudan. Also, vis-à-vis the other eschatological figures, the Mahdi was supposed to appear at approximately the same time that Jesus and the Dajjal were on earth. Where were they if Muhammad Ahmad was indeed the Mahdi? Furthermore, the Hadiths say that the Mahdi would kill al-Sufyani, not other Muslims as Muhammad Ahmad was doing. Fifth, the Mahdi was supposed to come in the midst of a chaotic time upon the death of a caliph. But the Ottoman caliph, Sultan Abdülhamid II, was very much alive, and chaos did not reign in the Ottoman domains—at least, not until Muhammad Ahmad had sparked it. Far from filling the earth with equity and justice, as would the true Mahdi, this charlatan in Sudan was filling at least part of it with pillage and looting. Traditions also described the coming of the Mahdi as resembling finding a treasure, but could anyone seriously describe Muhammad Ahmad in such glowing terms? Eighth, allegiance was supposed to be sworn to the Mahdi in Mecca, between the rukn and the maqam. However, Muhammad Ahmad had coerced or extorted loyalty and done so far from Arabia. Also, whereas the followers of the true Mahdi would be pious Arab Muslims from Syria and Iraq, Muhammad Ahmad's supporters consisted of al-ajam, "foreigners," who did not even speak good Arabic and awbash, "rabble." Tenth, there was no evidence Muhammad Ahmad was even remotely related to the family of the Prophet. Far from abiding by the Qur'an and Sunnah, he departed from them. The false mahdi, in an argument from politics and not religion, was undermining the peace and stability afforded by the Ottoman sultan-caliph. The God-given responsibility to defend the faith and keep the peace was imputed to the distant ruler in Istanbul (especially, it should be pointed out, by those on his payroll). Thirteenth and finally, his self-validating visions and ostensibly direct illumination from God made him unreliable, since he thereby rejected the consensus of all the Islamic scholars who had gone before.[21] Thus, Muhammad Ahmad was indeed not the true Mahdi but a mutamahdi, or "false mahdi."

For Muhammad Ahmad, the best defense was always a good offense. His responses to these derogatory fatwa were always addressed to the `ulama al-su', "ulama of evil," whose rejection was based more on their love of wealth and position than on legitimate Islamic scholarship and beliefs. One lethal weapon in the Sudanese Mahdi's armory was the doctrine of naskh or mansukh, "abrogation." This meant that he simply nullified any hadith that did not apply to him and so unfettered his Mahdiyah from the wooden letter of the text traditions regarding the Mahdi. Muhammad Ahmad also riposted that the religious scholars simply did not understand the deeper truths about the Mahdi and accused them of cherry picking traditions out of context in their misguided attempt to discredit him. Ultimately, his claims to be in direct, mystical contact with the prophet Muhammad, and thus indirectly with Allah, were irrefutable, albeit subjective.[22] But as long as Muhammad Ahmad was standing up for the disparate groups of Sudanese against Turkish and Egyptian oppression and for true Islam, as they saw it, and even more important, as long as he was winning on the battlefield, his Mahdism would be accepted. Most telling, for many in Sudan the Ottoman sultan was not the caliph of Islam but a tyrant and the Ottomans, far from being coreligionists, were aggressors and unbelievers. It did not hurt that in September 1882 a huge comet was seen in the skies, further proof to the already convinced that Muhammad Ahmad was exactly who he claimed to be. So the Ottoman anti-Mahdist agenda was largely doomed from the start. Perhaps if the Turks and their Egyptian subjects had been able to bring immediate and overwhelming firepower to bear on the Mahdi and his followers—*pace* the French in Algeria a few years earlier—the matter might have turned out differently. Istanbul was unable to do so, however, from a combination of diplomatic and logistical obstacles, neither of which would hobble the British when they decided to end the Mahdist state in Sudan once and for all at the end of the century. The worst the Mahdi did, though, was detach one province from the orbit of Ottoman control and, consequently, embarrass the sultan. His armies, whatever the claims and aspirations of Muhammad Ahmad or his successor Abd Allah, never truly threatened a march to overthrow the government in Cairo, much less Istanbul. Such is not the case for the al-Utaybi Mahdist uprising in Saudi Arabia in 1979.

THE SAUDIS VERSUS THE MAHDIST COUP MANQUE OF AL-UTAYBI

The stakes for the government of the Kingdom of Saudi Arabia were higher than those for the Ottoman Empire when they faced their Mahdist challenge because al-Utaybi and his Mahdi brother-in-law, along with their scores of armed followers, exploded onto the scene in the religious center of the country yet "presented more than religious fanaticism. It was indeed a serious political challenge."[23] Like the Ottomans, the Saudis engaged in a two-front war against the Mahdists: military and polemical. Unlike the Ottoman Turks vis-à-vis the European powers, particularly the British, however, the Saudis remained unhobbled by diplomatic or geopolitical concerns and were free to treat the uprising as a purely internal affair and thus to crush it without worrying about what any outside power might do.

The Saudi rhetorical struggle against al-Utaybi's people proceeded in tandem with the military one. Within days of the Mahdist rebels' ensconcing themselves in the Great Mosque of Mecca, King Abd al-Aziz had prevailed upon the ulama to issue fatwas denouncing al-Utaybi and company. This initial propaganda stroke's missive read as follows:

A group has locked themselves inside the holy mosque after morning prayer . . . and call for the taking of the oath of allegiance to someone they call "the Mahdi." They opened fire on people inside and out, killing some. . . . Do not kill them unless they kill some of you within the mosque . . . and do not kill them as if they were unbelievers.[24]

Fatwas such as this were published in the Saudi newspapers alongside articles and editorials labeling the actual alleged Mahdi, al-Qahtani, *al-Mahdi al-Maz`um* or *Mudda`an al-Mahdi*, both of which mean "the pretended mahdi." For good measure his supporters were branded *Khawarij*, or "separatists,"[25] perhaps the cardinal religio-political sin in Islam. The best summary of the official religious viewpoint toward this abortive Mahdist revolution can be found in the postmortem analysis of it published a few months after the rebellion had been crushed. The author was Shaykh Abd al-Aziz Baz, director of the Board of Islamic Research, Da`wah, and Religious Guidance for the government and probably the most esteemed religious authority in all the Kingdom.

Shaykh Baz's religious propaganda barrage had five main types of ordinance. First, he accused al-Utaybi, al-Qahtani, and all the Mahdists of "atheism" that "terrorized Muslims" and was "in violation of the Prophet's saying that he who carries arms against us is not one of us."[26] Second, since "Mecca is a holy place where fighting and bloodshed are not permitted," the Mahdists had contravened the Qur'an and the faith. Third,

as to their excuse that they wanted to proclaim the Mahdi, this was patently wrong, and invalid. It was an unauthenticaled allegation. . . . The question of the Mahdi is not of this world. No Muslim should claim for certain that anybody is the Mahdi. That would be unfounded, since only God knows about it, and there should be signs and portents as explained by the Prophet. Most important of these is that the Mahdi's regime would be based on the Shariah. In his rule justice will prevail where injustice had reigned supreme. He should also belong to the house of the Prophet, and possess certain facial characteristics, while his name and his father's should resemble the Prophet's and his father's.

Fourth, Shaykh Baz points out that "using dreams as the basis of claims is against the Shariah and cannot be adopted. God has given the Prophet and his people a complete religion and nobody has the right to depend on dreams to transgress the Shariah."[27] Finally, in a more political and prosaic vein, he states that "there is nothing wrong with this government. It has done nothing to warrant rebellion. It is those who deviate from the right path and fight Muslims who should be fought and killed wherever they may be. The Prophet has ordered us to obey the ruler and uphold unity."

Nonetheless, for all his censure of this Mahdist movement, Shaykh Baz takes pains to point out that belief in the Mahdi is a legitimate one:

However, denying the Mahdi completely, as some people have been doing, is wrong. There has been unanimous agreement that someday he will appear, but it is not right to state categorically that someone is the Mahdi unless all the evidence, signs and portents have been provided, as stated by the Prophet.[28]

So the Mahdi will come; but you, Sayyid al-Qahtani, are not him.

The Saudi government's troops, probably with Western help, finally dislodged, killed, or captured all the revolutionaries. And although some among the populace and perhaps even in the government religious establishment may have been ideologically sympathetic to al-Utabyi and al-Qahtani, at least in terms of their criticisms of the Saudi regime and its too cozy relationship with Westerners, the rebels' use of violence in a sacred space, as well as their foolhardy specifying of someone as the Mahdi, drove away if not silenced potential supporters.[29] Perhaps al-Utaybi's attempted *coup d'Mahdi* would have worked better had the protagonist been left as an ominous, anonymous judge of the regime, not expressly identified and so made a literal as well as figurative target for the establishment's fatwas and weapons.

CONCLUSION

Although historical data on counter-Mahdist schemas pales in comparison to that available for the Mahdist agendas themselves, what information does exist is instructive in a number of ways. The Muslim politicoreligious establishments of the Gujarati sultans and the Sa`diyan mawlays, as well as the officially secular one of majority Muslim, albeit republican, Turkey, responded to Mahdism with a robotic "crush, kill, destroy" approach.[30] This method may not have been subtle or rhetorically persuasive, but it did have one huge advantage: it worked. The Murabit regime's attempts to fend off Ibn Tumart's Mahdist Muwahhids was fashioned along the same lines, but the amirs of that state not only waited too long to unleash the military, they fumbled the chance to arrest Ibn Tumart, and thus his movement, early on. The prime lesson to be learned from the Murabit failure is "don't hesitate; incarcerate and terminate."

Notwithstanding their separation by a century, the counter-Mahdist approaches of the Ottomans and the Saudis appear uncannily similar. Both strategically attacked on not just the military but also the ideological front. The Ottomans did not succeed as well as the Saudis in their martial suppression of Mahdism, but as previously mentioned, neither were they as intimately threatened by such an uprising: Muhammad Ahmad aimed and succeeded at carving off a piece of the Ottoman Empire, whereas Juhayman al-Utaybi had a sword at the Kingdom of Saudi Arabia's very heart. In terms of propaganda warfare, the Ottoman and Saudi establishments both

- branded their respective Mahdists as rebels who wrongly killed other Muslims
- emphasized that the self-styled Mahdis they faced lacked the requisite characteristics of the true Mahdi, including the presence of other eschatological figures and the realization of justice and equity upon the earth
- denigrated these false mahdis' self-validation through visions and dreams[31]

- highlighted the fact that the extant governments were already Muslim and keeping the peace

Interestingly, it was not the nineteenth-century Ottoman imperial religious authorities but the late-twentieth-century Saudi ones that made a point of declaiming that despite the falseness of the Mahdist movement of the time, Mahdism itself remains a valid, legitimate belief in Islam, although one, according to Shaykh Baz, so hedged about with caveats and cautions that it is difficult to see how anyone could ever actually lay claim to the title (no doubt his point).

Since 1979 Mahdism has been relegated to the realm of theory and yearning. Books about the Mahdi saw an upsurge in publishing beginning after the Six Days' War in 1967 and accelerated following the al-Utaybi uprising and the establishment of the Islamic Republic in Iran. Now we seem to be on the cusp of another great leap forward of interest in, predictions about, and yearning for the Mahdi, sparked by American responses to the September 11, 2001 attacks. But until some individual ignores Shaykh Baz's warnings and specifies just who the Mahdi might be—a situation that would require direct ideological and probably military action—the virtual Mahdi or his supporters' writings can expect a refutation like the purely intellectual one provided by Ibn Khaldun: that Madhism is simply a Trojan Horse for pernicious Shi`i ideas; that it is just another means of uniting Muslims, and not even the best means of doing that; and that only the hoi polloi on the fringes of Islamic civilization would believe such a thing. Unfortunately for Muslim sultans, kings, and presidents today, not all their subjects accept Ibn Khaldun's enlightened, elitist dismissal of Mahdism.[32]

NOTES

1. For purists his full name was Wali al-Din Abd al-Rahman b. Muhammad b. Muhammad b. Abi Bakr Muhammad b. al-Hasan b. Khaldun. General sources on Ibn Khaldun include his *al-Muqaddimah*, edited by N.J. Dawood and translated by Franz Rosenthal (Princeton, NJ: Princeton University Press, 1967); Etienne Marc Quatremere, *Prolegomenes d'Ebn Khaldoun*, vol. 2 (Paris: Didot, 1858); Muhammad Mahmoud Rabi`, *The Political Theory of Ibn Khaldun* (Leiden: E.J. Brill, 1967); M. Talbi, "Ibn Khaldun," *EI2*; Aziz al-Azmeh, *Ibn Khaldun: An Essay in Interpretation* (London: Frank Cass, 1982); Amad al-Din al-Khalil, *Ibn Khaldun Islamiyan* (Beirut: al-Maktab al-Islami, 1985); Fuad Baali and Ali Wardi, *Ibn Khaldun and Islamic Thought Styles: A Social Perspective* (Boston: G.K. Hall and Co., 1981); Stephen Casewit, "The Mystical Side of the Muqaddimah: Ibn Khaldun's View of Sufism," *Islamic Quarterly* 29 (1985), pp. 172–85; Hodgson, vol. 2, pp. 476–484.

2. Talbi.

3. Hodgson, vol. 2, p. 476.

4. al-Azmeh, pp. 91ff.

5. See Rosenthal's "Introduction" to *The Muqaddimah*, p. ix.

6. I have translated the relevant extracts from the Arabic text in Quatremere, pp. 142–76.

7. In the first millennium of Islamic history the connections between Sufism and Shi`ism were quite close. See Seyyed Hossein Nasr, *Sufi Essays* (Albany: State University of New York Press, 1991), pp. 104–20: "Shi`ism and Sufism: Their Relationship in Essence and History." For the divorce between the two in the last 500 years, see Nasrollah Pourjavady, "Opposition to Sufism in Twelver Shi`ism," in DeJong and Radtke, eds., *Islamic Mysticism Contested*, pp. 614–23.

8. Which is the point of al-Khalil's book.

9. Sources include Nevill Barbour, "La Guerra Psicológica de los Almohades contra Los Almoravides," *Boletín do la Asociación Española de Orientalista*, vol. 2 (1966), pp. 117–30; H.T. Norris, *The Berbers in Arabic Literature* (London and New York: Longman, 1982), especially pp. 171–76, "Ideological Warfare against the Almoravids"; P. Chalmeta, "Al-Murabitun," *EI2*.

10. Norris, p. 167.

11. Ibid.

12. MacLean, p. 249.

13. Ibid., p. 250.

14. Garcia-Arenal, "Imam et Mahdi: Ibn Abi Mahallah," in Garcia-Arenal, ed., *Mahdisme et Millenarisme en Islam*, p. 179.

15. Yasamee, p. 99, quoting from the Ottoman archival documents: Basbakanlik Arsivi, Yildiz Esas Evraki, K36/2475/Z150/XI, Tezkere-i aliye-i hususiye, 10 Rebiülahir 305/13 Kanun-i evvel 303.

16. Ibid., pp. 91–92.

17. Ibid., p. 98.

18. Ibid., p. 91.

19. See Ibrahim, *al-Sira` bayna al-Mahdi wa-al-`Ulama*, particularly chapter 2 (translated as "The Ulama and Their Opposition to the Mahdist Revolt") and chapter 3, "The Ideological Viewpoint of the Ulama."

20. The division of Sudan between two *shuyuhk al-Islam*, "shaykhs of Islam," was part of the Ottoman Egyptian administration of the country. Holt, *The Mahdist State*, pp. 22ff.

21. Ibrahim, pp. 35–41.

22. Ibid., pp. 43ff.

23. Kechichian, p. 6.

24. Ahmad, *Rasa'il Juhayman al-`Utaybi*, pp. 30–31.

25. Mat`ani, *Jarimat al-`Asr*, passim.

26. Shaykh Baz did not, unfortunately, provide the hadith citation for this, however.

27. Other Sunni Mahdist claimants did, of course, use dreams and visions as legitimation, most notably Ibn Tumart and Muhammad Ahmad. Also Isma'il, the founder of the Safavid state in Iran, "experienced visions, seeing angels in the form of birds which in turn assumed human shape and conversed with him," according to Roger Savory, *Iran under the Safavids*, pp. 5ff.

28. All these quotations from Shaykh Baz can be found in his "Attack on the Masjid al-Haram," *Journal of the Muslim World League* 7, no. 3 (January 1980), p. 10.

29. Ayubi, p. 102.

30. Apologies to the robot from the old 1960s science fiction series *Lost in Space*.

31. I find no evidence that either Juhayman al-Utaybi or Muhammad al-Qahtani adduced dreams or visions as legitimation, but Shaykh Baz includes this charge in his brief against them.

32. Juan R.I. Cole, "Millennialism in Modern Iranian History," in Amanat and Bernhardsson, eds., *Imagining the End* (pp. 282–311), points out that this cliché of Mahdism being the belief system of those in "backwoods villages" has been disproved in the modern world by the example of the Islamic Revolution in Iran, which though not openly Mahdist was covertly so.

CHAPTER 4

The Virtual Mahdi Today

INTRODUCTION

Since the crushing of the abortive Mahdist-based rebellion in Saudi Arabia 25 years ago, Sunni Mahdism, like its Shi`i cousin, has gone largely theological, and thus theoretical, manifesting itself in books and on websites. Here Mahdism can be discussed and advocated and the coming of the Mahdi speculated upon, largely free from the threat of government suppression. After all, Mahdism *is* a legitimate Islamic belief. In 1976 the Muslim World League (*Rabitah al-`Alam al-Islami*) issued a fatwa stating so:

The memorizers and scholars of Hadith have verified that there are reliable and acceptable reports among the Hadiths on the Mahdi; the majority of them are narrated through numerous authorities. There is no doubt about their status as unbroken and sound reports. And the belief in the appearance of the Mahdi is obligatory . . . none denies it except those who are ignorant of the Sunnah and innovators in doctrine.[1]

Despite the beating Mahdist belief may have taken from the appearance of the false mahdi al-Qahtani and his spokesman al-Utaybi a scant three years after that missive, Mahdism to this day holds the imprimatur of most Sunni authorities. This has made it a rather safe topic for speculation in books and on websites, just not a wise career move in reality, at least not until recently.

If, as all the signs indicate is quite possible, a Mahdist claimant should arise in the near future, it will be in no small measure because of the groundwork laid for such a movement by its supporters the last quarter-century. The modern written Arabic "expressive literature"[2] on Mahdism amounts to the discourse of a sect within Islam, a minority sect to be sure, at least in terms of active expectations of the Mahdi's coming, but a viable and increasingly influential sect nonetheless. Especially when considering that the media's influence may very well outrank that of the political and religious establishments in the Sunni Arab world today[3]—the influence and alleged tendentiousness of the Arabic satellite channel al-Jazeerah[4] regarding the American invasion and occupation of Iraq serving as a case in point—Mahdist books and websites cannot be cavalierly dismissed as marginal, fanatical Islamic screeds. They are a rational means for Muslims of salvaging Mahdism in the face of the self-evident speciousness of all previous Mahdist claimants[5] and of extrapolating on the conditions necessitating the inevitable coming of the true, once and future Mahdi.

Books on Mahdism have been around almost as long as Islam itself, but after 1967 the number of such books published in the Arab world skyrocketed. At least 40 books on the End Time and the coming of the Mahdi have been published since then; this may seem like a small number until compared to the number put out by the Arab world's publishing houses between World War II and 1967, which was perhaps half a dozen.[6] Perhaps more tellingly, put this number into the context of the total numbers of books yearly published by the entire Arab world's 22 nation-states: the Arab world's nearly 300 million people represent 5 percent of the world's population, but publish only about 1 percent of the world's books. Thus, in this constrained literary domain, "a 'best-seller' may have a print run of just 5,000 copies."[7] Figures specifically for Mahdist books' sales are not available; they would fall under the rubric of books on religion, which comprise almost one-fifth of all published works in Arabic, a figure over three times higher than that in the rest of the world, where comparatively far fewer tomes on religion are published.[8] So when trying to gauge the popularity of Sunni Mahdist apologetic works, we cannot compare them to, for example, *The Da Vinci Code* or the works of Tom Clancy. In a much smaller publishing and reading universe, Mahdist books are quite popular.

The Six Days' War of 1967, in which Israel dealt the combined armies of the frontline Arab states a crushing defeat and which led to Israeli occupation of Sinai, the West Bank, and East Jerusalem, as well as the Syrian Golan Heights, was the seminal event that reopened the Mahdist Pandora's box in the twentieth century: since the likes of Nasser had failed to reglorify Muslim societies, perhaps it was time for the Mahdi to come and do so. However, probably of even greater importance were events such as the Islamic Revolution in Iran in 1978–79 and the al-Utaybi uprising in Saudi Arabia at the same time, which piled even higher the kindling of Mahdist anticipation and speculation; the Iran-Iraq War of 1980–1988, in which about a million (mainly Iranians) died; the first U.S. Gulf War of 1991, which evicted the armies of Saddam Hussein from Kuwait; the World Trade Center attacks of 2001 and the subsequent American overthrow of the Taliban in Afghanistan; and most recently the 2003 toppling of Saddam Hussein and then the U.S. occupation of Iraq. All these wars have together thrown barrels of intensely flammable Saudi crude on the pile of Mahdist expectations. It remains to be seen whether someone—perhaps Osama bin Laden, perhaps another charismatic Muslim leader yet to emerge onto the world stage—will toss a match onto this tinderbox. If and when someone does, the base of the flame will be fired by all those tomes on the Mahdi churned out in recent years.

MODERN ARABIC BOOKS ON THE MAHDI
AND ESCHATOLOGY

Perhaps the best window today into the modern Sunni Arab Mahdist mind is these books. Of the 40 or so published in Arabic since 1967, 33 are available. Twenty of these are Sunni, 13 are Shi`i.[9] Of course, it was the former that served as the primary source base for this topic. This chapter deals with the 13 of the 20 Sunni works that are pro-Mahdist. (The following chapter examines the remaining seven, which are anti-Mahdist.) Eight of those 13 explicitly mention the Mahdi in their title and deal primarily with him, one does so by another title,[10] and four discuss the Mahdi in the context of the other signs and figures of Islamic eschatology. Here are the works, in chronological order, with their titles translated:

1. Muhammad Ibrahim al-Jamal, *The Aggression and the Awaited Mahdi*, 1980[11]

2. Ibrahim al-Shawkhi, *The Awaited Mahdi: The Litany of the Signs of the Hour*, 1983[12]

3. Muhammad Salamah Jabbar, *The Signs of the Hour and Its Secrets*, 1993[13]

4. Hamzah al-Faqir, *The Awaited Hashimite*, 1993[14]

5. Basim al-Hashimi, *The Mahdi and the Messiah: Readings in the Gospel*, 1994[15]

6. Kamil Safan, *The Twenty-fifth Hour: The Dajjal, the Awaited Mahdi, Gog and Magog*, 1995[16]

7. Hamzah al-Faqir, *Three Whom the World Awaits: The Awaited Mahdi, the Dajjal, Messiah Jesus*, 1995[17]

8. Amin Muhammad Jamal al-Din, *The Lifespan of the Islamic Community and the Nearness of the Mahdi's Appearance*, 1996[18]

9. Fahd Salim *The Signs of the Hour and the Attack of the West before 1999*, 1996[19]

10. Basim al-Hashimi, *The Savior between Islam and Christianity: A Study in the Cooperation between the Mahdi and the Messiah*, 1996[20]

11. Abdal-Alim Abd al-Azim al-Bustawi, *The Transmitted Traditions on the Mahdi in the Scales of Tradition Criticism. I. The Awaited Mahdi in Light of True Hadith and Writings, the Sayings of the Ulama and the Opinions of the Various Sects. II. Encyclopedia regarding Weak Traditions on the Mahdi*, 1999[21]

12. Usamah Yusuf Rahmah, *The Nearness of the Hour: On the Occurrence of the Emergence of the Awaited Mahdi and the Descent of the Messiah (Peace unto both of them) and the Scenario of the Coming Events from Now until the Last Hour, in Light of the Prophetic Traditions*, 2002[22]

13. Ihyab al-Badawi and Hassan al-Zawam, *Osama bin Laden: The Awaited Mahdi or the Dajjal?* 2002[23] (This work, however, will not be analyzed until the final chapter.)

Of these thirteen, six were published in Cairo, four in Beirut,[24] and three in Amman, Jordan. Together and when examined in tandem with the increasing numbers of websites dealing with the Mahdi, also examined here, such sources represent the voice of the millions of Muslims yearning for the true Mahdi to come and set history aright.

THE WORLDVIEW OF MAHDIST APOLOGETIC WORKS

Since the Mahdi can be substantiated only from Hadith—fanciful efforts by some Mahdist writers notwithstanding[25]—all pro-Mahdist works deploy copious amounts of citations from traditions in their attempt to substantiate the truth of the Mahdi, as well as to delineate the major and minor signs of the End Time and extrapolate forward to the geopolitical context in which they will occur.

Two potential weak spots in Mahdist hadiths must be dealt with by his proponents. One is the fact that many of the traditions that treat of the Mahdi have, over the centuries, been classified by Muslim muhaddithun (hadith scholars) as "weak," meaning that there is a weak link in its chain of transmitters going back to the prophet Muhammad. Another and potentially far more damning one for Mahdists and their beliefs is the oft-repeated allegation that traditions about the Mahdi are forgeries interpolated into legitimate hadith collections by Shi`ites and other misguided Muslim propagandists over the centuries. Such sham hadiths are commonly described as *tazwir*, "forged"; *wad`*, "invented"; or *tadlis*, "fraudulent."

Defenders of the Mahdi deal with such potentially damaging criticisms in several ways. One is to claim that the sheer number of Mahdist hadiths overwhelms any question of any particular one's weakness or insertion by the pens of heretical Shi`i writers.[26] Another is to take issue with the very labeling of Mahdist hadiths as weak and simply, obtusely maintain that their chains are, on the contrary, *mutawatir*, "unbroken."[27] One can also argue that although most of the traditions heralding the Mahdi are singular (attested only once), most of these are not weak but sound.[28] Finally, one of the chief defenses of the Mahdi and the hadiths about him is to ascribe impure motives—particularly political ones, since Mahdism has such latent power to disrupt politics and spark revolutions—to anyone who denigrates such traditions.[29]

As noted previously, one of the most damning criticisms of Mahdism derives from its absence in the pages of the two most-revered collectors of tradition, al-Bukhari and Muslim. The pro-Mahdist expressive literature deals with this exclusion in two primary ways. One is to readily admit the Mahdi's lack of attestation in the two shaykhs of Hadith, but to quickly deem this fact outweighed, or at least balanced, by references to him in the other collections.[30] Alternatively, the Mahdi's apologists will contend that al-Bukhari and Muslim do indeed mention their once and future deliverer, but obliquely, in traditions such as "your imam is before you" or "a caliph will come from Quraysh to redistribute wealth."[31]

Besides the practice of quoting, defending, and rationalizing the various Mahdist hadiths, proponents of Mahdism will adduce notable Sunni ulama who, it is contended, believed in the Mahdi as well. Somewhat similarly to the manner in which hadiths are wielded to support the Mahdi, with the quantity of them trumpeted over their quality, Mahdists produce litanies of citations from alleged Mahdi-friendly scholars and religious figures. For examples, Ibn Taymiyah (d. 1328 CE), the famous antimystical scholar whose writings are actually the genesis of modern Wahhabism in Saudi Arabia,[32] has even been enlisted in the Mahdist cause as one who at least acknowledged the legitimacy of Mahdist traditions.[33] Another famous author cited is the prolific Egyptian intellectual Jalal al-Din al-Suyuti (d. 1505 CE), who does mention the Mahdi in his scholarship.[34]

In addition to these two notable Muslim religious figures, a constellation of lesser-known Islamic lights, but ones still allegedly luminous regarding the Mahdi, are strung together. Examples include Muhammad b. Ahmad b. Salim al-Saffarini (d. 1774 AH), a Damascus-based author of a number of works on Hadith and related subjects;[35] Muhammad b. Ahmad b. Uthman b. Qaymaz al-Dhahabi (d. 1348 CE), another Damascene scholar of history, the imamate, and traditions;[36] and Abd al-Wahhab al-Sha`rani (d. 1565 CE), a Sufi religious scholar of early Ottoman Egypt.[37] Citation of such a wide array of respected Muslim jurisprudents of the past seems to be part of the effort by Mahdist writers today to call as many corroborating witnesses as possible to the dock in order to back their case.

Anti-Mahdist writers often refer to the Mahdi as a "superstition,"[38] "fable,"[39] "fantasy"[40] or "delusion,"[41] a fact that Mahdism's proponents acknowledge but then attempt to refute.[42] Opponents of Mahdism who employ these derogatory terms do so, they claim, to warn of the dangers implicit in the lassitude supposedly engendered by those waiting on Mahdist deliverance. Supporters of the coming Mahdi riposte that he serves as a sign of hope, as well as a spur to pious Islamic practice.[43]

Another preemptive strike by Mahdist writers is to concede that some famous Muslim scholars have disbelieved in the Mahdi but then, of course, to rationalize away their doubt. For example, Ibn Khaldun's well-known denigration of Mahdism is grudgingly admitted, as is that of two more recent Muslim thinkers: the reforming Egyptian writer and mufti Muhammad Abduh (d. 1905) and Rashid Rida (d. 1935), the Syrian disciple of Abduh who advocated pan-Islamism and the restoration of the caliphate.[44] Abduh and Rida are both excoriated for allegedly arguing, as the gravamen of their anti-Mahdist polemic, that the only true Mahdi was, and is, Jesus.[45] The Mahdist writers' rebuttal is that the tradition upon which this claim is based is itself weak, and that Ibn Khaldun, though an influential genius, is not infallible.[46]

The composers of Mahdist works also downplay the criticism from Mahdism's opponents, in which the latter maintain that the belief is an alien import into Islam from the Jews, the Christians, or even unnamed "idolaters,"[47] the latter perhaps the Zoroastrians or other ancient Near Eastern peoples. In response to this Mahdist writers again take refuge in the accepted Mahdist traditions, implying that their very existence means Mahdism is integral to Islam.

Turning from preemptive attacks on presumed anti-Mahdist salients, believers in the Mahdi will question opponents' motives and attempt to take the rhetorical high ground by, for example, musing that the ulama and establishment leaders will most likely be supporters of the Dajjal when he appears, thus tarring Mahist doubters with that same broad brush.[48] Even non-Muslim critics of the Mahdi can come under fire, in particular al-Mustashriqun, the "Orientalists" or Western scholars who specialize in the Middle East and the Muslim world and have been the archvillains of many on the left since the publication of Edward Said's polemical masterpiece Orientalism in 1978. (Said, in a nutshell, argues that Western scholarship on Islam and the Middle East, so-called Orientalism, is merely an ideological rationalization of imperialism.) Sunni Arab Mahdists, taking their cue from Said, attack the likes of Dwight Donaldson for allegedly portraying all Mahdist traditions as fabrications,[49] or they excoriate those like the more familiar and influential Ignaz Goldziher,[50] who maintains that the concept of the Mahdi has its origins merely in the mutadhammarun, those "complaining" about Umayyad rule.[51]

Such theorizing is not alone as the target of criticism in pro-Mahdist tomes. Also attacked are modern geopolitical analysts, most notably Francis Fukuyama, whose The End of History and the Last Man argued that with the USSR's fall democratic capitalism was now the last word in human ideological struggles,[52] and Samuel Huntington, whose The Clash of Civilizations and the Remaking of World Order posited the post-Communist world clashes between civilizations, particularly between Islam and the West.[53] Fukuyama is held up as an example of someone who formulates nefarious Western plots to conquer the Middle East and, eventually, the entire world, whereas Huntington is said to be the pied piper of a secular theory of world conflict that seduces Muslim intellectuals away from the crucial task of combing through the Qur'an and Hadith for signs of The End.[54] Interestingly, old-line Orientalists and modern geopolitical writers are sometimes lumped into the same dismissable category in a neat rhetorical sleight-of-hand: "those who oppose the idea of the Mahdi are merely slavishly imitating Western thinkers"[55]—although Muslims have never, in truth, needed Western intellectual ammunition to level fusillades at Mahdism (as chapter 5 demonstrates).

Taking their cue from Ibn Khaldun and to a lesser extent Rashid Rida,[56] Sunni anti-Mahdist works often paint Mahdism as covert Shi`ism, and thus defenders of the Mahdi must establish their anti-Shi`i bona fides in order to respectably support Mahdism. Modern Sunni Mahdists, then, are quite critical of Shi`ism, although they will grudgingly give the Shi`a credit for not rejecting the Mahdi concept out of hand. For example, in an almost humorous case of the pot calling the kettle black, the Shi`a are said to be particularly prone to falling under the sway of false mahdis.[57] The Shi`i belief in occultation of the Hidden Imam or Mahdi is derided as an erroneous belief predicated on weak traditions[58] or on having been interpolated into Shi`i Islam and its traditions by heretics at the expense of the correct (i.e., Sunni) belief that the Mahdi will be born into this world and stride onto the stage of history at the opportune time. One theory pinpoints the source of this heterodox Shi`i doctrine in a specific person, one Abd Allah b. Saba, a Jewish convert to Islam in the early days of Islamic history. He is said to have been a false convert, a *mutamuslim*, who wanted to undermine the new dispensation with this irrational, eventually Shi`i concept of an occulted deliver.[59]

The polemical expressive literature between Mahdists and their opponents has thus come to contain a disputative subset in which Sunni and Shi`i true believers hurl invective at one another, each attempting to prove that it alone has the correct Islamic understanding and expectation of the Mahdi and, further, anathematizing the other side for its mulish intransigence in the face of such obvious proofs. Although this study is of Sunni Mahdism, a brief examination of two works from the Shi`i spectrum of Mahdist belief might prove instructive. Consider Abd Allah al-Gharaybi's *Traditions and Sayings about the Imam Mahdi*, published in 1988.[60] This book is a distillation of the Shi`i side in the modern Mahdist debate.

Al-Gharaybi makes a number of points. First, he maintains that Mahdism is truly Sunni, and not a Shi`i heresy, as some allege. More specifically, al-Gharaybi attempts to explain away some of the Sunni objections to Mahdism's Shi`i aspects. If the Mahdi were to emerge from occultation now, he would be over 1,200 years old, and unsurprisingly some Sunni commentators ridicule the doctrine. Al-Gharaybi, however, observes that recent scientific and medical research has demonstrated that there is no limit, at least theoretically, to human lifespans; the Qur'an (like the Bible) speaks of prophets like Noah living for close to a millennium;[61] and, of course, Allah can suspend natural laws whenever He desires. Al-Gharaybi argues that once points such as these are grasped, the Mahdi's hiddenness seems quite logical. Likewise, he contends that the Sunni community must move beyond its caricature of Shi`i Mahdism in which every so often someone goes to a cave and bellows, "Come out, O Mahdi!" The reality is that the Mahdi will emerge from Mecca. Al-Gharaybi does admit that some Sunni Mahdist apologists are somewhat correct when they level the charge that Mahdist belief produces only indolence and sloth among Muslims. But, he argues, waiting on a Mahdi who is already on earth and preparing to reemerge into the light of history, as opposed to one yet to be born, grow up, and assume his role, is far more beneficial to the Islamic community, both Sunni and Shi`i, in that it is far less likely to encourage apathy among Muslims than the alternative Sunni Mahdi. Al-Gharaybi goes on to warn that Sunnis and Shi`is need to come together regarding the Mahdi because the dislocations of the End Time are quickly approaching.

Al-Gharaybi's book is now 16 years old, but Arab Shi`is are still updating their Mahdist perspective and disseminating the results. For example, al-Shaykh Ali Kurani's *The Preparers of the Way for the Mahdi*,[62] published in 2003, makes many of the same arguments as al-Gharaybi's text, most importantly that the world geopolitical situation points to the imminent appearance of the Mahdi. Now while Sunni Mahdists would likely differ with Kurani's contention that the Ayatollah Khomeini (d. 1989), founder of the Islamic Republic of Iran, was quite possibly *na'ib al-Imam al-Mahdi*, the "deputy of the Imam Mahdi," most would agree with his eschatological timetable.[63]

Convergence between Sunni and Shi`i Mahdism, and what that might portend for the Islamic world as a whole, is examined in the final chapter. But any rapprochement between the Sunni and Shi`i branches of Islam, based on common expectations of the Mahdi, faces a major obstacle in that heretofore the overall tenor of the debate, at least in the Arabic-speaking Muslim world, is one largely of rancor from the Sunni side; so much so, in fact, that some Sunni Arab Mahdists are overtly and stridently anti-Shi`i (and thus, not surprisingly, anti-Iranian) in their eschatological prognostications.

Mahdism's proponents also occasionally acknowledge that some of the Mahdi's most vociferous supporters throughout the centuries have been the suspect Sufis and that some of their heterodox ideas might, just perhaps, have crept into Mahdist doctrines. But whereas one of the major critiques of anti-Mahdists is their contention that Sufism simply copied Shi`ism's errors regarding the Mahdi—such as by allegedly adding to what the Qur'an and Hadith say and for inserting fantasies and myths into the corpus of Mahdist doctrines,[64]—Mahdist believers sometimes adduce Sufis more favorably; for example, Sayyid Abu Ala al-Mawdudi (d. 1979), the famous Pakistani Pan-Islamist and neo-fundamentalist intellectual, is quoted as saying that "the Mahdi will in form resemble a Sufi."[65] In sum, then, whereas modern Sunni books on the Mahdi do give Shi`is and Sufis credit for at least not rejecting out of hand the doctrine of the Mahdi, they at the same time denigrate both groups for their allegedly incorrect beliefs regarding him.

THE REINTERPRETATION OF THE END TIME
FIGURES IN MODERN MAHDIST BOOKS

Once Modern Mahdist writers have reemphasized the legitimacy of Mahdism's roots in Hadith and corroborating commentators and have also dismissed the false Shi`i view of the Mahdi and, preemptively, the charge that such Shi`i belief automatically renders Mahdism illegitimate, they then move on to reconfiguring and recontextualizing the eschatological context in which the Mahdi will appear.

As mentioned in chapter 1, for centuries Muslim eschatological commentators have divided the signs and figures of the approaching end into two categories: major and minor. In general, the minor signs are types that prefigure or point to the End Time; the major ones will be proof that the end of history itself is drawing nigh. To paraphrase Winston Churchill, the minor signs are tantamount to "the end of the beginning," whereas the major signs truly mark "the beginning of The End." The appearances of the Mahdi, Jesus, and the Dajjal are three signs always deemed major; but others often mentioned in this same category are the sun rising in the West, Yajuj and Majuj, the Dabbah, and the consuming fire from Yemen. Infrequently the Mahdi is posited as neither major nor minor, but the crucial transformative link between the two categories.[66]

The minor signs include, but are not limited to, earthquakes, increased sexual immorality, strife within the Muslim community, great disparities in wealth, and the conquest of "Constantinople" (Istanbul since 1453) and Rome by Muslim armies.[67] Some Mahdist apologists further break down the most important minor signs into dozens of more specfic ones, a process that seems to involve a not inconsiderable degree of speculation and sensationalism.[68] Some of these signs may have already transpired; others are yet to happen.[69] But all of them are merely a warmup, as it were, for the main event: the appearance on the world historical stage of the likes of the Mahdi, Jesus, the Dajjal, and the Sufyani.

Whether the Mahdi is typified as a major or minor sign, he usually comes first in the eschatological chronology spelled out in the expressive literature of the Mahdist writers. All such writers agree in general with the traditional description of the Mahdi and his role in history: that he will resemble Muhammad in name and appearance; that he will be of the Prophet's family; that he and Jesus will eventually, somehow, cooperate against the forces of evil; that his primary task during his limited tenure on earth will be to fill the world with justice and equity, eliminating injustice and disparities of wealth and power. The modern Mahdist apologists do depart from these common bases to imbue their virtual Mahdi with their own preferred characteristics, however.

In terms of lineage and background, the Mahdi's family origins are said to be traceable simply to Fatimah[70] or to Fatimah through Hasan.[71] One might see such statements as evidence of the convergence of Sunni and Shi`i Mahdist views, except that other Mahdist loyalists take pains to point out that although descended from Fatimah, the Mahdi will be a rightly guided caliph and imam who is not Shi`i.[72] It is also sometimes asserted that that Mahdi must be specifically an Arab leader who eventually takes the reins of the entire Muslim world and then the entire planet. He must be *al-manzalah al-samiyah,* "of Semitic status,"[73] and so any non-Arab Muslim leader is ipso facto wrong when trying to claim such a status—as did, allegedly, the Ottoman Turkish sultan Abdülaziz (r. 1861–1876).[74]

The Mahdi's role is also fine-tuned by his modern devotees, fleshed out beyond the rather vague one as restorer of global justice and equity. On the psychological level, once he comes forth the Mahdi will move beyond his current status as abstract symbol of hope to Mulsims into that of an inspirational leader, filling believers' hearts with magnanimity[75] and liberating them from the grip of evil and its handmaiden anxiety, both individual and collective. Further, the Mahdi will reify such psychic yearnings in a number of ways. In what amounts to a rather gender-conflating metaphor, the Mahdi will, it is said, function as the "mid-wife" for the new, more just Islamic world order that is even now beginning its birth pains.[76] He will formulate a beneficial ideology that, when realized, will allow for the establishment of a divinely based program,[77] one that will elevate Muslims, religiously and politically, worldwide.[78] This divine agenda not only will restore Islam to its rightful place as the world's largest religion and master of the world[79] but also will engender the creation of a planetary Islamic polity, called by some Mahdist literature the *dawlah Islamiyah* (the Islamic state),[80] or alternatively the *dawlah Allah* (the state of God).[81] Whatever it is called, the operative and overriding religio-political principle will be true Qur'an-based laws and governance, replacing the extant *dawlat al-batil,* "illegitimate state,"[82] a term that could refer to the current world political system, modern Middle Eastern and Islamic regimes, or perhaps even the State of Israel.

Some Mahdist apologists advocate the creation of an army of *muwahhidun,* "proponents of the unity of God [*tawhid*]," in order to prepare the way for the coming of the Mahdi and, afterward, to serve as the hewers of wood and drawers of water in the Mahdist state that will be created.[83] The all-important concept of tawhid is posited as the primary ideology of Mahdism because the role of the Mahdi is to spread and enforce this belief system, without which Muslim success is not possible.[84] Of course, the overrriding importance of tawhid in Mahdist thought was first trumpeted by Ibn Tumart and his followers almost 900 years ago; and the concept still resonates today: although not yet Mahdist, Abu Musab al-Zarqawi's violent faction in Iraq until recently called itself *al-Tawhid wa-al-Jihad,* "Unity and Jihad."[85]

Once the Mahdi's rule is established (and the Mahdist scenarios speculating on just how this comes about will be explored later in this chapter), one of his primary goals will be to create a worldwide society in which wealth and power are more equally distributed than under the current (or, for that matter, any past) world system—which is, according to some Muslim writers, totally in thrall to Dajjal.[86] (There are, however, some Mahdists who eschew the Mahdi's quasi-socialist role and emphasize almost totally his political and military acumen.)[87] Sometimes Mahdist writers simply reiterate that traditions about the equalization of wealth and power asymmetries under the Mahdi, sans any elaboration of the methodology he will employ to get there.[88] Perhaps he will inspire everyone to share with others, and there will be no need for coercive redistribution.[89] Others, however, believe the Mahdi will basically serve as a global Robin Hood, specifically mandating wealth redistribution in order to rectify the vast disparities in living standards among groups and nations.[90] Some Mahdist apologists readily admit that the Mahdi will need help to achieve such a lofty goal, however, and that help will come in the form of the returned prophet Jesus.[91]

As with the Mahdi, there is a basic corpus of beliefs concerning Jesus upon which all Mahdist writers agree. He will descend to earth; repudiate Christianity and vindicate Islam by destroying all the world's crosses, killing all the world's swine, and reciting the Muslim profession of faith; cooperate with the Mahdi to overcome the forces of evil, in particular the Dajjal; and finally, die a natural death and be buried next to the prophet Muhammad.[92] As with their elaboration of the Mahdi over and above the bare bones information contained in hadiths, however, Mahdists today add their own spin on the return and role of Jesus. His descent, for example, is predicted as being upon the minaret of the white mosque near Damascus International Airport.[93] When will this happen? Most Mahdist writers think the event will occur prior to the Mahdi's emergence, probably after "the Jews" have rebuilt their Temple on the site of the al-Aqsa Mosque,[94] which by then will likely have been destroyed in a nuclear *Harmigiddun*, or "Armageddon."[95] (No repentant word yet from the Mahdist writer who claimed Jesus would return in autumn 2001, however.[96]) Others say that Jesus will not return until after the Mahdi has established his global state.[97]

What will be the nature of the relationship between Jesus and the Mahdi? One school of interpretation holds that Jesus will be the senior partner and the Mahdi his loyal lieutenant as *wazir muqarrab*, or "intimate advisor"[98]; furthermore, this view maintains that Jesus will be the more powerful because he alone will kill the Dajjal, possibly in Lydda (or Lod), not in Jerusalem.[99] Another Mahdist apologist perspective is that, to the contrary, the Mahdi will outrank Jesus because the latter will need the former's help to kill the Dajjal.[100] When they pray together afterward, Jesus will prostrate himself in the mosque behind the Mahdi.[101] A more ecumenical view is that the Mahdi and Jesus will be coarchitects and corulers of the "godly state," which will represent the "kingdom of God" on earth, the *malakut Allah*—a phrase that appears four times in the Qur'an[102]—and can be seen as the same "kingdom of God" of which Jesus spoke in the Gospels.[103] Thus, the Mahdist Muslim state will be the same one for which Christians are yearning and will allow the two historically opposed religious communities to live together peacefully at long last,[104] although this irenic view flies in the face of most Muslim eschatological exegesis, which seems to mandate conversion to Islam of all in the coming Mahdist state, including or perhaps especially Christians.

This discussion of Jesus vis-à-vis the Mahdi necessitates an exploration of an intriguing trend in modern Islamic eschatological discourse: the usage of the Bible and of Christian beliefs about the End Time in order to refine and recontextualize Islamic doctrines concerning the Mahdi, the Dajjal, and others. As David Cook so accurately and eloquently puts it:

> Apocalyptists are . . . so close to the edge of the necessity to constantly up-date and revise their predictions and scenarios, as around them Jews control the world, Muslims are humiliated and defeated, technology leaps and bounds forward, leaving Muslim societies rootless and disconnected, and treaties are signed with the archenemy Israel. The apocalyptic traditions available to the Muslims have not been able to provide a framework capable of absorbing these inexplicable changes, and so apocalyptists . . . have taken Christian apocalyptic expectations . . . [and] grafted onto them whatever can be salvaged from the wreckage of Muslim apocalyptic literature.[105]

Thus, the traditional conventional wisdom regarding Muslim disdain for the Bible—that it "never becomes of relevance to the legal issues within the Islamic community, nor generally, for any theological judgements"[106]— is no longer accurate, at least insofar as Madhist apologetics is concerned. No longer do Muslims, at least of the Mahdist variety, merely reiterate hadiths; in the past few decades, shaping them to fit a specfic geopolitical context has become paramount. Furthermore, not long after 1967 we begin to see, in the eschatological Islamic literature in general and in the Mahdist kind in particular,[107] an interpretive stew in which "classical Muslim apocalyptic, antisemitic [sic] conspiracy theories, and a great deal of Biblical material" are cooked up, then kicked up a notch by adding American evangelical glosses on the End Time passages in Daniel, the Gospels, and Revelation.[108]

For example, the many New Testament statements about a "Son of Man"[109] who will come at the eschatological denouement, usually understood by orthodox Christians to refer to post–Second Coming Christ, are reinterpreted as Jesus' predictions of the Mahdi.[110] Or in a slightly different vein, Mahdists approvingly cite the warnings in the Book of Revelation about the great battle of Armageddon,[111] alongside Qur'an and Hadith, with the name either Arabicized to *Harmagiddun* or reentitled *al-Malhamah al-Kubra*, "the great battle."[112] Some Mahdist writers see this titanic clash as a nuclear war between two great alliances. Interestingly enough, considering the rancor today in the Muslim world directed at the West in general and the United States in particular, a number of Mahdist scenarios posit the Mahdi allied with the Christian West against a common "Eastern" enemy, at least in the intial stages of the global battle for supremacy.[113] The

Mahdi will join forces with the Europeans and Americans, or more likely just the Americans, against the Russians, Chinese, and probably Iranians, who will be led by the Dajjal.[114] Later, once the Mahdi and his allies have triumphed, the West will betray him and attack his army, only to be defeated, thus leading to the Mahdi's global supremacy. The nuclear Armageddon will come either during the Mahdist and Western victory over "the East," or later in the aftermath of the American treachery.

The Mahdi's defenders also adduce a number of other references from that corrupted document, the Bible, to support their rather tortured exegesis: the Gog and Magog accounts;[115] the parable of the workers in the vineyard (presumably because Muslims—the community of the final Prophet—are analogized to the last group of workers hired, who nonetheless receive the same reward);[116] the day of the Lord, described by St. Paul (which mentions the "Rapture," so excoriated by liberal Christians and the problematic nature of which for Islam seems to largely escape, or get ignored by, approving Mahdist writers);[117] the Old Testament account of Jerusalem's besiegement and a concomitant great plague (equated with post–nuclear attack radiation poisoning);[118] and the famous apocalyptic warnings of Jesus.[119]

The pro-Mahdist literature not only utilizes the Christian and Jewish Scriptures but also positively cites a plethora of American Protestant leaders—or at least their eschatological musings. These leaders include the likes of Pat Robertson, founder of the Trinity Broadcasting Network, one-time presidential candidate in 1988, and "leader of the Gospel Fundamentalists"; Hal Lindsey, who began the modern Christian eschatological craze with his book *The Late Great Planet Earth* in 1970; Jerry Falwell, Baptist minister, president of Liberty University, and founder of the now-defunct Moral Majority; Jimmy Swaggart, the disgraced but now returned Pentecostal televangelist; and Billy Graham, the famous evangelist and counselor to U.S. presidents. Cyrus I. Scofield (d. 1921), publisher of a prominent study Bible in which eschatology figures prominently, is also included in this litany of non-Muslim corroborators about the End Time. So, too, are former presidents Richard Nixon (d. 1994) and Ronald Reagan (d. 2004), both of whom are said by Mahdists to have expected Armageddon and Jesus' Second Coming in the very near future.[120] Finally, some Mahdist apologists reach far back into history for another Western Christian validator regarding the imminent End Time: Nostradamus (d. 1566). The famous French Catholic seer (or fraud, depending on one's point of view) is cited to the effect that "great terror from the sky will strike the Middle East around the year 1999."[121] This may, of course, mirror the great interest in Nostradamus's apocalyptic predictions among Westerners prior to the turn of the recent millennium.

Besides classical Muslim eschatological traditions and borrowings from the Bible as refracted primarily through the aforementioned conservative and fundamentalist Protestant commentators, the modern Mahdist writer has an unfortunate tendency to incorporate anti-Semitic ideas into the End Time scenarios regarding the Mahdi's coming. Consider, for example, the reformulation of the "king of the south" mentioned in the book of Daniel,[122] where he is an evil ruler and conqueror who will "desecrate the [Jewish] Temple" and "set up the abomination that causes desolation."[123] Today's Mahdist literature refers to him as *al-rajul al-Ashuri*, "the Assyrian man," or *mahdi al-Sahyuni*, "the Zionist Mahdi," and sees him not as evil but as a garbled understanding of the coming Mahdi, wrongly portrayed as malevolent in the Jewish Scriptures because in the run-up to the End Time many Jews will follow the Dajjal, who will be opposed by the Mahdi.[124] However, just how this inverted, End Time understanding of the Mahdi is retrojected into a Jewish holy book written in the second century BCE (if not earlier) is never explained. This example nonetheless serves to illustrate that Mahdist writers are at least as prone to anti-Jewish conspiracy theorizing as their non-Mahdist brethren in the Muslim world.

The modern point of origin for such an Islamic worldview might well be traced to the writings of Mahmud Abu Rayya, a disciple of Rashid Rida, who around the time of World War II conflated the aforementioned Muslim trepidation about alleged Jewish attempts to undermine Islam in its early days with the modern state of Israel and its Zionist ideology:

A (Jewish) archetype was born here out of the internal Islamic questioning of the *Isra'iliyyat*[125] and the Palestine problem. . . . Drawn and abstracted from "the past" in order to be applied to contemporary history as an archetypal explanation, this idea was to have a long and variegated history in certain trends of later Islamic (especially "Islamist") thought. In official "establishment" circles, such as al-Azhar, the equation between the misbehaviour of ancient Jews . . . and the modern misbehaviour of Zionist Jews in Palestine became an intellectual paradigm for some.[126]

Mahdist circles may not be official or establishment, but their denizens have drunk as deeply at this well as have the muftis of al-Azhar, and perhaps more so. Mahdist prognosticators interpret Hadith to mean that Jews will be among the largest contingent of the Dajjal's followers, with his vanguard consisting of perhaps 70,000 of them, from Isfahan (Iran).[127] Also, theological criticism of Jews for not believing in Jesus' return, as do Christians and Muslims,[128] can all too easily elide into the anti-Jewish stereotype so beloved of some Islamists. Jews in Iran, particularly, are seen as a nefarious force allied with Christians and Communists to undermine Islam—and this even after the establishment of the Islamic Republic there.[129] Mustafa Kemal Atatürk, the Ottoman general who almost singlehandedly created the modern state of Turkey, is portrayed in this literature as the main reason for the fall of the Ottoman caliphate. He is said to have been dedicated to injuring Islam in this way by virtue of his allegedly being a *Dönme*, a descendant of those Jews who followed the seventeenth-century Jewish leader Sabbatai Sevi from Jewish messianism into Islam.[130] "The Zionists" are said to be helping undermine Islam not just by occupying Palestinian land but by aiding and abetting the Baha'i heresy, since the worldwide headquarters of Baha'ism is in Israel.[131] In the Great Battle that finally decides humanity's political fate and brings the Mahdi to planetary power, his pious Muslim armies will triumph over those of the Americans, Turks, and Israelis.[132] So, Judaism, through its political incarnation of Zionism, is seen as trying to hinder or oppose the Mahdi, with predictable results (or so the Mahdists hope).

The Dajjal whom so many Jews will allegedly follow will, say modern Madhists, come from "the East"—Iran, Russia, perhaps one of the former Soviet republics like Turkmenistan or Uzbekistan—or alternatively, from the Arabian Peninsula. He will escape or be freed from some form of angelic incarceration at the end of a time of great famine and drought and after either the conquest of "Constantinople"—modern Istanbul—or after Armageddon. The Dajjal will be the fountainhead of unbelief, error, and strife, performing miracles and eventually claiming divinity for himself. Besides Jews, his devotees will number devils, Christians, *batinis* ("esotericists," a term historically used to refer to Isma'ili Shi`ites[133]), and women. He will roam the earth for 40 days or 40 years but, despite his powers, be prohibited by God from entering four sanctuaries of the faithful: Mecca, Medina, Jerusalem, and Mt. Sinai. Jesus, perhaps assisted by the Mahdi, will finally kill him.[134]

It is in the view of the Dajjal that the anti-Shi`i and anti-Iranian predilections of some Sunni Mahdists come to the fore. One scenario, then, postulates that Iranian President Muhammad Khatami might very well be the Dajjal, since the Shi`i clerical hierarchy of sayyid, hujatollah, and ayatollah can easily be adapted to a claim of divinity (one step above ayatollah, presumably),[135] which the Dajjal will make. In this scenario Khatami will reveal his Dajjalate at an Islamic conference in Tehran in the not-too-distant future, after which he will lead the Shi`a Iranians in a nuclear attack on Bahrain and the eastern Gulf emirates, commencing the End Time events.[136] This would certainly seem to be, among other things, a good Sunni Mahdist argument supporting the U.S. nonproliferation stance toward the Islamic Republic.

The other, lesser eschatological figures are given much shorter shrift by Mahdist writers, no doubt because they are mere ancillaries to the big three of the Mahdi, Jesus, and the Dajjal. The Dabbah is acknowledged, and Mahdists largely follow the hadith accounts of it: emerging from somewhere in the Arabian desert the same day that the sun rises in the West, it will travel to Mecca and then proceed to roam the earth; and like the Dajjal, it will have *k-f-r*, the Arabic consonantal root for "unbeliever," inscribed on its forehead.[137] As for Yajuj and Majuj, there are a few more creative pro-Mahdist glosses applied than with the Dabbah. These groups are said, for example, to be post-Deluge[138] descendents of Japheth, son of Noah.[139] As time passed, the Japhethites somehow transmogrified into those hordes that Alexander the Great penned up, pending the Last Days. Modern Mahdist writers tend to identify these hordes as the modern Russians or Chinese that will, sometime after Jesus slays the Dajjal, stream forth across Eurasia until God, at Jesus' request, destroys them.[140] Finally, the Sufyani is warned about by some Mahdists in that he will take over the Middle East prior to the Mahdi's coming; he will probably come from Jordan. It is sometimes speculated that he will have lieutenants identified as *al-Abqa*, "the speckled/spotted," and *al-Ashab*, "the reddish"; the former was supposed to have been Yassir Arafat (d. 2004) while the latter will be an as-yet undertermined Jordanian.[141]

This is how literature today by pro-Mahdists portrays the important eschatological signs and personages surrounding their focus, the Mahdi himself. However, modern proponents of the Mahdi also go boldly where no Muslim has gone before, attempting to fit the traditions about their once and future deliverer into current Middle Eastern and world geopolitical trends and events.

"NEWSPAPER EXEGESIS": THE MAHDI'S COMING IN LIGHT OF TODAY'S HEADLINES

Before locating the Mahdi on today's world political and religious event horizon, his modern defenders first render their verdicts on self-styled mahdis throughout history. Going all the way back to the early days of Islam, the plethora of such movements identified by these writers[142] can be classified into three broad categories.

The first consists of those whose founders or leaders openly and presumably sincerely, but nonetheless falsely, claimed to be the Mahdi. Included here are the likes of Ibn Tumart, Muhammad Ahmad, and Juhayman al-Utaybi, although it was actually al-Utaybi's brother-in-law, al-Qahtani, who was supposed to be the Mahdi. The second grouping is said to encompass those whose creators used the idea of the Mahdi to delude people. These knowingly false mahdis are referred to as *musha`widhun*, "conjurers" or "swindlers," and *dajjalun* (plural of *dajjal*), "deceivers," and whose calculated deception differentiates from those individuals in the first category who probably honestly considered themselves mahdis.[143] Examples of such dajjals include the Bab and Baha'ullah, cofounders of the Baha'i movement, as well as Ghulam Ahmad Shah, originator of the Ahmadiyah sect—two new religions. The final category is that of individuals who did not personally attempt to claim the Mahdiyah but, rather, had it claimed for them by others. The prophet Jesus is the prime example here in that although it is undeniable that he was rightly guided by God, he never used the term about himself but, rather, was said to have fulfilled the relevant traditions by some in the Muslim community. Others that the Mahdist faction claim fall under this category are several eighth-century CE Umayyd caliphs (Sulayman b. Abd al-Malik and Umar b. Abd al-Aziz); Ubayd Allah, the first Fatimid caliph; al-Barelwi; and Ali al-Sanusi.[144]

Besides categorizing the false mahdis of the past, some Mahdists then go on to excoriate them. Ibn Tumart, for example, is ridiculed as a "liar and tyrant," and Ubayd Allah is denigrated as not merely a charlatan but *al-mahdi al-mulhid*, "the heretical mahdi."[145] The Baha'is and Ahmadis are dismissed as, at best, "error-ridden apostates"[146] and, at worst, as paragons

When will you reveal your light, O Awaited One. [*Source:* www. almujtaba.com]

of an era best summarized as the "century of Satan" (the nineteenth century), their founders demonized as modern Musaylimahs (the contemporary, self-styled prophetic rival to Muhammad)[147] or Kharijis.[148] And the 1979 al-Utaybi and al-Qahtani uprising in Saudi Arabia is dismissed as one of false mahdism, evidenced by the movement's failure, by its heinous use of force in Mecca, and by al-Qahtani's lacking the requisite physical characteristics.[149]

Obviously, no modern believer in the Mahdi considers any Mahdist claimant of the past to have actually been the true one. But Mahdist apologists will, of course, hasten to add that the historical abundance of aspiring Mahdis does not disprove the future historicity of this figure: operative here for Mahdism's tenacious supporters is *abusus non tollit usum*.[150] No number of false mahdis can change one iota the fact that he *will* come, eventually. (This Mahdist true-believer viewpoint parallels that of hardline Marxists who adamantly maintain, despite the failure of Communist societies worldwide and the total collapse of the vanguard of the revolution, the USSR, in 1991, that true Marxism "has not been tried yet.")

Of course, the Mahdi must come in large measure because true Islamic rule will have vanished from the earth, thus any and all extant regimes will be illegitimate, no matter how many claims of Muslim or Islamic they may make. For the Mahdist, as for the apocalyptist, "there are, therefore, three categories of ruler: prophets, tyrants, and the future Mahdi."[151] Some Mahdist writers further refine their political history, with two slightly different paradigms predominating. Both are an adaptation of a hadith in which Muhammad is said to have warned that after him would come caliphs, then amirs, kings, and tyrants.[152] One Mahdist gloss is to adopt this same paradigm, then predicatably plug in the Mahdist state at the end as the culmination and corrective thereof.[153] A variation on this theme has the post-Prophet polities as the caliphs, substitute sovereigns, then tyrannical kings, and finally the Mahdi's caliphate.[154] The only real difference between these Mahdist political theories is that the latter lumps amirs and *muluk*, "kings," together as mere impersonator rulers. Both Madhist paradigms look back—and in this they share a view with many fundamentalist Muslims—to the idealized, halcyon days of Muhammad and the early community as the standard against which all subsequent "Muslim" states are measured and found wanting, at least until the Mahdi comes.

Modern pro-Mahdist literature tends to steer clear of positively identifying the actual historical polities that allegedly fit these pejorative categories. However, it is not difficult to determine that the Umayyads and Abbasids would be considered amirs, kings, or substitute rulers—mere epigones of the *Rashidun*, the four "rightly guided" caliphs immediatlely post-Muhammad. And based on the positive views of the Ottoman Empire offered by Mahdist literature—that Istanbul was the seat of a legitimate caliphate under the Ottomans and that, for all its faults, under Ottoman leadership the Sunni Islamic world was at least "awake" and on the offensive[155]—it seems that

that empire is looked upon as the end of the span of kings, and not the much less legitimate tyrants. Mahdists will, however, specify that the current age is the penultimate one in history, that of so-called Muslim rulers who are in reality tyrants. All modern Arab and indeed Muslim states are subsumed under the heading of tyrannies (yet another perspective that Mahdists share with Islamic fundamentalists), since nary a one of them adheres to a truly Muslim agenda and administration.

In the Mahdist worldview the Ottoman state, if not a perfectly pious upholder of true Islamic law, was at least powerful on the world stage and an Islamic force to be reckoned with, unlike the Muslim Lilliputian polities that have succeeded it. The lion's share of the blame for the toppling of the Ottoman caliphate goes to that "agent of imperialism," the "crypto-Jew" Atatürk, who was helped by the Masonic order and the Iranians.[156] Mahdists still refer to "Constantinople" rather than Istanbul, seemingly as a way to denigrate the Islamic nature of the Turkish state; and so Mahdist eschatological thought posits that perhaps the city will be "re"conquered by "al-Rum" (the Romans), meaning the Americans and Europeans. The West's nefarious plot to recapture the old Byzantine capital has been in the works for centuries, kicking off its final phase in 1974 when the Greek-speaking portion of Cyprus tried to put itself under the rule of Athens, precipitating the Turkish occupation of one-third of the island, and has continued to this day with ventures such as the Turkish-Israeli joint security agreements of the 1990s. Mahdists even cite the rantings of the Russian nationalist Vladimir Zhironovsky—who constantly demagogued about the dangers of Turks and Muslims, hearkening back to 1453—and refer ominously to any visit by an Orthodox Patriarch to the West, particularly to America, as somehow part of this ancient, transcontinental plot.[157]

Mahdism's modern proponents also agree that the Muslim community has been in a state of angst and torpor for decades, if not centuries. This sorry state, the only cure for which is the Mahdi, overcame the entire, but particularly the Muslim, world over the last 500 years—the flip side, it seems, of the Western Christian expansion that began reaching critical mass with Columbus's discovery of the Americas in 1492. While the Ottoman Empire existed there was at least some secular power still held by Muslims—and with its caliphate, a modicum of religious legitimacy—and thus hope. But with the empire's downfall after World War I, the umma has been in a downward spiral. Ostensibly Muslim rulers, really mere kings, dictators, and tinpot tyrants, oppress their own people. In fact, the current age—the fifteenth one after the hijrah—is the blackest one in the history of Islam, with the *awtan*, "homelands," sundered, their resources plundered, and Muslims everywhere bereft of their own history, which has been appropriated by others[158] and given an alien tone of *unsuriyah*, "racism" or "nationalism," in which Islam and its heroes are subordinated to nationalistic identities. The Mahdist, for the most part, is thus obviously a devotee of Pan-Islam, the belief that Islamic identity should trump ethnolinguistic (Arabophone or Turkophone, for example) or artificial nationalistic (Syrian, Iraqi, Jordanian, or even Turkish) characteristics. And rather than striving to reverse this state of somnolence and decay, the vast majority of Muslims are slumbering through it. Even when some few do manage to awaken, they live heedless of Allah, devoting themselves to alien, mainly Western ideologies such as consumeristic capitalism, democracy, or Marxism. Most Muslims, then, in the Mahdist view are just as bad as the pre-Deluge inhabitants of the earth were in the time of prophet Nuh (Noah).[159] But God will be more merciful than he was in the time of Noah: He will send the Mahdi to awaken the Muslims and motivate them to arise from their lassitude and overcome the soporific angst of Western influence.[160]

But this will not come to pass until the Islamic world suffers through a number of *fitan* (singular *fitnah*)—"strifes," "civil wars," "social upheavals," and "discords," although in a useful double entendre for Mahdist writers the Arabic term also carries a sense of "temptations," "enticements," and "trials."[161] Drawing on traditions, the Mahdist model for the unfolding of these fitan is as follows: (1) *fitnah al-ahlas*, the "discord of pleasure"; (2) *fitnah al-sarra'*, the "discord of prosperity"; (3) *fitnah al-dahimah*, the "discord of the masses"; and (4) an unnamed inter-Arab conflict.[162] One Mahdist interpretive school holds that the first two such fitnahs have already occurred: the first was the Iran-Iraq War of 1980–1988; the second was the Iraqi occupation of Kuwait in 1990 and the subsequent U.S.-led war to evict Saddam's forces. In this view, the third conflict will occur in the near future when Iran attacks the eastern Persian Gulf states (Qatar, Bahrain, the United Arab Emirates, and perhaps Oman) for not acknowledging the power and legitimacy of the Shi`i false mahdi, the twelfth imam (who is, in all likelihood, actually the Dajjal). The fourth fitnah is then reinterpreted as the attack of the West, mainly the Americans, on the Dajjal-led Shi`is and his other useful idiots. This will result in a nuclear massacre of many Muslims.[163]

Some Mahdist sectarians have worked out elaborate chronologies similar in general outline, but of course differing in a number of details, for the unfolding of this fourth fitnah (the final one before the appearance of the Mahdi). al-Aqsa Mosque in Jerusalem will be destroyed, presumably by the Israelis, so that they can commence rebuilding the Temple of Solomon on that site. This Mahdist scenario is not as far-fetched as some, for in mid-2004 the following news article appeared:

Israel's public security minister warned that Jewish extremists could attack the al-Aqsa Mosque compound in Jerusalem, a site holy to Muslims and Jews, hoping to provoke violence and wreck Israeli plans to withdraw from the Gaza Strip and parts of the West Bank.[164]

The Western powers will send armies into Jordan and Palestine and surround Jerusalem in order to protect "the Jews." Al-Sufyani will emerge as an Arab leader in Jordan and, at least initially, receive Western assistance. He will be opposed by an Iraqi leader named Hasan or Husayn, but al-Sufyani will defeat him and conquer Iraq. (Obviously this scenario was devised before the U.S. deposed Saddam and occupied Iraq.) Simultaneously, in Palestine and the Occupied Territories al-Abqa'—a Palestinian leader—and his supporters will battle the followers of *al-mushawwah*, "the disfigured [one]." (This person was supposed to be the blind paraplegic Ahmad Yasin, the founder and leader of the Palestinian Islamist group Hamas, but he was killed by the Israelis in March 2004.) Whoever wins this internecine Palestinian power struggle will then be defeated by the Sufyani, who by that time will have become the de facto ruler of most Sunni Muslims in the Middle East.

At some point during al-Sufyani's ascent to power the Mahdi will have revealed himself in Arabia and will initially receive assistance from an African Muslim ruler,[165] perhaps President al-Bashir of Sudan. While the Arabs are occupied with the looming power struggle between al-Sufyani and the Mahdi for the Arab Muslim lands, Iran will conquer Bahrain and much of the eastern Persian Gulf and then, having obviously outwitted the American nonproliferation regime, as well as the International Atomic Energy Agency, will launch nuclear missiles at the Vatican. In retaliation, the United States will destroy much of Iran in a nuclear strike, after which Iranian president Muhammad Khatami will reveal himself as the Dajjal. Shortly thereafter Jesus will return and destroy the Dajjal at approximately the same time that the Mahdi and his army of followers will have rallied and defeated al-Sufyani and his minions.[166]

Two somewhat cognitively dissonant attitudes regarding Iran and its post-1979 Islamic Republic exist side by side in the minds of Sunni Mahdist writers. On the one hand, the Khomeini-inspired overthrow of the Shah of Iran, and the state thereafter established largely on the Ayatollah's radical principle of rule by the religious leadership[167] can be seen as necessary to save a Muslim, albeit heretical Shi`i, country from the nefarious influence of "Jews and foreigners." As such, the Islamic revolution in Iran was a positive development for the greater Muslim world insofar as it has irritated and rattled the West.[168] But it can also be depicted as evil in two respects: first, tactically, to the extent that the Islamic coup in Iran inspired the 1979 al-Utaybi false mahdism in Saudi Arabia; and second, strategically, in that it is but the latest example of Iranian Shi`i assaults on the Sunni world since at least the early sixteenth century CE, when the Shi`i Safavid dynasty (whose founder, Shah Isma'il, considered himself the un-Hidden Imam) took over in Persia (modern Iran) and launched a centuries-long struggle for Muslim territory, hearts, and minds with the Sunni Ottomans.[169] In reality, say some Sunni Mahdists, Shi`i Iran has always been led by the Dajjal, who will finally step out from behind the Oz-like curtain in Teheran in the near future,[170] although he will be far less benevolent than Dorothy's wizard.

Eschatological prognostication by pro-Mahdist writers in recent years has developed two approaches in terms of dating the events presaging and encompassing the Mahdi's coming and the End Time countdown. One is to actually, firmly set specific dates but retain a fog of ambiguity about the exact nature of the geopolitical context in which they will transpire; the other is to wax more detailed about the events, but to place the appearance of eschatological figures appearances only in rough chronological order, not pinponting just when all will come to pass.

Perhaps the easiest example of the latter approach is to aver that God alone knows when the beginning of The End will commence. This is on good authority, since the prophets Jesus and Muhammad said this very thing.[171] A related Mahdist tactic is to simply claim that these events will take place "soon,"[172] and that the time in which we live now generally fits the prophetic description of the time right before the onset of the eschaton: wars and rumors of wars; earthquakes; oppressive governments, tyranny, and dictatorship; aggression; corruption; immorality and sexual deviance; deceit; and inter-Muslim strife between politically and morally degenerate "petty states"[173]—the fulfillment of most, if not all, of the minor signs of the coming of The End.

One variation of this "the time is nigh" perspective is that practiced by Madhist writers who formulate a sequential timetable of the eschatological events and personalities, without precise dating. One Mahdist scenario, for example, foresees al-Rum—the Americans and Europeans, probably helped by the Israelis and Turks[174]—defeating al-Sufyani and his misled Arab forces in Syria (probably after the perfidious Westerners have repudiated an alliance with him) and then pressing their attacks to defeat al-Abqa' in Egypt, al-Ashab in Arabia, and yet another Sufyani epigone, al-Kundi, in North Africa. This will leave the Western Christian forces facing those of the Mahdi (who will have emerged in Arabia and rallied true Muslim Arabs to his banner), under a temporary truce. But the West will once again prove its distance from God by breaking the peace and attacking the Mahdi and his army of 70,000 with a huge force of almost a million men. The Mahdist regiments will triumph, however, and then move on to conquer "Constantinople" and then Rome, where they will find the Ark of the Covenant hidden in St. Peter's Basilica,[175] much to Indiana Jones's chagrin. The Ark of the Covenant may then be used by the Mahdi to gain the conversion of the Jews, who had heretofore opposed him.[176]

A more finely grained Mahdist scenario, but largely in this same vein, places the climactic Mahdist versus the West battle in Syria, between Aleppo and Antioch, and says that this will be World War III, after which besides taking the former capitals of the Roman Empire ("Constantinople" and Rome) the Mahdi and his multitude will liberate the entire world for

Islam. Then the Mahdi will reign as the just global caliph for seven or nine years, during which the Dajjal will emerge and Jesus descend to terminate him (one thing beyond the power of the Mahdi).[177] Note that in both of these eschatological paradigms no dates are provided, but only a rough ordering.

Another pro-Mahdist perspective does provide at least some firm dates. Jesus was to have descended in 2001 CE, just as the Dajjal was supposed to step onto the world stage. Although this mistaken assumption needs correcting, there is still time for Armageddon to take place on the posited date of 2010 CE; it consists of the West and the Muslims fighting and defeating the Communist world (and remember, the People's Republic of China is still officially Marxist-Leninist, despite its great profits from quasi-capitalist practices such as pirating Western music CDs) and the Shi'is. After this penultimate Armageddon, the Mahdi and the Sufyani will step into history. After the Mahdi and his loyal forces defeat the Sufyani's host, world war erupts between—you guessed it—the victorious Mahdist armies and the West, led by the United States. However, in a bit of interpretive legerdemain that makes the traditions more acceptable, this final war will be fought on ancient terms—with swords, on horseback—because the earlier Armageddon will have destroyed the more advanced, modern weaponry.[178]

An occasional Mahdist apologist will use Qur'anic analogies for the terrible effects of the modern weapons that will be used in the war by the United States and its Mahdist allies upon their enemies: "red death" will be caused by "stars falling from the sky," said to be nuclear weapons; and "white death"[179] will be biological, chemical, or nerve warfare.[180]

Finally, in terms of dating the End Time, some Mahdist writers rightly differentiate between the Hour of Resurrection and Judgment (which, of course, only God knows the time of) and the penultimate End Time that encompasses ongoing human history and the coming to power of the Mahdi, which can be calculated. Some modern Mahdists spin elaborate and highly questionable, if not absurd, webs of theological and historical computation in an attempt to do so. For example, since the world will last 7,000 years, and Adam was put here by God in 4990 BC, the world must end no later than 2010 CE. There are 63 years between the re-creation of Israel in 1947 CE (dating from the United Nations partition, rather than from the actual Zionist declaration of statehood in 1948) and Jesus' return, thus again pointing to the end in 2010. The Islamic community will last 1,400 years, and Jesus ascended at age 33, and Israel was reestablished in 1367 AH. Since Jesus will die at age 40, that provides an alternative scenario in which The End comes in 2007 CE (1367 + 40). Other formulas are these: the prophet Muhammad's birthdate plus the date the Islamic community's span ends (570 CE + 1430 AH = 2000 CE); the date of Muhammad's death plus the date of Jerusalem's Zionist occupation (633 CE[181] + 1367 AH = 2000 CE); the years of Jesus' ascension plus the year of Jerusalem's occupation by Jews (33 CE + 1967 CE = 2000 CE). Note that the Mahdist sectarians who strive for this degree of prognosticatory precision[182] do so by conveniently conflating the Christian or Common Era calendar with the Muslim one.

Of course, there is the penultimate end in Islamic eschatology, and the ultimate one. Once all the wars between the major powers cease and the Sufyani and the Dajjal are vanquished, along with the Christian West, the Mahdi will reign supreme as global "warlord,"[183] with Jesus at his side as the kinder, gentler face of this new planetary, albeit all-too-temporary, caliphate. This is the penultimate end, if such is not an oxymoron, tantamount to the kingdom of God expected by Christians, who little suspected that their dreams would be realized by this worldwide Mahdist state. In it there will be no modern Pharisees (the ulama), criminals, adulterers, or murderers; instead, only the childlike, poor and pious followers of Islamic law will remain.[184] This will be a golden age, ruled jointly by the benevolent, rightly guided duarchy of Jesus and the Mahdi. Eventually, however, they each will die a natural death. Then, at some undetermined point afterward, after unbelief and sin have regained the upper hand among the earth's inhabitants, the trumpet of death and then the ominous, terrible trumpet of resurrection unto Judgment will blow. But that phase of extra-historical eschatology no longer concerns the Mahdi.

MAHDIST WEBSITES IN ARABIC

As might be expected in today's electronic information-dominated world, the Mahdists have taken their propaganda battle to the chatrooms and websites of the Internet. Although the Arab populace with access to the Internet has doubled in the last six years, that simply means it has gone from practically nonexistent (.3%) to barely discernible (.6%).[185] By contrast, Sweden leads the world with almost 77 percent of its population online, and the United States (with, of course, a much greater population) is second with 69 percent.[186] But, in a parallel to the situation of the Arab publishing universe where the tiny numbers of Mahdist books published must be compared to the overall miniscule book publishing figures, Mahdist websites might seem insignificant—except when put up against the context of the total Arabic Internet, in which case they loom larger. And there are many websites dealing with the Mahdi in the Internet's dominant language, the world's most-spoken second language: English.

An Internet investigation of the term *al-Mahdi* using the search engine Google produces 4,220 results. Many of those, however, refer not to the expected Muslim deliverer but websites put up by an individual with "Mahdi" as part of his name; media stories about the head of the Ummah party in Sudan (who, being descended from Muhammad Ahmad, also has the surname al-Mahdi); or references to the militia controlled by the erstwhile Iraqi opponent of U.S. occupation, Muqtada al-Sadr's *Jaysh al-Mahdi*, "Army of the Mahdi." But once this chaff has been sifted, true Mahdist wheat remains. I have been able to identify, so far, at least two dozen pro-Mahdist websites: seven Arabic and seventeen English ones. There are, of course, almost certainly ones in other European languages (especially German, with its large minority Muslim population) and in Farsi and Turkish, as well as in Urdu, the language of Pakistan.

In general the Arabic websites on the Mahdi do not seem to present as developed and coherent apologia for their protagonist, at least not compared to books published on him. They are more sensationalistic and shallow; but insofar as they are probably trying to appeal to the online browser, who probably has a shorter attention span than someone who purchases a book, this should come as no surprise. At least one is, in fact, horrifically sensationalistic, with little other than its Mahdist expectations to differentiate it from Muslim fundamentalist or terrorist sites. This site, "*Muntadiyat al-Mahdi*" ("Gathering [Chat] Rooms of the Mahdi"),[187] has a picture of the beheaded American Paul Johnson, as well as a picture of the dead Saudi Islamist Abd al-Aziz Muqrin, followed by a list of Mahdist traditions and a question-and-answer section where the curious can email their queries about the Mahdi. The site "*al-Muntadi*" ("Gathering [Chat] Room") is a venue for Muslims to chat in Arabic about a whole host of topics, and one section deals with Mahdist hadith and also allows for questions and answers.[188] Another seems to do the same thing with another eschatological topic: the Dajjal.[189] Perhaps the most fascinating of the few Arabic Mahdist sites is "*al-Haridy*,"[190] which at first glance seems to be merely an irreverent satire of Arab culture and politics done totally in Egyptian Arabic dialect—until one finds the section talking about Osama bin Laden, in which he is described as "the Qahtani who drives people with his stick."[191] "The Qahtani" was a prominent figure in the messianic expectations of pre-Islamic southern Arabia and, in Islamic thought, was transformed into the brother of the Mahdi.[192] Osama bin Laden's possible Mahdist aspirations are fully explored in chapter 6 of this work, but it is fascinating that at least quasi-Mahdist tincture is beginning to be applied to the world's most famous terrorist.

MAHDIST WEBSITES IN ENGLISH

As for the English websites touting the coming of the Mahdi, the most prominent and ecumenically Muslim is probably one put up on Yahoo, "MahdiUnite."[193] MahdiUnite's aims are best understood in the site creators' own words:

Al Mahdi Unites Muslims of Shia and Sunni sects is a group aimed at fostering unity among all muslim schools of thought. Both Sunni and Shia Muslims believe

in the same Allah (s.w.t), they believe in all the prophets from Adam (a.s.) to
Prophet Muhammed (s.a.w.) and they all believe in the same Holy Quraan [*sic*]
that is in its pure and original form. On top of that, All [*sic*] muslims unanimously
agree in Al-Mahdi who will appear in the last days of this world to bring back all
the lost justice

Please join this group to get ready for the eventual arrival of the promised
Mahdi and contribute your articles on Ahaadith, Riwaayaat[194] and Holy qur'an
[*sic*] to unite all Muslim sects and work together for the general betterment of our
muslim [*sic*] ummah

Let us leave aside the ideology which divides Muslims. Let us leave aside the
attempt of imperialists to divide Muslims. Let us have big heart, let us concentrate
on the more important soci0-religious issues [*sic*] of the perct [*sic*] religion of Islam

Let us work together to defeat the enemy of Islam. And Peace Love

Of course, not all Muslims today "unanimously agree" about the coming
of the Mahdi, as we shall see in the following chapter. But this popular
pro-Mahdist site, which is consciously trying to unite the sundered Sunni
and Shi`i branches of Islam around the central figure of the Mahdi, repre-
sents the more populist aspect of the modern Mahdist movement, whereas
Mahdist books seem to be more the province of the intellectual elite. It claims
over 4,600 members have joined since its inception in 2002.

Another site, more didactic and less of a Mahdist-believer echo chamber
than MahdiUnite, is that of the reigning English-language champion proponent of the Mahdi, and indeed of all Muslim eschatological matters, the
Turkish pseudonymous writer Harun Yahya.[195] Veritable tomes on the
Mahdi and the looming signs of The End are posted there, and if you'd pre-
fer to relax at home with one of Yahya's books, just order it from his up-to-
date online bookstore (which looks suspiciously like a copyright-violating
version of Amazon.com's site). Yahya's interpretations of current events in
light of the Qur'an and traditions is too lengthy to encompass in its entirety,
but some of is major points are worth noting.[196] For example, the traditions
about the minor sign of worldwide sinfulness before the End Time clock
starts can "materialize only when suitable technological means are available,
as they are today (e.g., the press, publications, broadcast and satellite communication)." More significant, the solar and lunar eclipses presaging the
Mahdi's coming took place in 1981 and 1982 CE. Even the al-Utaybi movement of 1979 is said to have been predicted by Muhammad in hadiths as a
sign of the impending End Time. Like all eschatologists, Christian as well as
Muslim, Yahya conveniently splices together unrelated chapters of scripture
in order to make his point(s). A good example is his conflation of Surah al-
Qamar [54]:1 with Surah `Abasa [80]:25ff. The former says, "The Hour has
drawn near and the moon is split." The latter has the deity explaining, "We
pour down plentiful water, then split the earth into furrows. Then we make
grain grow in it." Yahya asserts that the American lunar expeditions of the
late 1960s and early 1970s, which included some digging into the moon's

surface for rocks and soil to bring back to earth, fulfills these two Qur'anic predictions of one of the signs of the last days. Finally, Yahya states that, according to the U.S. Geological Survey National Earthquake Information Center, there were over 20,000 earthquakes in 1999; and since several traditions foresaw frequent earthquakes as the End Time approaches, we are perilously close. This is an argument also made by Christian eschatologists,[197] who like Yahya conveniently fail to offer any statistics informing how many earthquakes occur worldwide in any given year because doing so might undercut their implication that earthquakes are taking place in unprecedented numbers. In fact, in some ways Harun Yahya has much more in common with modern conservative and fundamentalist Christian purveyors of The End than he does with his coreligionists: technical (especially Internet) savvy, slick presentation, convenient material access and ordering, and so on. But in the crux of the matter—belief in the coming Mahdi—he is firmly in lockstep with his Muslim Mahdist brethren.

Besides these two rather unique sites, the other 15 English-language sites on the Mahdi from a Sunni outlook[198] fall into three broad categories: (1) rather pedestrian restatements of Mahdist traditions; (2) online apologia, which may also reiterate the relevant hadith but then move beyond that into often-detailed, pro-Mahdist discussions; (3) Mahdist arcana: sites that approach the Mahdi from a decidely offbeat perspective.

In the first category are at least five sites that simply stress the hadith roots of Mahdist belief. One, posted by the Muslim Student Association at the University of Southern California,[199] is a bare-bones list of all Mahdist traditions from Abu Da'ud. Very similiar to it is "Everything about the Islam [sic],"[200] which is narrative and hardly analytical or apologetic at all. The other three leaven the litany of citations with at least some pro-Mahdist commentary. One entitled "Greater Signs of the Hour"[201] rehashes the eschatological events and personages and offers rather standard Sunni commentary on the Mahdist traditions dealing with them and, of course, with the Mahdi. This is also the case with "Al-Imam al-Mahdi,"[202] which despite its name is not overtly Shi`i. Much in the same vein is the Pakistani site "Who is Imaam Mahdi?"[203] This site, however, does stress that Jesus was not, and will not be, the Mahdi.

The second grouping of English-language Mahdist sites moves beyond mere restatement of traditions into occasionally quite lengthy defenses of the doctrine. "Identification of the Prophesied Imam Mahdi" says one of its aims is to prevent Muslims from falling under the sway of false mahdis, like the Bab or Iran or Mirza Ghulam (Ahmad) of India, at the same time reminding Muslims that "the prophecy of the Mahdi is one that will come to pass"[204] and expounding on the relevant traditions. "Who Is Imam Al-Mahdi?"[205] purports to be the "result for a long research in evaluating every Hadeeth (true or false)." Exegeting each Mahdist hadith, it does include analysis and also warns Muslims that while the Mahdi will certainly come eventually, "this prophecy . . . does not absolve the Muslim Ummah from its duty to strive in the cause of Allah, oppose injustice, and seek peace." The Madhist section of the website "CentralMosque.com"[206] unabashedly states regarding the Mahdi that "the *Ahadith* on this issue leave no room for rejecting or even doubting the concept." More than most such sites, and much more like the previously examined books on the Mahdi, this one tries to find modern equivalents of the conditions set for the Mahdi's coming in the hadiths. It goes on to detail why the Shi`a are wrong in their conception of the Mahdi and fulminates that "their Mahdi does not exist, except as a figment of their imagination." (One might safely speculate that CentralMosque.com adherents do not post many comments on MahdiUnite, or vice versa.) "Muslim-Uzbekistan" has on its site[207] a three-part article on the Mahdi by "Sheikh Salman al-Oudah" of Saudi Arabia. Besides being in general a firm defense of Sunni Mahdism and against false Shi`i doctrines, one passage in particular is important:

Some people go so far as to deny the hadith about the Mahdi altogether. Often they do this because of the great many ways the idea of the Mahdi has been abused throughout history, as if denying his existence will put an end to the problem. Sometimes, though, the reason for their denial is a lack of knowledge about the Sunnah. This is one extreme. Then there are those who embrace the idea of Mahdism with such force and excessive zeal that it consumes them. They are as much in error as those who reject the Mahdi altogether.

Another site, "IslamicForum," is not specifically about the Mahdi but contains a great number of posts and discussions on the topic from February to April 2004.[208] Some of the posts include quite knowledgeable details about the signs of the End Time, the falseness of past Mahdist claimants, and warnings about how to recognize the true Mahdi when he finally comes. The last two pro-Mahdist sites in this category are much more in-depth than the aforementioned. "Major Signs before the Day of Judgement"[209] by one Shaykh Ahmad Ali in Britain is almost an online booklet on the topic of the End Time, with emphasis on the Mahdi, Jesus, and Dajjal. Perhaps this site's major point is the falseness of previous self-styled mahdis, such as "Mohd-bin-Tomart"—Ibn Tumart—and Mirza Ghulam Ahmad, the founder of the Ahmadis. This site's shaykh states that "a list of some of the signs that will precede Imaam Mahdi and some that describe him have been gathered in this book so that we Muslims are not misled to believe in somebody claiming to be the Mahdi who is in fact a blatant liar." Finally, a book entitled "Al Mahdi, Jesus and Moshaikh [the Anti-Christ]," allegedly by the "late Grand Muhaddath"[210] of Morocco, Shaykh Abdullah ben Sadek, Ph.D. (d. 1993), has been posted as a pro-Mahdist site.[211] What differentiates this Mahdist apologia from others, whether online or hard copy, is that it states that prophet Jesus rather than the Mahdi will "receive the caliphate," and it explicitly claims that Israel was reestablished by Allah in order to provide a base of operations for the Dajjal prior to his defeat. In sum, these pro-Mahdist sites differ only quantitatively, not qualitatively, from their brethren books. Their view of the Mahdi is less in-depth but follows the same outline as the hard-copy works, whose core point is that no matter how large the plethora of false mahdis grows, the future historicity of the real Mahdi is in no wise vitiated.

The third cluster of online Mahdist sites is a melange of eccentric observations on the coming rightly guided one. For example, "VictoryNews-Magazine," a Muslim publication out of Queensland, Australia, has a first-person article by a Palestinian Ph.D. in molecular genetics, Ghada Ramahi, which details her mystical encounter with the Mahdi while on her recent hajj.[212] As she was about to be crushed by a crowd, she was saved by a man whom she described thus:

[H]is silhouette, eastern looking complexion, glittering black hair with a perfectly groomed rich black beard with very distinct 2–3 grey hairs in the centre of the cheek part. He was 38–42 years old. I saw him clearly, he was very distinguishable [distinguished?], tall, slender, handsome with serious (somehow burdened) look on his face, like a gaze in the far distance. He vanished in the crowd as I stood there trying to see how he could vanish and disappear while I kept my eyes fixed on him.

Perhaps Dr. Ramahi had internalized traditions about the Mahdi, which then manifested themselves at a particularly stressful time—a near-death experience. But this example shows that there is emotional, as well as intellectual, yearning for the Mahdi in the Muslim world. In an attempt to inculcate children with both the emotional and intellectual content of belief in the Mahdi, at least one site (originating in Indonesia, albeit at least partially in English) posts "Islamic Poems for Children (and the Young at Heart)."[213] Here is a poem entitled "Jesus, Al Mahdi and the False Messiah":

> The day will come when a man claims he is the messiah and brings
>   clouds full of rain.
> Written on his forehead there will be a sign for believers to read
>   and see.
> The sign will read KAFIR, if you see it you'll know
>   not to believe in him or to Hell you will go!
> This man will perform magic in a way never seen
>   that they'll appear as miracles sent from the unseen.
> But his magic is from Satan, the stoned cursed one
>   who longs for our souls when our lives are done.
> If he comes during your time, trust Allah and you'll see
>   He has not forsaken you, but sent Al Mahdi.
> At the Mosque on the Mount of Jerusalem fair
>   Al Mahdi will fight and make his stand there.

Then, at last such blessed relief will come
   as Jesus, the true Messiah descends—Mary's son!
When ad-Dajjal,[214] the false messiah, sees Jesus is here
   He will tremble then shrink—struck with fear.
But Jesus will call—ad-Dajjal can't get away
   For when he leaves the Mosque, the false messiah he'll slay.
Peace and truth will at least be restored
   As Jesus destroys the error surrounding his word.[215]
He will proclaim that Allah is one
   That he is his worshipper—not His son.

While this poem may not scan very well, it is a useful example demonstrating that Mahdist and eschatological Muslim beliefs, far from being the province of an intellectual or religious elite, are popular enough to warrant inclusion in didactic literature for children. Another take on the Mahdi, which likewise cannot be construed as in any fashion an intellectual one, is that of the Nation of Islam. "The Nation" is one of two major factions of the Black Muslim movement in America, founded by Wallace Muhammad (Wallace Fard) and Elijah Muhammad (Elijah Poole) in Detroit in the 1930s. In the 1970s one faction, led by Wallace Deen Muhammad, sought integration into mainstream Sunni Islam while the other, led by the intransigent Minister Louis Farrakhan, clung to the earlier, unorthodox, and some would say heretical teachings of the 1930s founders.[216] It is Elijah Muhammad's teachings on the Mahdi, as updated by Farrakhan, that presumably appear on the Nation of Islam (NOI) site "FinalCall."[217] Like all NOI doctrines, this one is a melange of Christian and Muslim ones. For example, the Son of Man that Jesus predicts will come after him is said to be the Mahdi. Jesus' statement that "as the lightning comes from the east and flashes to the west, so will be the coming of the Son of Man"[218] is no longer a metaphor under NOI exegetics; rather, it literally means that the Son of Man, the Mahdi, will come from the Middle East. In this view "Christ," "Son of Man," and "Mahdi"—three quite different terms—are conflated together to represent the coming deliver of "black" people from "white devils." And even farther out on the eschatological and Mahdist fringe is the site "Welcome to Submission"[219] and its treatment of "The Expected Messiah, Imam Al-Zaman,[220] or Mehdi [sic] and Jesus second coming, if any." This iconoclastic site says that the Messiah, Jesus, and the Mahdi all really refer to the same person, the one who "fulfills all the expectations of the Jews, Christians and Muslims of a unifying figure for all of God's messages." This sounds rather like a Unitarian's dream. But then the site goes on to explain that one Dr. Rashah Khalifa is this religious figure, which puts this group and its site even more outside the Muslim mainstream than Louis Farrakhan and the NOI. By the time Mahdist beliefs reach the likes of Khalifa and Farrakhan, they are passing over the boundary of orthodox Islam into the domain of heresy and separate religions. These heterodox doctrines about the Mahdi nonetheless help illustrate the power of the idea, even or perhaps especially on the margins of Islamic thought.

CONCLUSION

Books promoting the Mahdi and arguing that belief in him is not only legitimate but also necessary for Muslims run the gamut from overly ambitious, attempting to determine exactly when the Mahdi is coming, to more prudent, suggesting that the Mahdi is real but extreme caution should be taken when attempting to identify him. There are, of course, various shades of emphasis between these poles: the Mahdist doctrine is, if nothing else, a boon to those wishing to rekindle right belief and reestablish Islamic law; a wake-up call for apathetic Muslims; a corrective to the erroneous Christian beliefs about the coming Kingdom of Heaven and the Son of Man who constructs it.

The majority of the Mahdist published works examined here[221] fall under the category of hadith literalists as outlined in chapter 1; that is, most of them acknowledge to one degree or another that the promise of the Mahdi is absent from the pages of the Qur'an, yet they adduce traditions and Muslim scholars to support their belief in his future historicity. Furthermore, all in this category endeavor to determine at least the approximate date and time of the Mahdi's appearance and, to a lesser extent, of the other End Time figures on the world stage by sifting through the tea leaves of the current geopolitical scene.

Two other Mahdist apologetic writers fall into another category, that of pro-Mahdist figurativists.[222] These accept the importance of the Mahdi, Jesus, the Dajjal, the Dabbah, Gog and Magog, and the sun rising in the West—but they admit that a valid approach to such figures is to see them as *ramziyah*, or "symbolism." Thus, these figures may be literal, historical actors in the eschatological future, but it is just as likely that they amount to allegorical or metaphorical signs. Yajuj and Majuj might, for example, simply refer to the myriad evils that God will visit upon humanity in the run-up to the End Time. Or they might be eschatological code for "the Jews."[223] Likewise, in a more elaborate allegorical schema, Yajuj and Majuj are a disease attacking the body, which can be cured only by Jesus; both the Dajjal and the sun rising in the West are symbols of death; the Dabbah represents the final slamming shut of the door of repentance; the Mahdi corresponds to the struggle between a humankind's bestial nature and the spiritual one;[224] and Jesus symbolizes, simultaneously, both the awareness of death and the secret of life.[225] But these modernistic, allegorical works are the exception, not the rule, in the expressive Mahdist literature, since such a Western approach to scriptural interpretation is still largely forbidden in Islam,[226] where Qur'anic and hadith literalism remains, to put it mildly, regnant.

The overall apologetic approach of Mahdist sectarian writers surveyed herein can therefore be broken down into a six-part paradigm in which the writers

1. cite relevant, supporting traditions

2. adduce sympathetic ulama and scholars

3. refute opposition arguments, preemptively if need be

4. malign the Shi`ah position on the Hidden Imam

5. dismiss all previous Mahdist claimants as false

6. modernize the Mahdi and his co-eschaton figures by fitting them into current events

Websites defending the coming Mahdi are less systematic than full-length Arabic books on the topic; but what they may lack in analysis, they make up for in emotional, populist appeal. This is true of both the Arabic and English ones, though especially the former. Of course, "the main problem with analyzing the use of cyberspace is that is is virtually impossible to know who is taking advantage of the several million webpages which in some way mention Islam."[227] This holds true—on a much smaller scale, certainly—for the sites defending the eventual historical truth of the Mahdi.

Are Mahdist books and websites, then, merely the tip of a massive Mahdist iceberg of belief, or are they, rather, an attempt by a tiny, albeit fanatical, rump faction to wag the entire apathetic dog? We shall see, and almost certainly long before the cusp of the sixteenth Muslim century in 2076 CE. In the meantime, some examination must be made of the view of those Muslims who doubt the doctrine of the Mahdi.

NOTES

1. Sayyid Muhammad Rizvi, "The Concept of Messiah [sic] in Islam," available at www.ummah.org.uk/khoei/mahdi.htm; as well as at "Mahdi," available on the site http://answering-islam.org.uk/Index/M/mahdi.html.

2. On this topic of expressive literature see Fuad Khuri, *Imams and Emirs: State, Religion and Sects in Islam* (London: Saqi Books, 1990).

3. Mark Sedgwich, "Is There a Church in Islam?" *International Institute for the Study of Islam in the Modern World* Newsletter 13 (December 2003), pp. 40–41.

4. Correctly transliterated *a-Jazirah*.

5. On how at least one Sudanese Mahdist rationalized clinging to his beliefs after Muhammad Ahmad's death, see Muhammad Ibrahim Abu Salim and Knut S. Vikør, "The Man Who Believed in the Mahdi," *Sudanic Africa* 2 (1991), pp. 29–52. General social science works on apocalyptic sects tend to ignore Islam and Mahdism, but some of the essays in Jon R. Stone, ed., *Expecting Armageddon: Essential Readings in Failed Prophecy* (New York and London: Routledge, 2000) shed

some light on Mahdists' behavior, post-Mahdi; see in particular Leon Festinger et al., "Unfulfilled Prophecies and Disappointed Messiahs"; Joseph Zygmunt, "When Prophecies Fail"; J. Gordon Melton, "Spiritualization and Reaffirmation"; and Anthony B. van Fossen, "How Do Movements Survive Failures of Prophecy?" Also, for a more recent treatment there is Stephen D. O'Leary, "When Prophecy Fails and When It Succeeds: Apocalyptic Prediction and the Re-entry into Ordinary Time," in Albert I. Baumgarten, ed., *Apocalyptic Time* (Leiden: Brill, 2000), pp. 341–62.

6. This figures on Mahdist book publication numbers are those I have been able to glean from WorldCat and card catalog research.

7. See "Mass Media, Press Freedom and Publishing in the Arab World: Arab Intellectuals Speak Out," *Arab Human Development Report 2003* (20 October 2003), available at http://www.undp.org/rbas/ahdr/ahdr2/presskit/2_AHDR03E2_FINAL.pdf. A devastating indictment of the intellectual inbreeding of the Arab Muslim world is containted therein: "No more than 10,000 books were translated into Arabic over the entire past millennium, equivalent to the number of translated *into Spanish each year*" (emphasis added).

8. Ibid.

9. The easiest way to determine whether such a work is Sunni or Shi`i normally is to ascertain if the author discusses the *ghaybah*, or "occultation," of the Mahdi and his return from it. However, there are some signs that such a belief might be passing into Sunni Mahdism, as I explore in the final chapter.

10. This is *al-Hashimi al-Muntazar*, "the awaited Hashimite," referring to Muhammad's family. This is normally a Shi`i appellation, but it seems to be creeping into Sunni Mahdism.

11. *Al-I`tida wa-al-Mahdi al-Muntazar* (Cairo: Maktabat al-Madinah al-Munawwarah, 1980), 62 pp.

12. *Al-Mahdi al-Muntazar: Silsilah Amarat al-Sa`ah* (Amman: Maktabat al-Manar al-Zarqa`, 1983), 215 pp.

13. *Ashrat al-Sa`ah wa-Asrariha* (Cairo: Dar al-Salamah lil-Tiba`ah wa-al-Nashr wa-al-Tawzi` wa-al-Tarjamah, 1993), 143 pp.

14. *Al-Hashimi al-Muntazar* (Amman: Matabi` al-Ayman, 1993), 95 pp.

15. *Al-Mahdi wa-al-Masih: Qira'ah fi al-Injil* (Beirut: Dar al-Mahajjah al-Bayda', 1994), 104 pp.

16. *Al-Sa`ah al-Khamisah wa-al-`Ishrun: al-Masih al-Dajjal, al-Mahdi al-Muntazar, Yajuj wa-Majuj* (Cairo: Dar al-Amin, 1995), 249 pp.

17. *Thalathah Yantazuruhum al-`Alam: al-Mahdi al-Muntazar, al-Masih al-Dajjal, al-Masih `Isa* (Amman: Dar al-Isra' lil-Nashr wa-al-Tawzi`a, 1995), 96 pp.

18. *`Umr Ummat al-Islam wa-Qurb Zuhur al-Mahdi* (Cairo: Maktabah `Ali, 1996), 134 pp.

19. *Asrar al-Sa`ah wa-Hujum ul-Gharb qabla 1999* (Cairo: Maktabah Madbuli al-Saghir, 1996), 159 pp.

20. *Al-Mukhallis bayna al-Islam wa-al-Masihiyah: Bahth fi Ta`awun al-Mahdi wa-al-Masih* (Beirut: Dar al-Mahajjah al-Bayda', 1996), 167 pp.

21. *Al-Ahadith al-Waridah fi al-Mahdi fi Mayzan al-Jurh wa-al-Ta`dil. I. al-Mahdi al-Muntazar fi Daw` al- Ahadith wa-al-Athar al-Sahihah wa-Aqwal al-`Ulama' wa-ara al-Firqah al-Mukhtalah. II. al-Mawsu`ah fi Ahadith al-Da'ifah wa-al-Mawdu`ah* (Beirut: Dar Ibn Hazm, 1999), 847 pp.

22. *Iqtabarat al-Sa`ah: bi-Warid Zuhur al-Mahdi wa-Nuzul al-Sayyid al-Masih (alayhuma al—salam) wa-Sinariu al-Ahdath al-Mustaqbaliyah fi Daw` al-Ahadith al-Nabuwiyah min Alan wa-Hata Qiyam al-Sa`ah* (Damascus/Beirut: Dar Qutaybah, 2002), 335 pp.; this has an illustration of two airliners approaching the World Trade Center towers, with a Qur'an off to the side.

23. *Usamah bin Ladin: al-Mahdi al-Muntazar am al-Masikh al-Dajjal?* (Cairo: Madbuli al-Saghir, 2002), 295 pp.

24. Cairo and Beirut are the centers of book publishing in the Arab world. Beirut is also where almost all the Arab Shi`i books on the Mahdi I've been able to obtain have been published, no doubt because of the influence of Lebanon's large Shi`i population.

25. Such as the Shi`i effort by Muhammad Husayn al-Ridwi, *Al-Mahdi al-Maw`ud fi al-Qur'an al-Karim* (Beirut: Dar al-Hadi, 2001), 231 pp.

26. Such is the approach of al-Bustawi, vol. 1, pp. 367–77.

27. This is al-Shawkhi's tack, pp. 18–27; 44; 75ff; 103ff.

28. As per al-Faqir, *Al-Hashimi al-Muntazar*, pp. 10–15, and *Thalathah Yantazuruhum*, pp. 43ff.

29. Al-Jamal, p. 20.

30. Ibid.

31. Al-Shawkhi, pp. 29ff.

32. Some good sources on this seminal figure are Victor E. Makari, *Ibn Taymiyyah's Ethics: The Social Factor* (Chico, CA: Scholars Press, 1983), especially pp. 133–57 on his political theory; Emmanuel Sivan, *Radical Islam: Medieval Theology and Modern Politics* (New Haven, CT: Yale University Press, 1985), especially pp. 94–104; and for the Sunni Arab perspective, Aziz Azmah, *Ibn Taymiyah* (Beirut: Riyad al-Rayyis lil-Kutub wa-al-Nashr, 2000).

33. As by al-Shawkhi, pp. 34ff; al-Faqir, *Al-Hashimi al-Muntazar*, pp. 12ff, and *Thalathah Yantazurhum*, pp. 43ff.

34. Al-Shawkhi, pp. 67ff. On al-Suyuti's rather laconic, but clear acknowledgment of the Mahdi's future existence, see his *History of the Caliphs*, translated by Major H.S. Jarrett (Calcutta: J.W. Thomas Baptist Mission Press, 1881), pp. 5, 238.

35. Al-Din, pp. 41ff. Biographical data on al-Saffaini are available in Khayr al-Din al-Zirikli, *Al-`Alam. Qamus Tarajim li-Ashar al-Rijal wa-al-Nisa'i min al-`Arab wa-al-Musta`ribin wa-al-Mustashriqin* (Beirut: Dar al-`Ilm lil-Milayin, n.d.), s.v. "al-Saffarini."

36. Al-Faqir, *al-Hashimi al-Muntazar*, pp. 12ff, and *Thalathah Yantazuruhum*, pp. 43ff. Biographical data on al-Dhahabi are in al-Zirikli, s.v. "al-Dhahabi."

37. Background on this fellow is in Michael Winter, *Society and Religion in Early Ottoman Egypt: Studies in the Writings of Abd al-Wahhab al-Sha`rani* (New Brunswick, NJ: Transaction Books, 1982).

38. *Khurafah.*

39. *Usturah.*

40. *Takhayyul.*

41. *Wahm.*

42. Al-Faqir, *al-Hashimi al-Muntazar*, pp. 8–9, 12–15, and *Thalathah Yantazuruhum*, pp. 43–44; Salim, pp. 90, 113ff; al-Bustawi, pp. 23–59.

43. Al-Faqir, *Al-Hashimi al-Muntazar*, passim; Salim, passim.

44. On these two influential thinkers see Albert Hourani, *Arabic Thought in the Liberal Age* (London: Oxford University Press, 1962), especially "Muhammad

Abduh," pp. 130ff, and "Rashid Rida," pp. 222ff, and more pointedly, Malcolm Kerr, *Islamic Reform: The Political and Legal Theories of Muhammad Abduh and Rashid Rida* (Berkeley: University of California Press, 1966).

45. See above, chapter 1 of this book, p.

46. Al-Faqir, *al-Hashimi al-Muntazar*, pp. 12ff, and *Thalathah Yantazuruhum*, pp. 43ff; al-Bustawi, pp. 23ff; al-Shawkhi, pp. 30ff.

47. *Al-Wathaniyah.*

48. Salim, pp. 113–14.

49. Author of *The Shi`ite Religion: A History of Islam in Persia and Irak* [*sic*] (London: Luzac & Company, 1933).

50. See above, chapter 1 of this book, p.

51. Al-Bustawi, vol. 1 pp. 23–59, spells out some of these criticisms.

52. (New York: Free Press, 1992).

53. (New York: Simon & Schuster, 1996).

54. See Salim, pp. 11–26.

55. Al-Faqir, *Thalathah Yantazuruhum*, p. 44.

56. Al-Bustawi, vol. 1, pp. 23ff.

57. Al-Jamal, p. 19.

58. Al-Faqir, *al-Hashimi al-Muntazar*, p. 11.

59. Al-Bustawi, vol. 1, pp. 61ff. Background information on the tension between Islam and its Jewish antecedents is found in Ronald L. Nettler, "Early Islam, Modern Islam and Judaism: The *Isra'iliyat* in Modern Islamic Thought," in Ronald L. Nettler and Suha Taji-Farouki, eds., *Studies in Muslim-Jewish Relations: Modern Jewish Encounters. Intellectual Traditions and Modern Politics* (Amsterdam: Overseas Publishers Association, 1998), pp. 1–14.

60. *Ahadith wa-Kalimat hawla al-Imam al-Mahdi* (Dubay: Maktabat al-Hidayah al Islamiyah, 1988), 169 pp.

61. Surah al-`Ankabut [XXIX]:13: "Of old we sent Noah to his people: a thousand years save fifty did he tarry among them."

62. *Ahadith wa-Kalimat hawla al-Imam al-Mahdi* (Dubay: Maktabat al-Hidayah al-Islamiyah, 1988), 169 pp.

63. Besides al-Gharaybi and Kurani, the Shi`i books that I have been able to obtain are Muhammad Rida Hakimi, *Al-Imam al-Mahdi fi Kutub al-Umam al-Sabiqah wa-al-Muslimun [The Imam Mahdi in the Books of the Previous Communities and of the Muslims]* (Beirut: al-Dar al-Islamiyah, 2003), 357 pp.; Muhammad Husayn al-Ridwi, *Al-Mahdi al-Maw`ud fi al-Qur'an al-Karim [The Promised Mahdi in the Noble Qur'an]* (Beirut: Dar al-Hada, 2001), 231 pp.; Amir `Arab, *Al-Mahdi al-Muntazar: Haqiqah am Khurafah? [The Awaited Mahdi: Truth or Superstition?]* (Beirut: Dar al-Rusul al-Akram, 1998), 1040 pp.; Muhammad `Isa Da'ud, *Al-Mahdi al Muntazar ala al-Abwab. Qahir al-Masikh al-Dajjal [The Awaited Mahdi at the Doors. Conqueror of the Dajjal]* (?, 1997), 321 pp.; Abd al-Hamid al-Muhajir, *Fi Zuhur al-Imam al-Mahdi [On the Appearance of the Imam Mahdi]* (Beirut: Dar al-Kitab wa-al-`Itrah, 1995), 227 pp.; Basim al-Hashimi, *Dawlat al-Mahdi [The State of the Mahdi]* (Beirut: Dar al-Haqq, 1994), 172 pp.; Adil al-Hariri, *Al-Mahdi al-Muntazar fi Hadith al-Sunnah al-Mu`atabar [The Awaited Mahdi in the Traditions of the Sunni Interpreters]* (Beirut: Mu'assasat al-`Arif lil-Matbu`at, 1993), 96 pp.; Rida al-Sadr, *Al-Masih fi al-Qur'an [The Messiah in the Qur'an]* (Sur, Lebanon: Dar al-Arqam, 1993), 160 pp.; Mahdi Faqir Aymani, *Al-Mahdi al-Muntazar fi Nahj al-Balaghah [The Awaited Mahdi in True Understanding]*, translated [from the Persian?] by Basim

al-Hashimi (Beirut: Dar al-Kitab al-Islami, 1992); Muhammad Hasan al-Yasin, *Al-Mahdi al-Muntazar bayna al-Tasawwur wa-al-Tasdiq [The Awaited Mahdi between Fancy and Faith]* (Baghdad: Matba`ah Babil, 1987 [first edition 1978]), 116 pp.; Abd al-Rahman `Isa, *Al-Mahdi. Qiyadah wa-Fikr . . . wa-Wa`d Haqq [The Mahdi, Guidance, Concept and Promise of Truth]* (Halab, Syria: Dar al-Kitab al-Nafis, 1985), 112 pp.

64. Al-Bustawi, vol. 1, pp. 87ff, makes such general charges but fails to specify just what these additions are; nor does he explain how Mahdist teachings in the Qur'an can be "added to" when there aren't any. Jamal, pp. 19ff, is a bit more specific. For background on Sufism's putative borrowings from Shi`ism, consult In`am Ahmad Qadduh, *Al-Tashayyu` wa-al-Tasawwuf: Liqa' . . . am Iftiraq? [The Shi`ah and the Sufis: Encounter or Separation?]* (Beirut: Markaz Juwad lil-Saff wa-al-Tiba`ah wa-al-Nashr wa-al-Tawzi`, 1993), especially pp. 93–114 on the imamate and the Mahdi in the beliefs of both; Nasr, *Sufi Essays*, pp. 110ff; and Nasrollah Pourjavady, "Opposition to Sufism in Twelver Shi`ism," in DeJong and Radtke, eds., *Islamic Mysticism Contested*, pp. 614–23.

65. Al-Faqir, *Thalathah Yantazuruhum*, p. 74. Just where or when Mawdudi said this is not specified. On al-Mawdudi see Seyyed Vali Reza Nasr, *Mawdudi and the Making of Islamic Revivalism* (Oxford: Oxford University Press, 1996), especially pp. 139–40, where Mawdudi's denials that he himself was the Mahdi are discussed; and Khurshi Ahmad, *Mawlana Mawdudi: An Introduction to His Life and Thought* (Leicester: Islamic Foundation, 1979).

66. Al-Din, pp. 39ff.

67. See Ibn Kathir, *The Signs before the Day of Judgment*, pp. 79ff.

68. See, for example, al-Din, pp. 15–20.

69. This is, of course, the whole thrust of Hijazi's book *But, Some of Its Signs Have Already Come! Major Signs of the Last Hour* (Arlington, TX: al-Fustaat Magazine, 1995), which, despite its title, deals with both categories of signs. Even some Arab Mahdist writers agree, such as al-Shawkhi, pp. 6–7, 120–75.

70. Al-Din, pp. 43–46.

71. Al-Faqir, *Al-Hashimi al-Muntazar*, pp. 59–63, and *Thalathah Yantazuruhum*, pp. 48–53. Interestingly, in the former book, published earlier that the other, al-Faqir glosses that "this is according to Alid [Shi`i] hadith," a point he omits from the latter (later) work.

72. Al-Din, pp. 43–46; al-Jamal, pp. 19–22.

73. Remember that the Jewish people are not the only or even the largest group of Semitic people. The Arabs are Semitic as well, and there are far more of them— a fact that makes "anti-Semitic" a rather inaccurate description as utilized in modern sociopolitical discourse.

74. Al-Faqir, *al-Hashimi al-Muntazar*, pp. 20ff, and *Thalathah Yantazuruhum*, pp. 48ff.

75. Al-Shawkhi, pp. 111–19.

76. Al-Faqir, *Thalathah Yantazuruhum*, p. 6. Compare this to Jesus' words in Matthew 24:6ff, Mark 13:7ff, and Luke 21:9ff: "You will hear of wars and rumors of wars. . . . Nation will rise against nation, and kingdom against kingdom. There will be famines and earthquakes in various places. All these are the *"beginning of birth pains"* (New International Version [NIV]) (emphasis added).

77. Al-Shawkhi, pp. 111–19.

78. Al-Jamal, p. 20.

79. Al-Faqir, *Al-Hashimi al-Muntazar*, p. 9.

80. Al-Faqir, *Thalathah Yantazuruhum*, p. 6.

81. Al-Hashimi, *Al-Mahdi wa-al-Masih*, pp. 66ff, 103.

82. Salim, pp. 75ff.

83. Al-Din, pp. 55ff.

84. Al-Jamal, pp. 5, 20.

85. Steven Brooke, "The Rise of Zarqawi: Is He the Next Bin Laden?" *The Weekly Standard*, June 7, 2004.

86. Perhaps the best articulation of this belief in English is Ahmad Thompson, *Dajjal: The King Who Has No Clothes* (London: Ta-Ha Publishers, 1986). The confluence in this work between Islamic beliefs and paranoid conspiracy theorizing is almost breathtakingly fatuous. For example, the *K-F-R* (from the Arabic *kufr*, "idolatry") that will be stamped on the Dajjal's forehead is said to be the same symbol used on the tail fins of Israeli fighter planes. Only the Mahdi can combat the planetary scope and power of the Dajjal and his system, according to this book.

87. Al-Salim, passim, and al-Jamal, passim.

88. Al-Shawkhi, pp. 100ff; al-Din, p. 43; Rahmah, p. 157.

89. One is reminded of the account of Jesus feeding the 5,000 with five loaves of bread and two fish (Matthew 14:13ff; Mark 6:30ff; Luke 9:10ff) and the explanation thereof offered by some theological liberals: that Jesus did not actually miraculously replicate the bread and fish; rather, he inspired the multitude to share the food they were all hoarding for themselves.

90. Al-Faqir, *Al-Hashimi al-Muntazar*, pp. 45–50, and *Thalathah Yantazuruhum*, pp. 31–39.

91. Al-Hashimi, *al-Mahdi wa-al-Masih*, pp. 66ff.

92. Al-Jamal, pp. 21–22, 53–54; al-Faqir, *Thalathah Yantazuruhum*, pp. 89–96; Salim, pp. 41, 75ff.

93. Al-Jamal, pp. 53–54; al-Faqir, *Thalathah Yantazuruhum*, p. 92. Both authors refrain from speculating as to what this might mean in terms of frequent flier miles, however.

94. Al-Aqsa Mosque is one of two religious structures—the other being the more famous, gold-topped Dome of the Rock—built by Muslim conquerors of the Holy Land on the Temple Mount, the site of the Jewish Temple built by Solomon to house the Ark of the Covenant.

95. Salim, pp. 41, 59ff, 75ff.

96. Al-Din, p. 49.

97. Rahmah, pp. 157ff.

98. Al-Jamal, p. 54.

99. Al-Faqir, *Thalathah Yantazuruhum*, p. 93; Salim, p. 41; al-Din, p. 86.

100. Al-Jamal, p. 54.

101. Al-Shawkhi, pp. 176ff.

102. Surahs al-An`am [6]:75, al-A`raf [7]:185; al-Mu'minun [23]:88 and Ya'sin [36]:83.

103. The references to this phrase in just the Synoptic Gospels are too copious to list, except in general outline: Matthew, chapters 3–26 and passim; Mark, chapters 1–15 and passim; Luke, chapters 1–23 and passim.

104. Al-Hashimi, *Al-Mahdi wa-al-Masih and al-Mukhallis bayna al-Islam wa-al-Masihiyah*, both *passim*. Another comparative analysis, from a Catholic Christian perspective, is that of the Dominican Jacques Jomier, "The Kingdom of God in Islam and Its Comparison with Christianity," *Communio* 13 (1986), pp. 267–71.

105. "Hadith Authority and the End of the World: Traditions in Modern Muslim Apocalyptic Literature," p. 52.

106. Andrew Rippin, "Interpreting the Bible through the Qur'an," in G.R. Hawting and Abdul-Kader A. Shareef, eds., *Approaches to the Qur'an* (New York and London: Routledge, 1993), p. 252.

107. It is possible to examine and write about the Dajjal, for example, or the signs pointing to the End Time without focusing on the Mahdi, but it is rather more difficult to do the converse, for elucidating the Mahdi almost demands some discussion of the other eschatological actors.

108. Cook, "Muslims Fears of the Year 2000," *Middle East Quarterly* 5, no. 2 (June 1998), pp. 52ff.

109. Daniel 7:13; Matthew 12:8, 12:32, 13:41, 16:27, 19:28, 24:27, 24:30, 24:44, 25:31; Mark 8:38, 14:62; Luke 12:8, 18:8; Acts 7:56; Revelation 1:13, 14:14.

110. Al-Hashimi, *Al-Mahdi wa-al-Masih*, pp. 75ff.

111. Revelation 16:16.

112. Rahmah, pp. 145ff.

113. Cook says that "in the apocalyptist's world, the Christian is the historical here-and-now foe, while the Jew is the metahistorical foe," *Studies in Muslim Apocalyptic*, p. 315. Thus, tactical—or, as is the case here, strategic—alliances are possible with the former, but not with the latter.

114. See al-Din, pp. 6–7, 221–26; Salim, pp. 33–38; al-Hashimi, *Al-Mahdi wa-al-Masih*, pp. 86ff; Rahmah, pp. 145ff.

115. Ezekiel 38 and 39.

116. Matthew 20:1–16.

117. I Thessalonians 4:13–18, although al-Din wrongly cites it as being I Thessalonians 5.

118. Zechariah 14.

119. Matthew 24, Mark 13, Luke 21. On all these biblical citations see Salim, pp. 36–38; al-Hashimi, *Al-Mahdi wa-al-Masih*, pp. 92 ff; and al-Din, pp. 6–7, 21ff, 36.

120. Al-Din, pp. 34–42; Salim, pp. 36ff.

121. Salim, pp. 34ff.

122. Daniel 11:5ff.

123. Daniel 11:31.

124. Al-Bustawi, I, pp. 102–4, citing Sayyid Ayyub, *Al-Masih al-Dajjal, Qira'ah Siyasiyah fi Usul al-Diniyat al-Kubra [The Dajjal: Readings in the Fundamentals of the Great Religions]* (Cairo: Dar al-I'tisam, 1989), no page number provided.

125. The Jewish component of early Islamic traditions.

126. Nettler, "Early Islam, Modern Islam and Judaism: The *Isra'iliyyat* in Modern Islamic Thought," p. 11.

127. Salim, pp. 67ff; al-Shawkhi, p. 62; al-Faqir, *Thalathah Yantazuruhum*, pp. 73ff.

128. Salim, pp. 67ff.

129. Al-Jamal, pp. 11–14.

130. Salim, pp. 121ff. On the history of dönmes, see Gershon Scholem, "Doenmeh," *Encyclopedia Judaica*. On Atatürk as a "crypto-Jew," see Bernard Lewis, *Islam and the West* (Oxford: Oxford University Press, 1993), p. 185.

131. Al-Bustawi, vol. 1, p. 111.

132. Rahmah, p. 148.

133. See Daftary, *The Isma'ilis: Their History and Doctrines*, pp. 137–38.

134. Al-Jamal, pp. 50–55; al-Shawkhi, pp. 62ff; al-Faqir, *Al-Hashimi al-Muntazar*, pp. 24ff, and *Thalathah Yantazuruhum*, pp. 73ff; al-Din, pp. 62–63.

135. For a chart describing all the Muslim religious officals, see Lapidus, p. 262. Sayyid is not normally included in the Shi`i hierarchy, but it does refer to an alleged descendant of the prophet Muhammad.

136. Salim, pp. 11–17, 39–43, 113–14.

137. Al-Jamal, pp. 51–58; al-Din, pp. 101–2.

138. Genesis, chapters 6–9.

139. On the usage of biblical geneaological material by the Arabs and Muslims, see Irfan Shahid, *Byzantium and the Arab in the Fifth Century* (Washington, DC: Dumbarton Oaks Research Library and Collection, 1989), pp. 332–34, "Ishmaelism," and pp. 179–80, "Ishmaelism: A Cautionary Note."

140. Al-Din, pp. 13–14, 55, 95–100.

141. Salim, pp. 128ff.

142. Al-Bustawi, I, p. 89, quotes Ibn Taymiyah as having said that even by his time (fourteenth century CE) Mahdist claimaints had become so numerous that "many have been counted only by God."

143. Ibid., vol. 1, pp. 89ff.

144. Ibid., pp. 89–118.

145. Al-Shawkhi, pp. 50–62.

146. Al-Jamal, pp. 24–49.

147. See W. Montgomery Watt, "Musaylima," *EI2*.

148. Al-Faqir, *Thalathah Yantazuruhum*, p. 15; al-Jamal, pp. 24ff.

149. Al-Jamal, p. 16; Salim, pp. 87–90. Modern Mahdists' dismissal of al-Qahtani for not physically resembling the Madhi flies in the face of the exact opposite claims made for him by his mouthpiece brother-in-law, according to Ayman al-Yassini, *Religion and State in the Kingdom of Saudi Arabia* (Boulder, CO: Westview Press, 1985), pp. 124–29.

150. "Abuse does not take away the use."

151. Cook, *Studies in Muslim Apocalyptic*, p. 247.

152. See Lewis, *The Political Language of Islam*, especially chapter 3, "The Rulers and the Ruled," pp. 43ff.

153. Al-Shawkhi, pp. 103ff.

154. Al-Faqir, *Al-Hashimi al-Muntazar*, p. 33, and *Thalathah Yantazuruhum*, pp. 22–30.

155. Al-Din, pp. 60–61; Salim, pp. 12, 118ff; al-Bustawi, I, pp. 107ff.

156. Such ideas may owe their provenance to the Egyptian Muslim Brotherhood thinker Sayyid Qutb (d. 1966); see Emmanuel Sivan, *Radical Islam: Medieval Theology and Modern Politics* (New Haven, CT: Yale University Press, 1985), especially pp. 56ff; Ahmad S. Moussali, *Radical Islamic Fundamentalism: The Ideological and Political Discourse of Sayyid Qutb* (Beirut: American University of Beirut, 1992). The

most relevant primary sources would seem to be Qutb's *Dirasah Islamiyah* (Beirut: Dar Shuruq, 1982); *Fi Tarikh . . . Fikrah wa-Minhaj* (Jeddah: al-Dar al-Sa`udiyah lil-Nashr, 1967); and *Ma`alim fi al-Tariq* (Cairo: Dar al-Shuruq, 197?).

157. See Salim, pp. 125ff; Rahmah, pp. 150ff.

158. This most likely reflects the influence, even in the Muslim world—probably because it bolsters already held views of regional victimization—of Edward Said's *Orientalism* (New York: Random House, 1978). Two trenchant criticisms of Said's works can be found in Bernard Lewis's *Islam and the West*, chapter 6, "The Question of Orientalism" (pp. 99–118), and chapter 7, "Other People's History" (pp. 119–30).

159. For Qur'anic citations on the prophet Nuh, see Surah al-A`raf [7]:59ff; Hud [XI]:25ff; and Nuh [LXXI]. For the biblical story of Noah and the Flood, see Genesis, chapters 6–9.

160. Al-Jamal, pp. 10, 19; al-Shawkhi, pp. 120ff; al-Faqir, *Al-Hashimi al-Muntazar*, pp. 5–6, and *Thalathah Yantazuruhum*, pp. 5ff; al-Hashimi, *Al-Mahdi wa-al-Masih*, pp. 52ff.

161. Wehr, s.v. "fatana."

162. Al-Faqir, *Al-Hashimi al-Muntazar*, pp. 26–31, and *Thalathah Yantazuruhum*, pp. 15–21.

163. Salim, pp. 93–98; al-Din, pp. 21–26.

164. "Israel says holy site may be targeted," *Atlanta Journal-Constitution*, July 25, 2004, p. A4.

165. This may be a conscious reference to the curious but little-studied incident in early Islamic community in which some Muslims, perhaps ordered to do so by Muhammad, traveled to Abyssinia (modern Ethiopia) and were given refuge by the Christian king there. See W. Montgomery Watt, *Muhammad: Prophet and Statesman* (London: Oxford University Press, 1961), pp. 65–70.

166. Salim, pp. 110–51; al-Din, pp. 21ff.

167. In Farsi, *vilayet-i faqih*: literally "guardianship of [Islamic] jurisconsult," in which the religious leadership—the mollahs and ayatollahs in Iran—actually hold a superior position to the state, as something of a trusteeship pending the Mahdi's coming. This is why, for example, a Kurani can refer to Khomeini as the "representative" of the Mahdi.

168. Al-Jamal, pp. 5, 12–18.

169. On the rise and development of the Safavids, under whose tutelage Iran became majority Shi`i, see Lapidus, pp. 285–302, and on their stormy relations with the Ottomans, pp. 310ff; for a more detailed examination, see Hodgson, vol. 3, pp. 16–58.

170. Salim, pp. 12–14, 113–14.

171. Al-Hashimi, *Al-Mahdi wa-al-Masih*, p. 93. Jesus says this in Matthew 24, Mark 13, and Luke 21; specifically, for example, Matthew 24:36: "No one knows about that day or hour, not even the angels in heaven, nor the Son, but only the Father." Muhammad is not so specific, but Surah al-Qiyamah [XL] deals with the Resurrection of all human dead for judgment and implies that humanity will never be able to figure out just when this will occur, although signs such as the darkening of the moon and the uniting of it with the sun will be dead giveaways.

172. For Qur'anic backup see Surah al-Qiyamah [75]:34–36: "That hour is nearer to thee and nearer, it is ever nearer to thee and nearer still." Reverend

J.M. Rodwell, *The Koran Translated from the Arabic* (London: J.M. Dent & Sons, 1909).

173. Al-Jamal, p. 17; al-Shawkhi, pp. 120ff, 151; al-Faqir, *al-Hashimi al-Muntazar*, pp. 16–19, 23–59. Cf. I Timothy 3:1ff, where St. Paul says, "But mark this: there will be terrible times in the last days. People will be lovers of themselves, lovers of money, boastful, proud, abusive, disobedient to their parents, ungrateful, unholy, without love, unforgiving, slanderous, without self-control, brutal, not lovers of the good, treacherous, rash, conceited, lovers of pleasure rather than lovers of God" (NIV).

174. Rahmah, p. 148.

175. Al-Faqir, *Thalathah Yantazuruhum*, pp. 36–42, 52–74.

176. Cook, *Studies in Muslim Apocalyptic*, p. 175.

177. Rahmah, pp. 148–57.

178. Al-Din, pp. 20, 34ff, 95–104.

179. This might indicate the author had heard of or read the Frank Herbert non-*Dune* book *The White Plague* (NY: Putnam, 1983), which told the horrifying fictional story of a genetically engineered plague that killed only women and for which humanity had no defense.

180. This echoes Revelation 8:10–11: "A great star, blazing like a torch, fell from the sky on a third of the rivers and on the springs of water—the name of the star is Wormwood. A third of the waters turned bitter, and many people died"; and Revelation 9:1ff: "I saw a star that had fallen from the sky to the earth." The analogous Qur'anic passages are not so specific, but they do speak of the sky being rent asunder: Surahs al-Furqan [25]:22ff; al-Ma`arij [70]:7ff; al-Muzammil [73]:12ff; al-Mursalat [77]:2ff; and al-Infitar [82]:1ff.

181. Most Western and Muslim historians date Muhammad's death to 632 CE. But Mahdist writers take liberties here, as in so much of their treatment of tradition and history.

182. Salim, pp. 71ff; al-Din, pp. 24ff.

183. Cook, *Studies in Muslim Apocalyptic*, p. 172, uses the the term "glorified warlord" for the Mahdi, which I have adapted and made more expansive.

184. Al-Hashimi, *Al-Mahdi wa-al-Masih*, pp. 30–69.

185. According to Samer Younes, "What Future for Arab Countries?" *Gulf Daily News [Bahrain]*, July 16, 2004. For a rather dated but much more in-depth study of the topic see Jon B. Alterman, "The Internet," from *New Media, New Politics? From Satellite Television to the Internet in the Arab World* (Washington, DC: Washington Institute for Near East Policy, 1998).

186. See "Internet World Stats: Usage and Population Statistics," at http://www.internetworldstats.com/top25.htm.

187. At http://www.almahdy.net.

188. At http://www.montada.com/archive/index.php/t-145941.

189. At http://www.montada.com/archive/index.php/t-113190.

190. At http://www.haridy.com, registered to one Ahmed Salama in London.

191. Specifically, www.haridy.com/ib/archive/topic/13341-1.html.

192. See, of course, Cook, *Studies in Muslim Apocalyptic*, pp. 179–80.

193. At http://groups.yahoo.com/group/MahdiUnite/.

194. *Riwayat* is the plural of *riwayah*, "accounts" or "reports" of the prophet Muhammad's life and goings-on in the early Islamic community. As such, they are closely related to hadiths.

195. At http://www.harunyahya.com/.

196. For these go to this section of his site: www.harunyahya.com/mahdi.

197. On the basis of Matthew 24:7, Mark 13:8, and Luke 21:11.

198. Again, if one were to include all the pro-Mahdist sites in English that are Shi`i, the number would be even greater.

199. At http://www.usc.edu/dept/MSA/fundamentals/hadithsunnah/abudawud/036.sat.html.

200. At http://www.ancient-history.nl/Islam/The%20Signs%20Before%20the%20Day%20of%20J . . . .

201. At http://www.islamworld.net/hour/Two.txt.

202. At http://www.1ummah.org/encyclopedia/mahdi.html.

203. At http://www.islaam.org/Al_Mahdi/who_is_imam_mahdi.htm.

204. At http://www.irshad.org/islam/prophecy/mahdi.htm.

205. At http://www.islamicweb.com/history/mahdi.htm.

206. At http://www.central-mosque.com/signs/ImamMahdi.htm.

207. At http://www.muslimuzbekistan.com/eng/ennews/2002/04/ennews07042002.html.

208. At http://forums.gawaher.com/index/ph/?showtopic=6096&.

209. At http://inter-islam.org/faith/Majorsigns.html.

210. That is, interpreter of Hadith.

211. At http://compuex.com/ad101/mahdi.html.

212. At http://victorynewsmagazine.com/ImamMahdiAJHelpsThoseWhoCall.htm.

213. At http://www.islamic-paths.org/Home/English/Discover/Poems/Content/Children/Jesu. . . .

214. It is actually al-Dajjal, as we have seen, but the author of this poem is transliterating the Arabic as if it were being spoken, in which case the letter *d* in Arabic is one that overrides the *l* sound of the definite article.

215. The error inserted by Christians into the New Testament, according to Muslims—that Jesus is the Son of God. See Surahs Imran [III]:73ff and al-Ma'idah [V]:109ff.

216. See "Black Muslims and the Nation of Islam" at http://www.apologeticspress.org/rr/rr1996/r&r9602b.htm and, for more in-depth examination, C. Eric Lincoln, *The Black Muslims in America* (Grand Rapids, MI: W.B. Eerdman's, 1994).

217. At http://www.finalcall.com/artman/publish/article_1323.shtml.

218. Matthew 24:27.

219. At www.submission.org/millennium/mahdi.html.

220. "Imam of Time," a term sometimes used by Shi`is for the Hidden Imam or Mahdi.

221. Al-Shawkhi, al-Faqir, al-Hashimi, al-Din, Salim, al-Bustawi, and Rahmah.

222. Jabr and Kamil Saf`an.

223. Saf`an, pp. 35ff.

224. For the Christian perspective on this inner dichotomy see St. Paul's Epistle to the Romans 7:14–8:17.

225. Jabr, pp. 133ff.

226. The best summary account of modern approaches to the Qur'an is that of Toby Lester, "What Is the Koran?" *The Atlantic Monthly*, January 1999, pp. 43–56.

See also, however, Michael Schub, "That Which Gets Lost in Translation," *Middle East Quarterly*, 10, no. 4 (fall 2003), available online at http://www.meforum.org/article/573.

227. Daniel Martin Varisco, "Islam Takes a Hit," *International Institute for the Study of Islam in the Modern World Newsletter* (June 2004), pp. 42–43.

CHAPTER 5

Modern Muslim Anti-Mahdists

"Because you realized that you could not live by the book alone, you encouraged the invention of hadith to help you govern the Empires you had gained. But is it not the case that many of these hadith contradict one another? Who decides what you believe?" "We have scholars who work on nothing else but the hadith," replied the Sultan. . . . "I agree with you. They are open to many interpretations. That is why we have the ulema to ascertain the degree of their accuracy. We need them. . . . Without these traditions, our religion could not be a complete code of existence."
—Tariq Ali, *The Book of Saladin*, pp. 117–18.[1]

While Mahdism remains alive and well in the Sunni world today, there are Muslims who nonetheless oppose the belief. Like their pro-Mahdist coreligionists, they are publishing books and building websites to promote their views. Admittedly, the anti-Mahdist forces are less prolific than the pro-Mahdist ones. To date only seven Sunni books denigrating Mahdist doctrine have come to light, and websites arguing against Mahdism number only in the single digits (all in English). But the very fact that opponents of Mahdism are beginning to feel the need to express their views indicates that Mahdism is a growing force in Sunni Islam. Remember that the Roman pagan philosophers began to write books attacking Christianity as early as the second century CE, not because the Christians were numerous—even by the time of the first Christian emperor, Constantine, in the early fourth century they represented less than 10 percent of the empire—but because their religion was gaining adherents, especially among the upper classes, and so was deemed a threat. An analogous situation might very well be developing in the Sunni Muslim world regarding Mahdism.

ANTI-MAHDIST BOOKS

The primary source for this chapter consists of the following Arabic books:

1. Abd al-Qadir Ata, *The Awaited Mahdi between Truth and Superstition*, 1980[2]
2. Abu Muhammad Harbi, *The Trenchant Critique of the Book of the Engineer from al-Azhar (True Illumination of the Book "The Lifespan of the Islamic Community and the Nearness of the Mahdi's Appearance")*, 1998[3]

3. Muhammad Farid Hijab, *The Awaited Mahdi between Religious Doctrine and Political Meaning*, 1984[4]

4. Abd al-Karim al-Khatib, *The Awaited Mahdi and Those Who Await Him*, 1980[5]

5. Shaykh Abd Allah b. Zayd al-Mahmud, *No Awaited Mahdi after the Messenger*, 1981[6]

6. Abd al-Mu`ta Abd al-Maqsud, *The Awaited Mahdi in the Balance*, 1980[7]

7. Adab Mahmud al-Hamsh, *The Awaited Mahdi in Transmissions of the Sunnis and the Twelver Shi`is: A Critical Study*, 2001[8]

A number of observations about these anti-Mahdist works are in order. First, three works were published in Cairo and one in Alexandria, in Egypt. In addition, one each was published in Jordan, Qatar, and Algeria (but note that the anti-Mahdist book was published in Algiers before the outbreak of the ongoing civil strife there between repressed Islamists and the government). Thus, none was brought out in a country with a substantial Shi`a population, unlike the Mahdist apologetic works, of which four of thirteen were published in majority-Shi`ah Lebanon. This may indicate that apprehensions about Mahdism are stronger in Arab countries with large Shi`a populations. As for dates of publication, five of the seven anti-Mahdist tomes came out in the early 1980s, likely reflecting the uneasy aftermath of the Islamic Revolution in Iran and, even more pointedly for Arab Sunni Muslims, the al-Utaybi uprising of 1979. But by far the most in-depth of the Mahdist oppositional works is al-Hamsh's lengthy 2001 volume of over 500 pages, which is quite unlike the others, none of which is more than 134 pages and, in fact, four of which are fewer than 100 pages each. Noteworthy, too, is that in his book al-Hamsh claims to have surveyed 750 books on the Mahdi written over the last 11 centuries. If that many tomes on the Mahdi pro and con have been penned, belief in the Mahdi is even more powerful within Islam than previously imagined.

MALIGNING THE MAHDI: SEIZING THE TERMS OF THE DEBATE

The rhetoric employed by the Mahdi's doubters is more varied and polemical than that of his devotees. Moving beyond the rather pedestrian "superstition," "fable," "fantasy" and "delusion," antagonists denigrate Mahdism as *nazariyah khurafiyah*, "superstitious theory," or *khurafah siyasiyah irhabiyah*, "terroristic political superstition";[9] *wad` al-qassas*, "invention of fiction writers"; *tadlil*, "misguidance";[10] *shirk*, "polytheism";[11] and even `*amaliyah al-islah al-niha'i*, "the ultimate reform movement."[12] Also, Mahdism has been called *qadiyah ghaybiyah*, a "transcendental/hidden matter,"[13] which may be a double entendre belittling its alleged Shi`i origins. Rather less tendentiously, Mahdist doctrine is also identified as a political ideology that when triumphant receives the appellation *thawrah*, "revolution," but when failed is dismissed as pernicious *fitnah* or a variation thereof: *ta'amur*, "conspiracy"; *inqilab*, "coup d'etat"; `*isyan*, "rebellion"; *shaghab*, "riot"; or *tamarrud*, "insurrection."[14]

Perhaps the gravamen of anti-Mahdists is found in their attacks on Mahdist traditions and those who gullibly accept them. As Mahdism's supporters pointed out in their apologia, the doctrine's detractors do label Mahdist beliefs and traditions as invented, forged, or fraudulent. But opponents also disparage Mahdist hadiths as *sina`ah*, "manufactured";[15] *al-ahadith al-mazlumah*, "iniquitous traditions"; *mulaffaq*, "concocted" in terms of their texts; and *majhul*, "anonymous" and/or *mujarradan*, "denuded," in terms of their chains of authority.[16]

Those who reject Mahdism also engage in ad hominem attacks on its supporters and on the early Muslims who created and compiled the doctrine's bedrock traditions. Mahdists are derided as *ahl al-bad`*, "people of innovation"; *ahl al-da`wah*, "people of progaganda"; and *ahl al-zayg*, "people of deviation."[17] *Mughalah*, "excess," especially of the Sufi or Shi`i brand, is said to be the source of Mahdist absurdity and the wellspring of the *ad`iyah*, "impostors" or "braggarts" across the span of Islamic history who deluded themselves and others into thinking they were mahdis.[18] Also, any sects of Islam which promote belief in the Mahdi are scorned as *jama`at ilhadiyah*, "heretical groups."[19]

Finally, in terms of rhetoric, ant-Mahdists will sometimes strenuously avoid calling the Mahdi by that name and instead utilize a number of Shi`i and Sufi terms: *al-qa'im*, "the established or upright one"; *al-qa'im al-muntazar*, "the awaited upright one"; *al-gha'ib al-muntazar*, "the awaited hidden [one]"; *al-imam al-mukhtafi*, "the concealed imam"; and *al-insan al-kamil*, "the perfect man" (the last a Sufi label for the prophet Muhammad as the archetype of humanity).[20] Using such terms for the Mahdi seems an attempt to stress the non-Sunni roots of the concept and thereby to vitiate its appeal.

MALIGNING THE MAHDI: ATTACKING THE PROVENANCE OF MAHDISM AS A DOCTRINE

Some in the Mahdist Doubting Thomas camp trace the belief's provenance to hoary pre-Islamic, even pre-Christian and pre-Jewish, ideas about a dying and reappearing god so prevalent in the ancient Near East. In this vein they trot out the Sumerian fertility goddess Inanna or Ishtar;[21] the sleeping son of the Hittite weather god, Telipinu,[22] awakened each spring by bees; the Akkadian king Sargon (d. 2316 BCE), said to be returning some day;[23] Mani (d. 277 CE), the Persian prophet who synergistically combined Zoroastrianism, Christianity, and perhaps even Buddhism;[24] the Persian Sasanian dynasty's (226–634 CE) presumed expectation of the return of their eponymous founder; and various and sundry Zoroastrian cults that survived into Islamic times.[25]

Alternatively, Mahdism is said to have derived from Jewish thought and as such is non-Islamic. Biblical passages such as "they will beat their swords into plowshares. . . . Nation will not take up sword against nation";[26] "out of you will come for me one who will be ruler over Israel";[27] and "from Judah will come the cornerstone . . . from him every ruler"[28] are said to be proof texts for the idea of a *mukhallis*, "deliverer" an idea that then wrongly passed into Islam. For in the anti-Mahdist world-view either Jesus or the prophet Muhammad was the one spoken of in these Old Testament passages, but the Jewish people failed to recognize either of them.[29] This oversight was then passed on to some in the early Islamic community and transformed into the expectation of the Mahdi, a dangerous error that survives to this day.

Another anti-Mahdist line of attack alleges that Mahdism derives from erring Muslims aping the Christian view of Jesus' return, rather than hewing to the more prosaic view of that returned prophet as purely human. And in fact an implicit charge of Mahdism's opponents is that Muslim expectations of the Mahdi have been unduly influenced in recent decades by the Christian agitation about the beginning of the third millennium.[30] Interestingly, and somewhat surprisingly, the skeptics do not then go on to pillory their coreligionists for heavy dependence on the Bible and modern Christian eschatological works.

Some mention is even occasionally made in Mahdist-denier works of less likely influences on Mahdism, such as the Hindu belief in the return of the god Vishnu at the end of every age of the universe[31] or the alleged expectation in Mongolia that Genghis Khan will rise again.[32] Yet another font of Mahdism can be posited: medieval and Renaissance political philosophy; specifically, the Platonic idea of a philospher-king as updated by the medieval Arab Muslim philosopher Abu Nasr al-Farabi (d. 950 CE) was fused with the ancient Near Eastern deliverer concept and leavened, in early modern times, with Niccolo Machiavelli's (d. 1527) idea of the ruthless, ambitous prince or ruler. The result was the modern view of the Mahdi.[33] And at least one anti-Mahdist writer finds Francis Fukuyama to blame: his book *The End of History* contributes to Mahdism by enticing misguided Muslims to look for the imminent end of the world.[34] Fukuyama, recall, is also excoriated by pro-Mahdists for allegedly helping fuel Western imperialism.

But most who compose books attacking Mahdism find pre- or non-Muslim influences necessary but not sufficient to explain away the belief. Its true origins are said to lie in the internecine rivalries among Kharijis, Shi`is, and Sunnis, exacerbated later in Islamic history by the nefarious Sufis.[35] Perhaps the most dispassionate criticism is that Mahdism arose in the late seventh and early eighth centuries CE (late first and early second centuries AH) when critics of Umayyad and later Abbasid rule lacked any alternative outlet for expressing displeasure with these regimes. Following a line of thought in Western scholarship that has been largely supplanted, one critique of Mahdism holds that the Abbasids exploited the yearning for the Mahdi, as well as the desire of the Persians in the new Islamic realms for more power, in order to topple the Umayyads.[36] This is in reality a rather one-dimensional and superficial view of the quite complex ethnic, religious, socioeconomic, and political tensions in the late Umayyad and early Abbasid Islamic world of the mid-eighth century CE.[37]

Anti-Mahdist writers today, then, take a rather reductionistic (less charitably, a simplistic) view of the roots of Mahdism. Positing that the idea first developed among those who had "suffered political defeat"[38]—that is, those who thought Ali and then his male offspring alone should hold the caliphate—this idea became institutionalized into the Hidden Imam concept among the Shi`a, whence it spread into the newly developing Sufi mystical orders in the Islamic world of the time. And following Ibn Khaldun, Mahdist critics today maintain that it was from these Sufis that Sunni Islam adopted the doctrine of the Mahdi.[39] Mahdism is thus seen as an infection or disease that incubated among the Shi`a, was transmitted to the Sufis through intentional physical and mystical vectors, and then disseminated throughout the larger Sunni world through casual contact.

This view is not totally without historical merit. Particularly following the Mongol invasions and conquest of much of the Islamic Middle East in the thirteenth century CE, Sufis and Shi`is in Persia, especially, began to incorporate each other's ideas and practices.[40] Whether belief in the Mahdi actually spread from Shi`ism into Sufism, or vice versa, may never be settled. From a Sunni anti-Mahdist perspective, however, the similarity of mystical terms and personages employed by Sufis and Shi`is is a damning indictment, regardless of which side originated them. Some Sufi orders, for example, believe in a mahdistic figure called the *qutb*, or "pole."[41] This fellow is figuratively if not quite literally the axis around which the earth turns. Below him, so the Sufis say, are a number of *awtad*, "pillars,"[42] usually five, followed by a larger grouping of *abdal*, "substitutes," as well as *nuqaba*, "leaders."[43] All these mytical hierarchies below the qutb are in effect intercessory saints—something not to be tolerated by opponents of Mahdism. Likewise for the terms that Sufis sometimes use for their leaders and Shi`is for their Hidden Imams, including the Mahdi: *qa'im al-zaman al-bab*, "establisher of time's gate," or *sahib al-zaman*, "lord of time."[44] All these mystical appellations and the theorizing accompanying them are a colossal waste of time, in the anti-Mahdist view, however: they are fairy tales at best and satanically inspired fantasies at worst.[45]

Specific Shi`a sects are sometimes singled out for censure in the matter of Mahdism.[46] Despite Ibn Taymiyah's aforementioned claim that only God knows how many Mahdist claimants and sects there have been, attempts to count and categorize them are nonetheless made, especially by opponents. For example, by one mode of reckoning there are 24 Shi`a Mahdist groups,[47] the most influential of which are said to have been the Fatimids, Twelvers, Isma'ilis, Zaydis, and Druze. (The "Fiver" Zaydis are the Shi`i sect predominant in Yemen to this day, whose imams ruled the area for much of its history. The Druze are a Lebanese offshoot of the Shi`ah, worshipping the eleventh-century CE Fatimid caliph al-Hakim as the deity.[48]) The Fatimids, in particular, are subject to a great deal of anti-Mahdist Sunni derision. They seem to be resented because of their two-centuries-long reign in Egypt and their lasting, pernicious influence upon the larger Islamic world. For example, al-Suyuti's acceptance of Mahdism in his works like *Tarikh al-Khulafa* (*History of the Caliphs*) is considered a result of lingering Isma'ilism in Egypt, long after the overthrow of the Fatimids. In general, from a Mahdist cynic's perspective, any group claiming a real live Mahdi in its midst is ipso facto illegitimate. In fact, the Fatimid founder Ubayd Allah was a covert "Magian" or Zoroastrian, and his followers and successors were dangerous *zanadiqah*, "free thinkers"[49]—tantamount to a charge of atheism in the modern Arab Sunni mindset.[50] *Zandaqah*, "free thinking," is a charge that has been levied against nonestablishment critics quite often in Islamic history.[51] In fact, the Fatimids are accused of going outside the pale of Islam by deifying their imams and caliphs, especially al-Hakim. However, it was actually only their offshoot Druze who did this; but to a Sunni anti-Mahdist, much like to a Sunni Islamist, all Shi`a are the same in terms of religious error.[52] And the Fatimids are the Shi`i copiers *par excellence* of the Sufis' overblown, metaphysical hierarchies of holy men.[53]

The main pernicious influence of Shi`ism in general upon Sunnism is, of course, in the wholesale transmogrification of the Hidden Imam into the Mahdi.[54] Just slightly less egregious is the ridiculous Shi`i concept of *ghaybah*, "hiddenness" or "occultation." One can find this doctrine nowhere in the Qur'an, and so it is equally false regardless of whether the Imam is Hidden in a cave in Iran or Syria or in an adjoining dimension. Likewise for the idea that the Imam or Mahdi is *ma`sum*, or "infallible."[55] The usual critical suspects are trotted out here: how can a man live for over a millennium? how could the Muslim community possibly gauge the infallibility of a claimant to the Imamate or Mahdiyah? The Shi'a are also in error, argue disbelievers in the Mahdi, regarding their glorification of the blood line of Muhammad, their denigration of some of the early caliphs, and their reliance on allegorical and mystical, rather than literal, readings of the Qur'an and traditions.[56]

As alluded to earlier, the anti-Mahdist view is that whereas the Shi`a were the font of heretical Mahdism, the Sufis were its conveyor belt into Sunni and orthodox Islam. Two tendencies in Sufism predisposed adherents of that aspect of Islam toward Mahdism, Mahdism's opponents maintain: one was *al-mughalah*, an "excess" of obeisance regarding their orders' shaykhs, or leaders, who are sometimes equated with a mystical qutb;[57] the other is the pretentious idea of *wilayah*, or mystical "friendship [with God]."[58] The first concept seems to have developed in Islam originally among an early proto-Shi`a group called the Rafida, who came to regard their imams as not merely divinely inspired but actually infallible.[59] It then made its way into Sufism. Modern critics of Mahdism reject this notion with the simple question: if there are human beings with such power, what is left for God to do?[60] The second idea, though it may have its provenance in an honest, well-meaning attempt to enter God's presence through contemplative prayer,[61] is nonetheless a satanic innovation or fantasy.[62]

In what may amount to damning with faint praise, Mahdism's detractors will sometimes point out that in Sufism the Mahdi began as a rather anodyne religous figure, not a political one as in Shi`ism,[63] and that it is only in the last century or so of Islamic history that "Sufi Mahdism" has erupted onto the political scene, with Muhammad Ahmad in Sudan, Muhammad b. Ali al-Sanusi in Libya, and Muhammad b. Abd Allah Hassan in Somalia. But as previously mentioned, the latter two of these never actually claimed to be the Mahdi, thus largely vitiating this anti-Mahdist point.

One Sufi who should receive the lion's share of the blame, according to anti-Mahdist ideologues, for injecting satanic innovations into Sufism and thus indirectly into Sunni Islam is Muhyi al-Din Ibn al-`Arabi (d. 1230 CE), the famous Andalusian mystic and scholar. He is branded the leader of *al-malahidah al-falasifah*, the "philosphical apostates," who promoted non-Islamic ideas like *wahdat al-wujud*, "the unity of existence,"[64] a virtual pantheism totally opposed to tawhid, God's divine unity.[65] Ibn al-`Arabi is also said to have fancied himself a potential Mahdi.[66]

Thus, anti-Mahdist Arabic books published in the last quarter-century have, as the first prong of their agenda, attacks on the provenance of Mahdism: its alleged non-Islamic roots in pagan, ancient Near Eastern, Judeao-Christian, or Shi`i and Sufi beliefs.

MALIGNING THE MAHDI:
ATTACKING MAHDIST PROPAGANDA

Moving on from savaging the allegedly non-Islamic origins of Mahdism, detractors of the doctrine then denigrate the Mahdists' proof texts. First, of course, anti-Mahdists point out that the Qur'an contains no references to the Mahdi or, for that matter, even to a mujaddid. In fact, they allege that the Muslim scriptures contain specfic passages that argue against the Mahdi, such as "God does not change the condition of a people until they first change what is in their hearts";[67] "today I have perfected your religion for you and completed My favor to you";[68] "perfected is the word of your Lord in truth and justice";[69] and the whole account of Alexander the Great imprisoning the hordes of Yajuj and Majuj.[70] The first three, so the anti-Mahdist reasoning may go, imply that the Islamic community has all it needs, and so a divine deliverer would be superfluous; the last passage may be listed because it implies the Qur'an is dismissing such eschatological figures as mere fantasies. Mahdism's opponents also point out that whereas Jesus is prominently mentioned in the Qur'an, the Mahdi is not. (Anti-Mahdists have also been know to state categorically that the Dajjal is mentioned in the Qur'an, too—a mistake that calls into doubt their scriptural acumen.[71]) As for eschatological prognostication, non-Mahdists may also contend that the Arabic scriptures say little about political events after the prophet's time, except arguably for some nebulous mention of conflicts between the "Israelites" and two other peoples: "the people who destroyed the Temple of Solomon" and the Palestinians.[72] Thus, not only Mahdism itself but also its adherents' ill-considered attempts to determine the time and place of the deliverer's appearance are clearly misguided.

After adducing the Qur'an to support their side, Mahdist critics turn their ire on the traditions about the Mahdi. The absence of the Mahdi from al-Bukhari or Muslim is the first line of attack.[73] Curiously, these critics seem to adduce this point less than the pro-Mahdists do in their preemptive strikes; anti-Mahdists appear more comfortable basing their opposition on a lack of Qur'anic corroboration. Even some of the eschatological hadiths that are backed up by the Qur'an, such as the Yajuj and Majuj accounts, are pilloried by Mahdism's detractors. Hadith compilers who included Yajaj and Majuj are likened to people gathering firewood by night—not very discriminating, that is. And this refers to an eschatological hadith with a Qur'anic basis; how much easier it is for a Mahdist doubter to deride one that lacks such legitimacy.

Thus, offending non-Qur'anic eschatological traditions, those about the Mahdi, are disparaged both generally and specifically. In sum, the charge is made of their being weak at best and outright forgeries at worst, almost certainly Shi`a-tainted, if not created, and then blindly repeated by ignorant ulama over the centuries.[74] Of course, the Jewish agent Abd Allah b. Saba is blamed for smuggling Mahdism into Islam through Shi`ism.[75] Interestingly, both the pro- and anti-Mahdist camps trot out Ibn Saba for corrupting Islam: the former, however, spins his influence as part of an ongoing Jewish and now Zionist or Israeli plot against Islam that only the Mahdi will be able to surmount, whereas the latter blames him for injecting the false doctrine of Mahdism itself into the Islamic body politic in the first place.

Furthermore, argue the Mahdi's detractors, allegedly sound traditions are not clear, and the purported clear ones are not sound.[76] One tally has it that the unambiguously clear ones number only 10, but that these are not trustworthy at all.[77] In reality, then, Mahdist hadiths represent not the actual utterances of the prophet Muhammad but, rather, factionalization among the ulama over the centuries; mutually contradictory traditions illustrate this clearly, although concrete examples of such are not provided. And apart from these unbelievable traditions, there is absolutely no good Islamic reason to believe in the Mahdi.[78] By undermining the scriptural and, more relevant, hadith foundations of Mahdism, its opponents hope to cause the entire doctrinal edifice to collapse.

In this vein, specific traditions are singled out and deconstructed. For example, how could the Mahdi fill the entire earth with justice when even the Almighty's final messenger, Muhammad, could not do so? As for the Mahdi resembling the Prophet physically, with a prominent hooked nose and receding hairline, don't many of his Arab descendents share these same characteristics? And what about God lengthening time, as necessary, until the Mahdi comes? Even the hadith compiler who included this one has his doubts,[79] so why should Muslims today trust it? The Mahdi's alleged descent from Fatimah is suspect, too, since many of those traditions are weak. Other traditions, such as that of the Prophet supposedly saying, "Myself and Ali and Hasan and Husayn and the Mahdi are all descended from Abd al-Mutallib,"[80] are not just weak but atrociously bad. Similarly, the prophetic account of the Mahdi and his army fighting al-Sufyani and his minions is totally contrived. The chain of transmission for the hadith about loyalty being sworn to a Muslim leader in Mecca between the rukn and the maqam is more solid, but it says nothing about the Mahdi. Finally, any so-called Mahdist tradition that mentions a group conquering from the East and preparing the way for the Mahdi is obviously invented.

Taken as a whole, the doubters' view of Mahdist hadiths is that they are *mutakhallifah*, "detritus"—more stories about hadiths than hadiths themselves.[81] The rest are fabrications, probably by the Shi`a, which makes them *ahadith al-mazlumah*, "evil traditions,"[82] or *batilah*, "worthless,"[83] and so demanding nothing but refutation and rejection.

To do so, anti-Mahdists employ a strategy similar to that of pro-Mahdists: adduce famous Muslim scholars and religious figures, but this time only the ones who are said to have renounced Mahdism. Generally, this involves the assertion that "most" ulama throughout Islamic history have rejected Mahdism, tempered by the grudging admission that some have nonetheless accepted the idea of a mahdi-as-reformer[84]—as a mere mujaddid, that is. In this vein, the four critics of Mahdism most often called to the dock are Ibn Taymiyah, Ibn Khaldun, al-Suyuti, and Rashid Rida. Ibn Taymiyah, the progenitor of Wahhabi Islam, is cited approvingly for his condemnations of the Sufis' quasi-worshipful obeisance to their shaykhs, which presumably fuels Mahdism, and for his broadsides directed at Ibn Arabi, as well as his fulminations against "satanic innovations," which presumably include at least some of the more grandiose beliefs about the Mahdi.[85] Ibn Khaldun is of course applauded for his insight that it was *ghulat*, Ali's supportive "extremists," and their Shi`a descendants who infected Islam with Mahdist doctrines. Anti-Mahdists are willing to concede, however, that Ibn Khaldun was a historian, not an expert on hadiths.[86] Al-Suyuti's alleged contention that any group claiming a mahdi is thereby rendered ipso facto illegitimate (the Fatimids being a case in point) is also a favorite of Mahdist detractors.[87] And Rashid Rida is said to have rejected Mahdism on the basis of the contradictory nature of the supporting traditions.[88]

The third and perhaps most compelling anti-Mahdist salient is the one aimed at the historical product of Mahdism: the outbreaks of revolutions and rebellions led by those claiming the belief applied to them.

MALIGNING THE MAHDI CLAIMANTS IN BOOKS

In the anti-Mahdist worldview, the most damning criticism of Mahdism is probably the carnage, bloodshed, and divisions of the Islamic community engendered by self-styled mahdis over the centuries. The high-profile nature of such movements in the last century, as well as the relative diminution of Islamic religious leaders' influence, may have convinced anti-Mahdists to expend as much, if not more, effort attacking historical Mahdist irruptions as they do denigrating traditions.

Of course, all previous "Mahdist" movements have been the work of *ad`iya'*, "impostors" who donned *athwaban za'ifah*, "forged cloaks," and succeeded in hoodwinking many. The roll call of such religious charlatans lists actual Mahdist claimants as well as their spokesmen. For the early period of Islamic history, this would include men such as Abd Allah b. Saba, the Jewish convert who claimed Ali would return as Mahdi; any Umayyad or Abbasid caliph who used the honorific title "al-Mahdi"; and Abu Tahir Sulayman (d. 944 CE), leader of an offshoot branch of the Isma'ili Shi`a in Bahrain, known as the Qarmatians, who was trying to summon the Mahdi, in addition to fighting the Abbasid caliph.[89] The middle centuries saw such mock Mahdism exemplified by Ibn Tumart and the Muwahhids. In the modern period, maintain anti-Mahdists, there are the examples of unspecified Mahdist wanna-be's in Egypt, following Napoleon's conquest; the Bab and Baha'ullah, founders of Baha'ism; Ghulam Ahmad, founder of the Ahmadiyah; Muhammad Ahmad of Sudan; three Islamic resistance leaders who, as noted in chapter 1, never actually claimed the Mahdiyah: Shaykh Shamil of the Caucasus region of southern Russia, Muhammad b. Ali al-Sanusi of what is now Libya, and Muhammad b. Abd Allah of Somalia; and finally Juhayman al-Utaybi.[90]

Al-Utaybi's 1979 attempt to spark an overthrow of the Saudi regime by designating his brother-in-law the Mahdi comes in for particular vituperation in anti-Mahdist works. This movement is compared to the two "rapes" of the Ka`bah in Mecca: the first by Abd Allah b. al-Zubayr in his battles with the Umayyad caliph Marwan in the seventh century CE, when he used catapaults to hurl stones at the site;[91] and the second perpetrated by Abu Tahir Sulayman who, in 930 CE, led the Qarmatian Shi`a to not only attack and plunder Mecca but to steal the black stone from the Ka`bah. For those opposed to Mahdism, then, al-Utabyi's ill-considered and illegitimate attack on and in Islam's holiest city not only demonstrates yet again the susceptibility of the simple-minded to Mahdist blandishments and the lengths to which self-styled Mahdis will go but also proves the evil power of Mahdism as a *dhari`ah*, "pretext," for political discontent.[92]

So from the Mahdist skeptics' perspective, a survey of historical "Mahdist" movements shows at least seven negative aspects. First, everyone who ever claimed to be the Mahdi has been killed or died. Second, the belief inevitably produces a great deal of strife and bloodshed with the Muslim community. In fact, third, all fitnahs in the Islamic world can be attributed to some form of Mahdism (a dubious assertion in reality). Fourth, the Mahdi concept is almost always used in a demagogic fashion as a means of stirring the masses by leaders who tend to be Shi`i, greedy, or ambitious, and this despite the fact that many if not most historical irruptions of Mahdism were actually stoked by and among Sunnis. Fifth, Mahdism creates new factions in Islam (the last thing the community needs) and exacerbates already existing ones. Sixth, it prevents the Islamic world from actually enacting true reforms. Finally, the false doctrine of the Mahdi weakens Muslims by drawing them away from more useful activities like prayer, fasting, and charity with its false promise of a deliverer to fix all Muslim problems, individual and collective.[93]

On the other side of the ledger, anti-Mahdists will grant that Mahdism might have two positive aspects, but ones still far outweighed by its negative ballast. One positive characteristic is that, the sword of rebellion being double-edged, belief in the Mahdi can be utitilized not just by the power-hungry and deluded but by those honestly searching for an oppositional ideology to topple an oppressive regime and institute a more Islamic, and thus presumably more just and equitable, government. The implication is that Mahdism might be more appropriate in this regard than an alien, Western ideology such as nationalism, communism, or perhaps even democratic capitalism. In this view if such a movement fails, those who crush it disparage it as a mere fitnah; if it succeeds, the winners will lionize it as a more respectable thawrah,[94] even, presumably, if led by a man claiming himself to be the Mahdi. The other nominally constructive consequence of Mahdism is in its narcotic effect: the belief does inure its adherents to their pain and unjust situation in this life insofar as they defer their hope of improvement until the Mahdi's coming.[95] This view of him tends to predominate among the Shi`a, but Sunnis are not immune to it, for "millions" of them look to his coming as a means of imploring Allah to better their lot in life.[96] So Mahdism is something of a crutch of piety, in the anti-Mahdist view. However, both of these positive aspects are far outweighed by the harm Mahdism has done to the Islamic community over the centuries.

Besides pointing out the deleterious effects of Mahdist outbreaks throughout Islamic history, Mahdism's opponents sometimes focus on Mahdists' inveterate attempts to calculate the precise time and geopolitical context of their namesake's coming. The cardinal Mahdist sin in this respect is said to be failing to differentiate between those events mentioned in the traditions that have already occurred, and those that have yet to transpire. (This is a charge levied in the Christian community, too, at some of the more sensationalistic interpretations of the Book of Revelation.) For example, hadith references to al-Sufyani would fall into the former category, since according to many interpreters they were obviously fulfilled by the Umayyad caliph Mu`awiyah b. Abi Sufyan; but any mention of the Mahdi would have to be lumped under the latter category.[97] Nor should the two classes be conflated, which pro-Mahdists do all the time, whether ignorantly or, more likely, intentionally. A biblical, not Qur'anic, prohibition against these attempts to divine the eschatological signs is adduced by the anti-Mahdist camp: "The words are closed up and sealed until the time of the end. . . . None of the wicked will understand, but those who are wise will understand."[98] So not only Mahdists, but their opponents, find useful propaganda material in the Bible.

The Shi`a and the Sufis are also denounced for their prognosticatory endeavors regarding the Mahdi and the other eschatological portents and figures. They stand accused of resorting to consulting *munajjimun*, "astrologers," in order to date the Mahdi's appearance.[99] Ibn al-Arabi, in particular, is charged with misusing the ancient practice of *hisab al-huruf*, the "science of letters," and the assigning of numerical values to letters of the Arabic alphabet in order to do his eschatological calculations.[100] Other Mahdists, in their zeal to prove the truth of their promised deliverer and set his appearance's date, have erred in the same fashion.[101] From the anti-Mahdist view, even if one accepts *arguendo* that belief in the coming Mahdi is legitimate, claiming to be able to figure out when this will happen is ridiculous; and of course even more absurd is the assertion that he is about to appear or is already here. Were that true, we would need to see on the world stage the two other major End Time personalities, Jesus and the Dajjal—two figures whose manifestation would, to put it mildly, be hard to keep secret.[102]

Mahdism, then, for its detractors within the Muslim world is a fantasy, akin to something from *The Thousand and One Nights*.[103] Belief in the Mahdi is not required of Muslims, as is belief in angels, jinn,[104] life after death, and the Fire of Judgment. Muhammad and Jesus are the true and final imams, not the fictional Mahdi, and Muhammad was the last messenger who will ever be guided by God.[105] So why does Mahdism survive as a belief among many, if not most, of the world's 1.3 billion Muslims?

Its disbelievers put forward three reasons for the refusal of Mahdist belief to die. First, the youth of the Muslim world, few of whom any longer study the Qur'an assiduously, have little defense against such currents of thought, especially when its tenets of equality and justice mesh well with the redistributionist envy fueled by seemingly similar ideologies like socialism and communism,[106] much in vogue among some sectors of the Muslim world prior to the collapse of the USSR. Second, "enemies of Islam" promote Mahdism as a means of weakening the Islamic world. In premodern times this meant the Shi`a sects. But from the late nineteenth century until the late twentieth the primary exploiter of Mahdist belief has been Zionist Israel. Sufficient proof of this lies in the fact that the Israelis safeguard the worldwide headquarters of the Baha'i faith in Haifa.[107] Why else would "the Jews" be so tolerant and protective of an Islamic heresy, if not to undermine Islam? And so it is an easy anti-Mahdist leap to the conclusion that Mossad would logically fund or support in any way possible the huge split in the Muslim world that would be created by anyone claiming to be the Mahdi. Now, in the early twenty-first century, the United States may be supplanting Israel as the main non-Muslim sponsor of discrediting Mahdist movements, a point examined in-depth in this book's conclusion. The final reason for Mahdism's survival into modern times is that it has been largely transformed into a political ideology, a permanently available oppositional movement with immediate legitimacy among many Muslims, especially in terms of its call for justice and equality.[108] This should come as no surprise, since Mahdism has always been at least as much political as it is religious, if not more so.[109] Faith in the Mahdi, then, is not so much a fixed doctrine[110] as it is an empty vessel into which challengers to any unpopular regime can pour their frustrations and produce a heady brew of rebellion or revolution.

To the Mahdi's debunkers, the cure for this doctrinal sickness depends upon one's position on the modern political-ideological spectrum. A modernist opponent of the Mahdi might maintain that Mahdism will continue as a belief and as an episodic political headache for Muslim governments for the foreseeable future so long as it is viewed as a valid oppositional political paradigm.[111] Once it has been discredited enough times in this respect—though no one is quite sure how many defeated Mahdist uprisings or inept Mahdist regimes that might take—it should dissipate. The more traditional, religious-minded Muslim critic of Mahdism would argue that expelling the doctrine from the Islamic body politic will be achieved only once Muslims and their religious leaders truly study the Qur'an and turn away from such fantasies back to the true Islam.

ANTI-MAHDIST WEBSITES

As mentioned earlier, the Mahdi's skeptics' websites are less numerous than those of his supporters, but if anything no less vociferous. To date the few anti-Mahdist sites are almost all in English, which may reflect the fact that the more Westernized a Muslim becomes, the more likely, though by no means certain, it becomes that he or she will turn against the doctrine as an anachronism in the modern world.

As of this writing there appear to be only a few sites in English run by Sunni Muslims devoted to debunking the Mahdi idea. (Of course, there are also a number of Arab Shi`a sites that exhaustively argue that no previous Sunni Mahdi could possibly have been the real one,[112] sites where, for example, Muhammad Ahmad of Sudan is discredited at length.[113]) Like the pro-Mahdist sites these range from the laconic to the verbose, though in general they are rather less in-depth and lengthy than those supporting the Mahdi. A bare-bones Pakistani site, for example, considering the question "What is the significance of *Imam Mahdi* in Islam?" replies:

There are some *Ahadith* which mention the coming of a *Mihdi* [sic]. All these *Ahadith* are baseless and critics know that they were concocted by the Abbasids against the *Umayyids* to justify their stance. The celebrated Muslim scholar *Ibn Khaldun* has convincingly refuted them in his treatise "The *Muqaddamah* [sic]."[114]

There are those for whom this curt dismissal of Mahdism does not settle the matter. They can find a more comprehensive posting and discussion of Mahdism at "IslamicForum,"[115] where the topic appears to be a lively one among both Sunni and Shi`a and evern some seemingly secularized Muslims. The most thorough and determined anti-Mahdist site appears to be allaahuakbar.net.[116] Shi`ism, the Mahdavi movement of Sayyid Muhammad Jawnpuri, the Ahmadis and Qadiyanis—all are brutally debunked by the strict Sunnis who run this site. Perhaps their approach, which neatly sums up the view of most Muslims who consider the Mahdi a dangerous myth, is best understood when read in their own words:

Any one who sees an optical illusions [sic] declared himself a Mahdi. Like Mirza Gulam Ahmed Qadiyaani, Syed Mohammed Jaunpuri, Wallace Fard Muhammad, Elijah Poole (Muhammad) . . . Deviant Groups like Baha'is, Shi'ah, etc. There are many who have called themselves Mahdi. . . . Allaah [sic] can only help us from these so called Mehdis, it is really becoming difficult to make a choice when we receive them left, right and centre. When someone has a personality disorder, he talks strange things. . . . Many have claimed that they are Imam Mahdi. . . . Many Muslims have been trapped by this claim. . . . May Allah protect Muslims from the fraudulent doctrine of these Deviant Movements. . . . O Allah! Bring Ignorant Muslims who have been trapped by them, back to the fold of Islam, let them see what is right and what is wrong and then give them the hidayah[117] to follow the right path.

Although these Allaahuakbarites do state that the Mahdi will come at the end of time, according to true Hadith, they nonetheless make it clear that the doctrine has led many astray over the centuries and so their opposition to any historical manifestation of Mahdism, as well as their denigration of such, puts them squarely in the de facto, albeit not technically de jure, anti-Mahdist camp.

The most profane—but perhaps the most humourous and, at least from a Westernized, modernist Muslim viewpoint, the most effective—anti-Mahdist missive might be that posted at "MuslimWakeup!"[118] This posting consists of a short play in which two Pakistanis—one Sunni, one Shi`i—argue and even fight over whose Mahdi is the true one, this against a backdrop of encroaching American imperialism. One of the most salient passages is this:

Reza: So you admit it! You're waiting for the Mahdi too!

Abu Bakr: Yes, well, frankly, there are signs—you know, siiiiigns, like the idea in the Quran . . . you know, the Quran that you don't believe in you non-Muslim heretic infidel homosexual! There are signs that we have regarding the arrival of the Mahdi. He will come, it is said when the blue pigeon starts chirping under the 7th treet from the left of the Bakery on Quaid e Azam road, Hafizabad, Punjab. After the bird has chirped . . . Dajjal's donkey—absent Dajjal of course—will emerge from the woods. At that point a great army—of the truest believers—will begin gathering underneath the 7th tree from the left side of the Bakery. The Mahdi will then finally emerge seven minutes after when sixteen leaves from the eighth stem from the bottom have fallen. When he arrives he will invoke all the powers at his disposal . . . and call to Isa Alayhissalam,[119] then he will descend and kill all the Jews and Christians and convert all the Greek women to Islam so that we may marry them.

Not very politically correct, perhaps, but this is wickedly sardonic regarding not just the attempts to predict the Mahdi's coming but also the differences between Sunnis and Shi`is (Abu Bakr represents the former and Reza the latter). One suspects that, at least for Westernized Muslims, this sort of satire is more injurious to the doctrine of Mahdism than are all the learned disquisitions on traditions found in all the books on the topic.

CONCLUSION

Six of the seven books surveyed in this chapter fall under the rubric of Qur'anic and Hadith Anti-Mahdist Literalists.[120] These authors appear to be rather orthodox, traditional Sunni Muslims whose objections to the Mahdi are grounded in the doctrine's lack of a Qur'anic and hadith basis. The remaining skeptical work,[121] which emphasizes political and intellectual aspects of Mahdism, appears to fit under the category of Anti-Mahdist Figurativist.

The overall approach of these books hostile to Mahdism is basically a tripartite one. First is scriptural unsubstantiation: the Qur'an makes no mention of the Mahdi, and the traditions purporting to predict his coming are false or counterfeit. Second is guilt by association: Mahdist beliefs are strongest among the heterodox Shi`a, and so therefore the belief is off-limits to Sunnis. Third are historical examples: all self-styled mahdis throughout history, without exception, have produced only negative effects. Therefore, the belief and the doctrine is one to be avoided by discerning Sunni Muslims. The websites opposing the Mahdists basically follow this same line of attack but add the further element of ridicule. It will be interesting to observe whether online discrediting of Mahdism grows as more and more Muslims, particularly Sunni Arabs, manage to find a way to access the Worldwide Web or Mahdist expectations increase in the run-up to the turn of the next Muslim century: the year 1500 AH begins in 2076 CE.

There are signs that such hopes are beginning to burgeon already and that likely candidates to claim the Mahdiyah are being sought out—or, perhaps even more ominously, testing the waters themselves—here in the first decade of the twenty-first century. That portentous possibility is explored in the next, and final, chapter of this work.

NOTES

1. (London: Verso, 1998).

2. *Al-Mahdi al-Muntazar bayna al-Haqiqah wa-al-Khurafah* (Cairo: Dar al-`Ulum lil-Tiba`ah), 74 pp.

3. *Al-Sayf al-Abtar ala Kitab Muhandis al-Azhar (Kashf Haqiqah Kitab `Umr Ummat al-Islam wa-Qurb Zuhur al-Mahdi)* (Cairo: Maktabah Madbuli Saghir, 1998), 97pp.

4. *Al-Mahdi al-Muntazar bayna al-`Aqidah al-Diniyah wa-al-Madmun al-Siyasi* (Algiers: al-Mu'assasah al-Wataniyah lil-Kitab, 1984), 123 pp.

5. *Al-Mahdi al-Muntazar wa-Man Yantazurunuhu* (Cairo: Dar al-Fikr al-`Arabi, 1980), 134 pp.

6. *La Mahdi Muntazar ba`d al-Rasul Khayr al-Bashir* (Qatar: Ri'asat al-Mahakim al-Shari`ah wa-al-Shu'un al-Diniyah, 1981), 96pp.

7. *Al-Mahdi al-Muntazar fi al-Mayzan* (Alexandria: Matabi`a al-Thaqafah, 1980), 85 pp.

8. *Al-Mahdi al-Muntazar fi Riwayat Ahl al-Sunnah wa-al-Shi`ah al-Imamiyah. Dirasah Hadithiyah Naqdiyah* (Amman: Dar al-Fath lil-Nashr wa-al-Tawzi`, 2001), 553 pp.

9. Al-Mahmud, pp. 16–20, 51ff and passim.

10. Muhammad, passim.

11. Al-Khatib, pp. 133ff.

12. Ata, pp. 70ff.

13. Muhammad, passim.

14. Hijab, pp. 7ff, 112ff.

15. Al-Mahmud, passim.

16. Muhammad, passim.

17. Al-Mahdmud, passim.

18. Al-Khatib, passim.

19. Ata, pp. 10ff.

20. Hijab, pp. 11–16.

21. See *Merriam-Webster's Encyclopedia of World Religions [MWEWR]*, "Ishtar," p. 512.

22. Ibid., "Anatolian Religions," pp. 49–53.

23. See H.W.F. Saggs, *Civilization before Greece and Rome* (New Haven, CT: Yale University Press, 1989), pp. 40–41.

24. *MWEWR*, "Mani," p. 689, and "Manichaeism," pp. 689–90.

25. Hijab, pp. 17–26, and al-Khatib, p. 33, mention these possible ancient sources for Mahdism. See also *MWEWR*, "Zoroaster," pp. 1164–65 and "Zoroastrianism," pp. 1165–66.

26. Isaiah 2:4.

27. Micah 5:2.

28. Zechariah 10:4.

29. Ata, pp. 19–21.

30. See Hijab and Ata, both passim.

31. See Ward J. Fellows, *Religions East and West* (New York: Holt, Rinehart and Winston, 1979), pp. 69–127, on Hinduism and its cyclical view of history.

32. On Genghis Khan not just as a returning messianic figure but as a full-blown deity, see Klaus Sagaster, "Chinggis Khan," and Walter Heissig, "Mongol Religions," both in *The Encyclopedia of Religion*.

33. This unique interpretation is found in Hijab, pp. 23ff.

34. Harbi, pp. 9–12.

35. Al-Khatib, pp. 15ff; Ata, pp. 19–27.

36. Hijab, p. 107.

37. See Moshe Sharon, *Black Banners from the East: The Establishment of the `Abbasid State—Incubation of a Revolt* (Jerusalem: Magnes Press, 1983); Muhammad Qasim Zaman, *Religion and Politics under the Early `Abbasids: The Emergence of the Proto-Sunni Elite* (Leiden: Brill, 1997); and Elton Daniel, "Arabs, Persians and the Advent of the Abbasids Reconsidered," *Journal of the American Oriental Society* 117, no. 3 (July–Sep. 1997), pp. 542–48.

38. Hijab, pp. 47–52.

39. Al-Khatib, passim; `Ata, pp. 64ff; Muhammad, pp. 79ff; al-Mahdum, pp. 3ff.

40. See Nasr, *Sufi Essays*, especially pp. 116ff; Pourvady, "Opposition to Sufism in Twelver Shi`ism," in DeJong and Radtke, eds., pp. 614–23; and Kamil Mustafa al-Shaibi, *Sufism and Shi`ism* (London: LAAM, 1991).

41. See Abd al-Razzaq al-Qashani, *A Glossary of Sufi Technical Terms*, translated by Nabil Safwat (London: Octagon Press, 1991); Baldick; and Nasr, p. 66.

42. Literally, in Arabic, "tent stakes"—a not unfitting image for what they do. So following in this vein, the qutb would be the main tent pole.

43. On abdal and nuqaba see Louis Massignon, *Essay on the Origins of the Technical Language of Islamic Mysticism*, translated by Benjamin Clark (Notre Dame, IN: University of Notre Dame Press, 1997); al-Shaibi; Baldick.

44. On the various permutations of al-qa'im, see Moojan Momen, *An Introduction to Shi`i Islam: The History and Doctrines of Twelver Shi`ism* (New Haven, CT: Yale University Press, 1985); W. Madelung, "Ka'im al-Muhammad," *EI2*.

45. Hijab and al-Khatib, passim.

46. Ata, pp. 27–36.

47. Hijab, pp. 71–86.

48. On both these groups see Daftary, pp. 68ff and 195ff; Khuri, pp. 113–24, 131–42 and 189–210. On the political history of the Zaydis in Yemen and the Druze in Lebanon see William Spencer, ed., *Global Studies. The Middle East* (Dubuque, IA: McGraw Hill, 2004), pp. 198ff and 120ff. In al-Qadi Husayn b. Ahmad, al-`Arshi, *Bulugh al-Maram fi Sharh Misk al-Khitam* (Cairo: Matba`at al-Birtirim, 1939), one learns that at least 16 Zaydi imams in Yemen were given the title "al-Mahdi." Obviously, at that level of frequency, the term has lost most of its eschatological significance.

49. Al-Khatib, pp. 24ff.

50. Al-Mahmud, p. 19.

51. See Louis Massignon, "Zindik," *SEI.*

52. Such slipshod (or intentional?) categorization of Shi`a sects is not strictly a modern phenomenon. It goes back at least to the twelfth century CE, according to Herbert Eisenstein, "Sunnite [*sic*] Accounts of the Subdivions of the Sh`a," in Frederick DeJong, ed., *Shi`a Islam, Sects and Sufism: Historical Dimensions, Religious Practice and Methodological Considerations* (Utrecht: M.Th. Houtsma Stichting, 1992), pp. 1–9.

53. Hijab, p. 78; Ata, pp. 27ff.

54. Al-Mahmud, pp. 3–5.

55. Al-Khatib, pp. 18–19; al-Mahdmud, pp. 29–31.

56. Ata, pp. 53ff, 64ff.

57. This tendency is particularly powerful in African Islam, among Sufi orders such as the Tijaniyah and the Qadiriyah. See Mervyn Hiskett, *The Development of Islam in West Africa* (London: Longman, 1984); Louis Brenner, *West African Sufi: The Religious Heritage and Spiritual Search of Cerno Bokar Saalif Taal* (Berkeley: University of California Press, 1984); Jamil M. Abun-Nasr, *The Tijaniyya: A Sufi Order in the Modern World* (Oxford: Oxford University Press, 1965); and Abun-Nasr, "Tidjaniyya," *EI2.*

58. Muhammad, pp. 13–14.

59. See Zaman; W.M. Watt, "The Rafidites: A Preliminary Study," *Oriens*, vol. 16 (1963), pp. 110–21; and E. Kohlberg, "The Term 'Rafida' in Imami Shi`i Usage," *Journal of the American Oriental Society* 99 (1979), pp. 1–9.

60. Al-Khatib, p. 103.

61. Nasr, p. 108, defines *wilayah* as "the ever-living spiritual presence in Islam which enables men to practise the spiritual life and to reach a state of sanctity."

62. Al-Khatib, pp. 54ff, 124ff.

63. Hijab, pp. 87ff.

64. William C. Chittick, *The Self-Disclosure of God: Principles of Ibn al-`Arabi's Cosmology* (Albany: State University of New York Press, 1998) is perhaps the best elucidation of this and related ideas.

65. Al-Khatib, pp. 63–69; 98–103; 110ff.

66. Ibid., pp. 111ff.

67. Surah al-Ra`d [III]:11.

68. Surah al-Ma'idah [V]:3.

69. Surah al-An`am [VI]:116.

70. Surah al-Kahf [18]:90ff.

71. On all these lines of attack, see Hijab, pp. 28–40; al-Khatib, pp. 18, 37; Muhammad, pp. 73ff; and al-Mahmud, pp. 6ff.

72. Ata, pp. 22ff, makes this rather convoluted argument. He provides no specific Qur'anic citation, but Surah al-Isra' [17]:3–8, an account of two armies sent against the ancient Israelites, would seem a likely candidate. N.J. Dawood, in his Qur'an translation, *The Koran* (London: Penguin Books, 1990 [1956]), p. 197, has a note identifying the two hostile camps as the Assyrians and the Romans.

73. Al-Khatib, pp. 130–32; al-Mahmud, pp. 6ff.

74. Al-Khatib, pp. 48ff; Muhammad, passim; Ata, p. 55.

75. Hijab, pp. 79ff; al-Khatib, pp. 32ff.

76. Al-Mahmud, pp. 39ff.

77. Al-Hamsh, p. 531.

78. Ibid., pp. 6ff.

79. Al-Tirmidhi, who refers to this tradition, among others, as *hasan sahih*—employing two usually mutually exclusive categories for the same hadith.

80. Muhammad's grandfather.

81. Muhammad, pp. 21ff; al-Mahmud, pp. 39–55; Hijab, pp. 42ff.

82. Muhammad, p. 21 and passim.

83. Al-Hamsh, p. 532.

84. Muhammad, p. 73; Hijab, pp. 42–56; al-Mahmud, pp. 19ff.

85. Al-Khatib, pp. 57–58; al-Mahmud, p. 56.

86. Ata, pp. 59–61; al-Khatbi, pp. 34, 41–47, 109; al-Mahmud, pp. 34–36, 63–64.

87. Al-Khatib, pp. 25–26. This is drawn from al-Suyuti, *Tarikh al-Khulafa'*, pp. 4ff, 426ff.

88. Al-Mahmud, p. 62.

89. On this group see Daftary, pp. 116–18 and 160ff.

90. Al-Khatib, pp. 28–33; Ata, pp. 11ff, 27–36, 45–52; al-Mahmud, pp. 21, 58–61; Hijab, pp. 53–56, 87–102.

91. See Madelung, *Religious and Ethnic Movements in Medieval Islam*, part 1, "'Abd Allah b. Al-Zubayr and the Mahdi," pp. 291–305.

92. Ata, pp. 10ff; Hijab, pp. 7–8.

93. Al-Mahmud, pp. 3–72; al-Khatib, p. 133; Ata, p. 10; Hijab, pp. 103–23.

94. Hijab, pp. 103–4. For background, see Lewis, *The Political Language of Islam*, p. 96: "Its [fitnah's] use is invariably negative. . . . *Fitna* was the term used by the first Muslim writers who discussed the French Revolution of 1789, and did not like it. When Muslim writers, in the course of the nineteenth century, began to speak more favorably of revolutions, they coined new words or reconditioned old words . . . the positive term for revolution was *thawra*, which in classical [Arabic] usage variously meant 'rising,' 'excitement,' 'rebellion,' or 'secession.' It is now the universal Arabic term for good or approved revolutions."

95. Al-Khatib, p. 39 and passim.

96. Al-Hamsh, p. 524.

97. Ata, pp. 55ff.

98. Daniel 12:9, 10. Ata, p. 43, employs this passage.

99. Al-Khatib, p. 39.

100. Ibid., pp. 110ff. For background see A. Bausani, "Hurufiyya," *EI2*. Hisb al-Huruf probably has Jewish cabalistic origins and is not overly dissimilar from the

approach taken to biblical (Old Testament/Scriptures) prophecy by the likes of Michael Drosnin in his bestseller *The Bible Code* (New York: Touchstone, 1997).

101. Hijab, p. 69.

102. Harbi, pp. 69ff.

103. Al-Mahmud, p. 31.

104. *Jinn* are spirit beings in Islam who are not necessarily evil or demonic, referenced numerous times in the Qur'an: Surah al-An`am [6]:101, 113, 129ff; al-A'raf [7]:38, 179; al-Hijr [15]:27; al-Naml [27]:17, 139; al-Kahf [18]:51; al-Sajdah [32]:13; Saba' [34]:12ff, 41: al-Saffat [37]:158; al-Rahman [55]:15. See also W.M. Watt and Richard Bell, *Introduction to the Qur'an* (Edinburgh: Edinburgh University Press, 1970), pp. 153ff.

105. Al-Mahdmud, p. 31.

106. Ata, pp. 16–17.

107. When the Baha'i movement ran afoul of the Qajar government in Iran in the nineteenth century, the Ottoman Empire, which then ruled what is now Palestine and Israel, accepted Baha'ullah as an exile; his movement is centered in the same area to this day.

108. Hijab, pp. 103–23.

109. Al-Mahmud, pp. 30ff.

110. Ata, pp. 64ff.

111. Al-Khatib, passim.

112. The two best examples are probably http://www.yamahdi.com/ and http://www.al-mahdi.org/.

113. At www.yamahdi.com/links/pages/Pseudo_Mahdi/.

114. At www.renaissance.com/pk/janq1499.html.

115. At http://forums.gawaher.com/index.php?showtopic=18934&hl=mahdi&.

116. At http://www.allahuakbar.net/. *Allahu akbar* is, in Arabic, "God is greater" (or "greatest") and a key phrase in Muslim prayers and worship.

117. *Hidayah* is "guidance" and comes from the same Arabic root—*hadaya*—whence comes al-Mahdi, "the rightly or divinely guided one." This would appear to be an intentional slam at Mahdists.

118. At http://www.muslimwakeup.com/mainarchive/000468.php.

119. "Isa" is of course Jesus. "Alayhissalam" is the badly transliterated Arabic *alayhi al-salam*, "upon him be peace"—the phrase that always follows the mention of a great prophet like Muhammd or Jesus.

120. Ata, Muhammad, al-Khatib, al-Mahmud, Harbi, and al-Hamsh.

121. Hijab.

CHAPTER 6

Conclusion: Who Will Be the Next Mahdi?

One cannot predict the advent of millenarianism any more than one can pre-dict tornadoes. All one can do is observe that, when certain conditions over-take certain individuals with certain mythologies or theological expectations, certain outcomes commonly, but not inevitably, ensue.
—Dale Allison, *Jesus of Nazareth: Millenarian Prophet*, p. 82

TAKING STOCK

Before moving on to an examination of the prospects for anyone claiming the Mahdiyah in the future—specifically, sometime in the twenty-first century, before or around the year 2076, which is the advent of the six-teenth century AH—it would be useful to assess what has been learned about Mahdism so far. First, the doctrine is a deeply entrenched one in Sunni and Shi`i Islam despite its absence from the Qur'an and its prove-nance in suspect traditions. Furthermore, the idea of the Mahdi, though similar to that of the Messiah in Judaism and Christianity, is nonetheless quintessentially Muslim and thus should be treated as such. Second, a survey of eight of the most well known and well documented Mahdist movements over the past millennium reveals a number of interesting points, of which the most important for modern times are that (1) contra conventional wisdom in the field, belief in the Mahdi is as vital in Sunni as in Shi`i Islam; (2) Mahdism tends to build up and manifest on Islam's peripheries (geographical in the past, but perhaps cultural, socioeco-nomic, or intellectual today); (3) jihad is central and indeed indispensable to such movements; and (4) there is probably no more potentially power-ful Islamic ideology for overthrowing a regime than Mahdism. Third, opposition to manifestations of Mahdism is most effective when fighting on two fronts: military and rhetorical (especially religious). Fourth, although no actual Mahdist claim has been attempted in the last quarter-century, at least in mainstream Islam, the numerous books and websites touting the Mahdi and trying to determine when he will appear indicate that the belief burns brightly in Sunni Islam and that should a Mahdiyah be declared, many would be at least willing to consider the assertion. And fifth, those Sunni Muslims opposed to the doctrine of the Mahdi base their unbelief on its lack of Qur'anic basis, its alleged Shi`i origins, and the destruction wrought by all the false mahdis throughout Islamic history, none of which appears to have dissuaded in the slightest the Mahdi's true believers. As one of the staff members of the aforementioned pro-Mahdist website Harun Yahya.com website put it, "Someone's declaring himself to be the Mahdi is the clearest proof that he is not the Mahdi."[1]

Mahdism has a number of characteristics, no one of which is alone sufficient to totally define its eclectic power and pervasiveness. Its most critical detractors would, for example, have Mahdism branded only as a superstition or fantasy or perhaps even as a sign of psychosis, much like the alleged appearances of the Virgin Mary that took place in Cairo after the Six Days' War ended in such shattering defeat for the Arab states.[2] Less derogatorily, Mahdism can be portrayed as an extreme example of dissatisfaction with the lack of social justice in the Islamic world and its deferral to the next world (or at least to the next fair and legitimate dispensation of history, that of the Mahdi and Jesus).[3] Not psychotic, perhaps, but it is nonetheless merely escapist, in this view. Relatedly, Mahdism might be defined largely as the struggle of the ignorant, disenfranchised, heterodox or heretical peoples of the peripheries against the establishment, the sophisticated, normative center. Mahdism from this perspective is thus tantamount to

popular piety once represented by wonder-workers, wandering dervishes, and local pilgrimage rites. Unorganized, unorganizable, the masses of Muslims who . . . look expectantly for signs of the world coming to an end . . . [and who] represent a volatile, occasionally politicizable, element that responds more to emotion and charisma than to specific doctrines and policies.[4]

Despite the terminology used here that may apply to the marginalized, but not necessarily the Mahdist marginalized, in Muslim society—the Muwahhids or Sudanese Mahdists were hardly "unorganized," and they did not establish states based solely on "occasionally politicizable . . . emotion and charisma"—this author makes an important point that is relevant to Mahdism's usual points of origin. Whereas in the past, for an Ibn Tumart or Muhammad Ahmad, the Islamic edges would have been primarily geographical but still encompassing of other categories (socioeconomic, political, etc.),[5] today the "Mahdist fringe" might be primarily intellectual and otherwise intangible, rather than geographical, though nonetheless just as real to a Mahdist. A Wahhabi Muslim in Medina, inquiring online about the coming of the Mahdi, would be such an example. Those who inhabit such fringes of certain political and religious traditions sometimes devolve into conspiracy theorizing,[6] a category under which fall at least some elements of Mahdism: a Manichaean worldview in the figurative, not literal, sense; real or perceived victimization; scapegoating others, such as Jews and Free Masons, for their problems; shoddy documentation of claims; and acceptance of outlandish conjecture. Conspiracy theories in general and Mahdism in particular "tend to flourish especially among those buffeted by circumstances, including those inhabiting the fringes of political life. . . . [T]hey help a people unhappy with current circumstances to explain their predicament while avoiding responsibility for it."[7]

This victimized, conspiratorial side of Islam has increasingly been channeled into Mahdism over the last few centuries of history as Islamic polities fell behind and then were subjugated by European powers; as the Ottoman Empire disintegrated, with a great deal of European help; as Western ideologies seduced many Muslims, Arab and otherwise, away from the true faith; and in the latter part of the twentieth and the early twenty-first centuries CE, as the American empire has made its salients into the Middle East and Muslim world. In its sullen but determined opposition to all these developments—but particularly, for our time and the near future, the last one—Mahdism greatly resembles its more infamous brother, Islamic fundamentalism.[8] For both, history is a variation on the theme of "one damned thing after another,"[9] with the Islamic wrinkle that in recent centuries history has inexplicably been primarily the narrative of one damned Western (European or American) thing after another, especially in the Muslim backyard. And not just military "things," either, though no doubt still damnable: perhaps even more pernicious than British, French, or Yankee forays into Islamic lands has been the intellectual imperialism of Enlightenment-spawned modernity, which has dethroned God and put the coregents of secularism and science-technology on the throne of the world, entertained by the jester of yet another European-hatched ideology: nationalism.

Islamic fundamentalists and Mahdists agree on the strategic problem: the world is dominated by "Christian" powers, especially the United States, while the faith and society of the Final True Religion groan under imperialism, both real and intellectual. But Islamic fundamentalists think that individual and societal self-reformation, based on a return to the "fundamentals" of Islam—the Qur'an, Hadith, Islamic law, and emulation of the early Muslim community—will rectify the situation, mainly by repietizing Muslim individuals and society and thus empowering them to drive back and eventually overthrow Western powers. Mahdists, in contrast, are not so sanguine about the solution. They think that the Islamic world will never be reenergized sufficiently on its own to best the armies and the real and ideological seductions of the West. Only the Mahdi, with a little help from his prophetic friend Jesus, will be able to make that happen. So, the difference between Islamic fundamentalism and Mahdism is really, at root, one of degree and not of kind. Put another way, fundamentalist Islam can be seen as a river that during parts of its course flows near a cliff hanging over the raging sea of Mahdism. When the riverbed is near this cliff, it might take very little to wear away the soil and allow the waters of fundamentalism to pour themselves into Mahdism.[10]

HINTS OF SUNNI MAHDISM TODAY

While Mahdism has gone virtual in the last 25 years, there are signs that the discontent, angst, and anger in the Sunni Muslim world are reaching such a fever pitch that expectations for the coming of the Mahdi are percolating and rising to the surface. So although it is probably still true that "this new 'Mahdi-ism' has not captured the minds of the public at large, but remains in the domain of the Islamic radicals,"[11] we cannot count on this remaining the case indefinitely.

One group that has, for several decades, fully expected the imminent arrival of the Mahdi is the Naqshabandi Sufi order. Their overall shaykh Nazim Adil al-Haqqani has, in recent decades, traveled yearly to Sri Lanka to look for signs of the Mahdi's coming.[12] The leading Naqshabandi shaykh in Lebanon, also named Nazim, was in the 1980s and 1990s not only predicting the Mahdi's looming appearance but also claiming to be in constant mystical contact with him, since the Mahdi had been born in Saudi Arabia in 1941 and has ever since been living in a cave in that country's Empty Quarter.[13] By one count the Naqshabandis now have as many as 50 million members—and if Mahdism is this powerful in such a large mystical subset of Islam, its latent power is ever greater than supposed.[14] However, it is worth noting that

whilst Sheikh [sic] Nazim does not want his pupils to *act* as if the world is about to end, he does want them to believe it. . . . [T]he attitude . . . was illustrated by a pupil who held up a pen. . . . [T]he pen was the world. It could be used, but was held at a distance so that it did not have a hold on his heart. He held it; it did not hold him. . . . [I]n a sense they are not concerned if the Mahdi never comes.[15]

What would happen if someone actually acted on such a Mahdist belief? Well, he might find himself in prison, like the Turk in Medina several years ago arrested by the Saudi police for wandering about the city proclaiming that he was waiting for the Mahdi.[16] No information is available on the sentence meted out by the Saudi authorities to this optimistic Turkish Mahdist.

On a much more serious and ominous level, al-Qaeda[17] has recently deemed it necessary to tamp down the fervor of Mahdist expectations among its followers and sympathizers. Al-Qaeda's 2003 Arabic statement *God Does Not Entrust Knowledge of the Mahdi to Anyone before His Appearance* seems to have been aimed at doing exactly that.[18] Its most salient sections are worth quoting:

Many Muslims think an Islamic state will only be established with the appearance of the Mahdi, and so they remain quiescent and implore God to hasten the

Mahdi's appearance and so they seize upon any Hadith mentioning him . . . and so they also abandon their efforts and just wait for deliverance. . . . Other Muslims disavow the belief in the Mahdi and attempt to eliminate it.

However, this belief does have a firm foundation in Hadith. . . . [and] so perhaps the reasons for the disagreements over the Mahdi come from (1) the extreme state of weakness and disarray Muslims find themselve in, and/or (2) belief in illusions or fantasies.

While there are over 50 Hadith on the Mahdi, the truth is that many are weak or hard to understand . . . [and] as for the physical descriptions of the Mahdi, they are all irrelevant. Likewise for the saying that he will have the same name as the Prophet, because tens of thousands of Muslims have that same name. . . . The truth is, *no one knows yet who will restore the caliphate and restore the ummah to prominence* [emphasis added].

While no one but Allah may know, one may be forgiven the suspicion that the al-Qaeda members who posted this statement are being disingenuous about who they expect to be the restorer of the caliphate and of the Islamic community's prominence—none other than the organization's founder himself, Osama bin Laden. Note also that the qualifier "yet" implies that this restorer can and will be recognized. But before delving into the possibility that the world's foremost terrorist cum Muslim freedom fighter, depending on one's perspective, might attempt a Mahdist putsch, it would be fruitful to examine the psychological makeup of messianic leaders.

POTENTIAL MAHDIS ON THE COUCH

No one has ever attempted a full-blown psychological profile of Mahdist claimants throughout history. Since this work is primarily a history written by a historian, that record shall remain intact. Nonetheless, the extensive extant literature on non-Muslim charismatic and messianic religious leadership might shed some light on what sort of Muslim[19] might attempt to don the Mahdi's mantle in the twenty-first century.

Charisma is of course the sine qua non of a successful Mahdist claim, and the starting point for a discussion of that topic is Max Weber's definition:

Charisma is a certain quality of an individual personality by virtue of which he is set apart from ordinary men and treated as endowed with supernatural, superhuman, or at least specifically exceptional powers or qualities . . . not accessible to the ordinary person, but regarded as of divine origin or as exemplary, and on the basis of them the individual is treated as a leader.[20]

Weber goes on to state that "within the sphere of its claims, charismatic authority *repudiates the past, and it is in this sense a specifically revolutionary force* [emphasis added]."[21] Once the fetters of tradition are broken, a Mahdi and his followers are free to move in geographical, ideological, and religious directions that were theretofore forbidden. Indeed, a Mahdist movement would not come into existence at all if its creator and fulfiller were unwilling to go against the grain and make such a daring declaration. But the message of Mahdism, though necessary, will always be insufficient to propel itself to success absent political and military victories.[22] How far would Ibn Tumart or Muhammad Ahmad have gotten without defeats of their enemies, the al-Murabits and the Ottomans? And how much headway did Juhayman al-Utaybi's public address announcements testifying to Muhammad al-Qahtani's Mahdiyah make when they were besieged by Saudi troops and obviously losing the military struggle? Charisma, even Mahdist charisma, requires real-world validation.

Although the Mahdi is not in the true sense a prophet, the distinction between messianic leaders and charismatic religious leaders is useful when applied to an Islamic context.[23] Both types seem to derive from a common background that includes elements such as a sense of not belonging exclusively to any group; mystical experiences and visions; and a sense of mission that inspires and energizes followers.[24] Are there any Mahdist claimants who do not exhibit such characteristics? But the charismatic prophetic type is more like the modern New Age or pseudo-Hindu guru, whereas his messianic counterpart is the ascetic, uncompromising enforcer of the laws of the monotheistic God.[25] Of course, the messianic brand does not lack charisma, and the charismatic is not totally devoid of the messiah complex. The point is the source of each's legitimacy: for the messianic, it is an external deity; for the charismatic, it is his own internal divine voice. Of course, for a follower even of a Mahdi, who's to know the difference? This is where his congruence with the Traditions and, more important, his military successes validate his claims.

Dale Allison, in his book *Jesus of Nazareth: Millenarian Prophet*, provides a litany of characteristics common to millenarian movements and their leaders,[26] which could be quite useful when applied to an Islamic venue in which at least some are waiting for the Mahdi:

1. appeal first of all to the disaffected and unfortunate in a period of social change that threatens traditional ways and symbolic universes

2. interpret the present and near future as times of atypical or even unprecedented suffering and/or catastrophe

3. a divinely-wrought comprehensive righting of wrongs, constituting a 'holistic solution,' is regularly envisaged

4. such reversal will come soon

5. revivalistic . . . deepen[ing] the piety of the faithful and stir[ing] up religious faith among the indifferent

6. promote[s] egalitarianism

7. tend to divide humanity into two camps, the saved and the unsaved

8. breaking of hallowed taboos associated with religious customs

9. nativistic because they emphasize the value of an indigenous cultural heritage or selected portions of it. Often that heritage is threatened by the domination of a foreign culture

10. often replace traditional familial and social bonds with fictive kin

11. mediate the sacred through new channels

12. involve[s] intense commitment and unconditional loyalty

13. more often that not coalesce around a charismatic leader

14. central beliefs . . . are formulated as fresh revelation, and they are authenticated by a prophet's miracles

15. sometimes take a passive political stance in expectation of divinely-wrought deliverance

16. expect a restored paradise which will return the ancestors

17. sometimes insist on the possibility of experiencing the coming utopia as a present reality

18. often grow out of precursor movements

19. ha[ve] to come to terms with disappointed expectations, since the mythic dream or end never comes.

It is safe to say that the Mahdist movements surveyed in chapter 2 of this work exhibit most or all of these characteristics, with the possible exception of number 14 and the definite exception of number 15. A "passive" Mahdist movement in terms of historical manifestation is almost an oxymoron in Sunni Islam, though modern virtual Mahdism may in a sense qualify. As for new revelation, a Mahdi never claims to be receiving this, for that would mark him as outside the bounds of orthodox Islam, wherein Muhammad is the *khatm al-awliya*, "seal of the saints," after whom there are no communiques from Allah. A Mahdi who claims to be receiving visions and divine messages is always careful to explain that they merely validate and refurbish the original message of Muhammad received in the Qur'an. In sum, then, this litany of millenarian marks can be applied as a template to any charismatic Muslim leader we might suspect of harboring Mahdist dreams or delusions. And in the world of 2005—and in the forseeable future—that means Osama bin Laden.

DOES ANYONE THINK BIN LADEN IS THE MAHDI?

Of all the charismatic leaders in all the cities and towns in all the Islamic world, the one most likely to be considered or to consider himself Mahdi material is undoubtedly, at this juncture in history, Osama bin Muhammad bin Laden. (He did not begin regularly using "bin Muhammad" as part of his name until after the 9/11 attacks, it seems. Is this just coincidence, or

"Osama bin Laden: Holy Warrior of Islam." [*Source:* Department of Defense]

is it an attempt to harmonize with Mahdist traditions?) In fact, Mahdist expectations seem to run in his family: bin Laden[27] supposedly "told Pakistani journalist Hamid Mir that, at his death, Muhammad bin Laden [Usamah's father] had set aside $12 million to contribute when the Hazrat Mahdi[28]—the 'rightly-guided one'—returned at the end of time to 'revive the glory of Islam.' "[29] If this money wound up as part of son Osama's personal fortune, the father may not be disappointed. Even if not, such largesse indicates that expectations for the Mahdi ran strong even in a family allied closely to the Wahhabi Saudi ruling family.

That bin Laden alone in the early twenty-first century has the stature even to attempt a Mahdist claim is of little doubt. "All revolutionary jihadist armies respect him."[30] Even before he engineered the 9/11 attacks, some of his compatriots and followers in Afghanistan considered him a "saint."[31] And perhaps not merely a saint. A number of the Muslim prisoners at the Guantanamo Bay facilities who were with bin Laden in Afghanistan have told interrogators that when he prayed, he was surrounded by a divine glow and that this possibly indicates he is the Mahdi.[32] In fact, Mahdist hopes seem to have grown so high among al-Qa`idah members and sympathizers that the organization's leadership deemed it necessary to issue the aforementioned statement tempering them. Nevertheless, "wishful thinking" about the coming of the Black Flags from the East, Mahdist harbingers, persists and in fact is becoming increasingly evident in some Muslim circles.[33] In July 2004 an al-Jazeerah TV broadcast claimed a group calling itself "The Holders of the Black Banners" demanded the freeing of Iraqi prisoners in U.S. and Kuwaiti prisons.[34]

What of Osama bin Laden's status in the non-jihadist world? Polls taken not long after the 9/11 attacks showed that as much as 25 percent of the population in Pakistan and Palestine considered the attacks legitimate under Islamic law.[35] This indicates at least some sympathy for bin Laden's cause, it is safe to say. Two Arabic books published since the attacks give more insight into bin Laden's stature in the Sunni Muslim world. *Usamah bin Ladin and the Phenomenon of Religious Violence in the World. Why?*[36] does not make any Mahdist claims for bin Laden, but it does justify him as the main enemy of America and "the Jews" and as *al-namudhaj*, "the model," for hundreds of millions if not billions of Arabs, Muslims, Chinese, Cubans, Koreans, Vietnamese, Africans, and even Europeans[37] who hate the United States and Israel for their `unjuhiyah*, "hubris." Bin Laden, then, is simply the *ta`bir*, "manifestation" or "expression" of the planet's oppressed masses.[38] Perhaps his visage will soon replace that of Che Guevara on WTO protesters' t-shirts. The other Arabic book on bin Laden actually broaches the issue of Mahdism: *Usama bin Ladin: the Awaited Mahdi or the Dajjal? The War of Extermination and the Barons of the CIA.*[39] This is the first book in modern times that openly discusses the possibility that a particular person is the Mahdi and admits that many Muslims consider bin Laden to be him, though ultimately its authors disagree. (Arab Muslim authors have not been quite so reticent about identifying the Dajjal, however, as we have seen.) After the usual condemnations of President Bush and the United States for its *al-harb al-salibiyah al-jadidah*, "new war of the cross"[40]—that is, Crusade—the authors latch onto a theory popular in France and the office of U.S. representative Cynthia McKinney, Democrat from Georgia, namely, that the CIA actually manipulated bin Laden into attacking the World Trade Center towers in order to thereafter rationalize and justify America's war on Islam. 9/11 is also portrayed as the day that kicked off the countdown to the End Time.[41]

Of course, those who even briefly entertain the notion of Osama al-Mahdi are certainly a minority of the world's Muslims. Even if only 1 percent of the global Islamic population of 1.3 billion is willing to consider the idea, however, that amounts to a potential supporting pool of some 13 million individuals. And there are many more millions—non-Muslims as well as Muslims—who while decrying bin Laden's methods nonetheless sympathize with his Mahdi-esque agenda of opposing American "imperialism" and standing up for the self-styled oppressed of planet Earth. As an eminent British magazine on international affairs recently put it:

The *jihadi* groups draw their strength from a common pool of self-righteous anger at what they see as the humiliation of Muslims at the hands of the West. Judging from the "chatter" on militant Islamist websites, the passion that fuels Islamist terror is growing. The main reason for this is the perception, widespread in the Muslim world, that America's wars in Afghanistan and Iraq, along with its support for Israel, are tantamount to a war on Islam.[42]

Is the situation ripe—or dire—enough for at least some of the world's Muslims to push Osama bin Laden over the threshold from populist anti-imperialist to full-blown Mahdi? How many of the aforementioned characteristics of millennarian movements are in place today in at least some parts of the Islamic world? Consider each:

1. Yes, the Muslim world is in a "period of social change that threatens traditional ways."

2. Yes, bin Laden and others "interpret the present and near future as times of . . . suffering and/or catastrophe."

3. Yes, "a divinely-wrought comprehensive righting of wrongs," Mahdism, "is regularly envisaged."

4. Yes, many in the Islamic world expect the Mahdi to "come soon."[43]

5. Yes, influential Islamic fundamentalism is certainly "revivalistic."

6. Yes, "egalitarianism" is a basic tenet of Islam, and even more trumpeted today in an age of relative deprivation of Muslim societies.

7. Yes. Long before George Bush said, "You are either with us or against us," Ibn Taymiyah had articulated for Islam the Manichaean division of the world into *Dar al-Islam* and *Dar al-Harb*: the "world of Islam" and, literally, the "world of war" or unbelievers; this idea is firmly entrenched in Islamic political ideology to this day.

8. Somewhat, for no major "taboos associated with religious customs" have been broken yet, but bin Laden's declaration of fatwas, when he has little or no official Islamic sanction to issue them,[44] is a movement down that slippery slope.

9. Yes, "an indigenous cultural heritage . . . is threatened by the domination of a foreign culture"; not just the French but many of the world's Muslims feel this way.

10. No, not yet. "Replac[ing] traditional familial and social bonds with fictive kin" is not prevalent yet, though suicide bombings that extoll dedication to a cause, even unto death, over one's family might be close.

11. No, neither bin Laden nor any other charismatic Muslim leader today is openly claiming to "mediate the sacred through new channels"—again, at least not yet.

12. Yes, "intense commitment and unconditional loyalty" are mainstays of groups like al-Qa`idah, Hizbollah (the Lebanese Arab Shi`i organization), and Hamas (the Palestinian Islamist group).

13. Yes. "Coalesce[d] around a charismatic leader" is the very definition of al-Qa`idah.

14. No. No "central beliefs . . . are [being] formulated as fresh revelation.

15. No, Islamist or jihadist groups almost never take a "passive political stance in expectation of divinely wrought deliverance"; they will much more likely take matters into their own active hands.

16. Yes, "expect a restored paradise which will return the ancestors." This movement among Muslims is called *Salafiyah*[45] because it prioritizes the renewal of

Islam through return to the presumed halcyon days of *al-salaf al-salih*, "pious
ancestors," and is still a powerful intellectual current.

17. No. No one yet seems to be "insist[ing] on . . . experiencing the coming utopia
as a present reality."

18. Perhaps. If and when Mahdism reappears it will of course "grow out of precursor movements," such as Salafism, but odds are it will not claim origins in
any earlier Mahdist movement, for by definition any previous such outbreak
is ipso facto illegitimate; bin Laden, for example, "did not support either the
raid [?] or the ideology of Juheiman al-Utaiba."[46]

19. No. Since Mahdism is not yet a reality, there are no "disappointed expectations" with which to have to come to terms.

The tally, then, is eleven yes, two maybe, and six no. But one characteristic
listed, number 15, is frankly irrelevant to a Sunni Muslim context, for only
the Shi`ah have ever adopted political passivity while awaiting Mahdist
deliverance. Thus, if the precursors for the advent of Muslim millenarianism are even roughly analogous to those for its cousin monotheisms
Judaism and Christianity, we now see over half of them firmly in place
today. All it would take for a Mahdist claim to materialize—and to be
taken seriously by millions—would be for bin Laden to announce on his
next al-Jazeerah-taped interview that the Prophet had invested him as
Mahdi and that the inevitable opposition of the religious establishments of
the American lapdog regimes in Riyadh, Cairo, and especially Baghdad
was just what the Mahdi was predestined to face. His charismatic power
is certainly great enough for him to at least attempt a grab at the Mahdi's
ring of power. And since the first goal of the Mahdi will be to set up an
"Islamic Union" as a base of operations,[47] bin Laden would be following
exactly in a Mahdist mode were he to call for such a polity's creation.

Were this to happen, what would be the reaction of Shi`i Muslims?
Most, of course, would reject any Sunni Mahdist claimant out-of-hand as
merely an impostor of the Hidden Imam. But would all do so? The bad
blood between Sunnis and Shi`is in the modern world consists of more
than just the name-calling outlined in anti-Mahdist books. It manifests itself
in the actions of Abu Musab al-Zarqawi, decapitator extraordinaire, who
"favors butchering Shias [*sic*], calling them 'the most evil of mankind . . .
the lurking snake, the crafty and malicious scorpion, the spying enemy,
and the penetrating venom.' American military officials hold Zarqawi
responsible not only for assassinating Shia religious leaders in Iraq, but
also for the multiple truck bombings of a Shia religious festival this past
March, which killed 143 worshippers."[48] Yet there is also a countertrend in
Sunni-Shi`i relations, in which the Islamic activism and anti-Americanism
of the two sundered branches of Islam are beginning to surmount their
differences. In particular, although in theory the Sunni yet-to-come Mahdi
has little to do with the Shi`i coming-again Hidden Imam, in reality
the critique of extant "Muslim" regimes and indeed of the entire world

geopolitical situation, which can be centered around the Mahdist ideal, has provided an avenue of rapproachement between Sunnis and the Shi`a.[49]

In the realm of doctrine, both postrevolutionary Iranian Shi`ism and Sunni Mahdism have in recent years evoked "a new type of eschatological movement without a specific person as the leader."[50] In Iran, Khomeini's establishment of the Islamic Republic is said by proponents (few of whom actually live in Iran now, it seems) to have created the prophesied Mahdist worldwide state in microcosm prior to the actual appearance of the Mahdi or Hidden Imam.[51] That does not mean the Shi`a expectation of the return of the Hidden Imam as the Mahdi has in any way lessened, however. The constitution of the Islamic Republic of Iran, established in 1979, Article 5, states that only because the Hidden Imam is in occultation must political leadership reluctantly devolve upon the *fuqaha*, "experts in [Islamic] jurisprudence."[52] Enshrining this waiting on the Mahdi has a long history in Persia cum Iran: the Safavids, who conquered Persia in the early sixteenth century and were the dynasty responsible for converting Iran to Shi`i Islam, kept two horses permanently stabled for the Mahdi and Jesus to use upon their return.[53]

Muqtada al-Sadr, the Americans' *bete noire* in Iraq until recently, echoed these Shi`i Mahdist yearnings, and indeed incited them, by calling his followers *jaysh al-Mahdi*, "the army of the Mahdi." Al-Sadr comes from a family of religious leaders and styles himself *hujjat al-Islam* (literally, in the original Arabic, "proof of Islam"), tantamount to *hujjat Allah* or in Persian *hojatollah*, one rank below *ayatollah*, the highest ranking religious official.[54] He is alleged to have claimed the "impending reappearance" of the Mahdi, and that "the Americans invaded Iraq to seize and kill the Mahdi. His Supporters chant Sadr's name at rallies to imply that he is the "son of the Mahdi." Sadr has stated that the army "belongs to the Mahdi" as an explanation of why he cannot disband it."[55] So al-Sadr is certainly invoking the absent, but imminent, Mahdi in a modern political and military dispute. Just how it is that the infidel Americans know the Mahdi is about to reappear is never explained by al-Sadr; perhaps his famous lack of actual religious training helps explain this curious oversight. It will be interesting to see if al-Sadr retains his Mahdism should he actually join the political process in Iran.

Al-Sadr seems to be a proponent of what has been called Islamic populism, created by the Ayatollah Khomeini and given form in Iran's Islamic state.[56] The overall agenda of this worldview in many ways parallels the programs advocated by Sunni Islamists like Sayyid Qutb: pan-Islamic tawhid supplanting nationalism; the Islamic community as the demoralized captive of Western ideologies; and the needs of social justice for the masses.[57] In fact, this Muslim cross-sectarian confluence of goals has reached the point where

almost as if receiving inspiration from the historical vision of the Shi`a, Sunni Islamist movements today are moving to distance themselves from the oppressive state and denouncing 'suborned clergy' who serve the interests of the state and not of Islam. . . . [C]ontemporary Sunni Islamist movements have actually now moved toward a more 'Shi`ite' view of the unjust state: acceptance of the principle that unjust governance in Islam not only should not be tolerated . . . but in fact requires the believer to resist it. The theology of these Sunni Islamist groups is often accused of being 'Shi`ite' by authoritarian regimes who feel their legitimacy thus threatened.[58]

Of course, this "the enemy of my enemy is my friend" policy may not translate into acceptance by the Shi`a of a Sunni's claim to the Mahdiyah, but it does provide an opening for an "ecumenical" Islamist leader such as bin Laden who, unlike al-Zarqawi, "prides himself on being a unifying figure and has made tactical alliances with Shia groups, meeting several times with Shia [sic] militants."[59] In fact, this author strongly suspects that the reason U.S. forces have been unable to run down bin Laden is that he is nowhere near the Afghan-Pakistani border but has instead been in Iran for some time, given safe harbor by the ayatollahs because their and his common interests, particularly mutual hatred of the United States, far outweigh their comparatively petty religious differences.

One way that Osama bin Laden might keep al-Qa`idah energized and even achieve Mahdist immortality would be to emulate (perhaps unintentionally, if U.S. bombs kill him unbeknownst to the world at large) Sayyid Ahmad Barelwi, who, it might be remembered, disappeared in battle and was then posthumously declared Mahdi by his devotees.[60] Such Mahdism is hardly one that the Muslim and non-Muslim world alike would need to concern itself with. Yet no one should count on Osama bin Laden going that quietly into the night.

If he does, however, and we never wake up to the nightmare of an Islamic Mahdiyah of Arabia where bin Laden controls the world's largest oil spigot, it is only a matter of time—just about 70 years, as a matter of fact—until some other charismatic Muslim leader manifests the remaining unfulfilled attributes of that powerful brand of Islamic millenarianism we call Mahdism. For million of Muslims worldwide Mahdism remains a cherished and important part of their Islamic faith. By the same token Mahdism has been an incredibly potent source of revolutionary and often violent regime change from Morocco to India. The secular intelligentsia of the United States, and even more so of Europe, might wish to to pretend otherwise, just as Western intellectuals were slow to admit, and some even now refuse to admit, the dangers of Islamic fundamentalism. But to do so regarding Mahdism would be not only historically and intellectually dishonest but profoundly irresponsible and indeed even more dangerous. Because when Mahdism reoccurs, and it will, almost certainly it will greatly outstrip today's merely Islamic fundamentalist–based terror on several levels: revolutionary power, mass appeal, Islamic legitimacy, and political, as well as military, threat to Middle Eastern and Muslim governments as well as to the United States and the West. For Mahdists, remember, are not bound even by the loose fetters of tradition and rules of engagement that might constrain a mere fundamentalist Islamic leader. All the rules are off when a Mahdi is on the stage. We know a jihadist bin Ladin was responsible for the mass killings of September 11, 2001. Is there any doubt that an Usamah al-Mahdi would hesitate to detonate a nuclear weapon in the United States in order to usher in the Final Battle? Or that he might send smallpox-laced followers to criss-cross American airports, hoping thereby to advance Allah's timetable of The End?

Dealing with any such overt Mahdist movement will require not just the application of overt as well as covert military power, but perhaps just as important a preemptive delegitimization of any attempted donning of the Mahdi's mantle. This would work only if Muslim ulama and scholars attacked the aspiring Mahdi on the basis of, for example, incompatibility with the Mahdist hadiths. In this vein Osama al-Mahdi could be countered by a fatwa pointing out that (1) his Yemeni birth contradicts the Hijazi one predicted; (2) his murder of other Muslims in Tanzania, Kenya, New York, and Afghanistan is unIslamic; (3) the Dajjal and Jesus are both missing on the world stage, and both are supposed to appear on earth when the Mahdi does.[61]

Let us hope that if such a grim eschatological play is ever acted out, our leaders in Washington are not "good secular sorts, [who] view so mundanely the causes of holy war"[62] but, rather, politicians, intellectuals, and military leaders who truly understand how to deal not just with holy wars but, rather, with the radical power of the holiest war: that of the Mahdi.

NOTES

1. Personal email communication from Ebru Bayrak of the Harun Yahya Mahdist website to the author, October 3, 2004.

2. See Sadiq Jalal al-`Azm, *Naqd al-Fikr al-Dini* [*Criticism of Religious Thought*] (Beirut: Dar al-Tali`ah lil-Tiba`ah wa-al-Nashr, 1997 [1969]), especially pages 97–115.

3. See Jane Smith and Yvonne Haddad, *The Islamic Understanding of Death and Resurrection* (Albany: State University of New York Press, 1981), especially p. 70; Louise Marlow, *Hierarchy and Egalitarianism* (Cambridge: Cambridge University Press, 1997) p. 27; and Tamara Sonn, "The Islamic Call: Social Justice and Political Realism," in Nimat Hafez Baranzangi, M. Raquibuz Zaman, and Omat Atal, eds., *Islamic Identity and the Struggle for Justice* (Gainesveille: University Press of Florida, 1996), p. 71.

4. Richard W. Bulliet, *Islam: The View from the Edge* (New York: Columbia University Press, 1994), p. 205.

5. Ibid., p. 9, where Bulliet observes that even in the early days of Islam the periphery could be a social one.

6. See Daniel Pipes, *The Hidden Hand: Middle East Fears of Conspiracy* (New York: St. Martin's Press, 1998); and Ahmad Ashraf, "Conspiracy Theories," *Encyclopedia Iranica*.

7. Pipes, pp. 303, 305.

8. Whereas some in the field still adamantly oppose the juxtaposition of the terms *Islamic* and *fundamentalism*, I find the phrase quite useful and acceptable. See my article "Islamic Fundamentalism," in *Encyclopedia of Fundamentalism* (Routledge, 2001), as well as Sivan, *Radical Islam*, and Ahmad S. Moussalli, *Moderate and Radical Islamic Fundamentalism: The Quest for Modernity, Legitimacy and the Islamic State* (Gainesville: University Press of Florida, 1999); Bassam Tibi, *The Crisis of Modern Islam: A Preindustrial Culture in the Scientific-Technological Age*, translated by Judith von Sivers (Salt Lake City: University of Utah Press, 1988); Johannes J.G. Hansen, *The Dual Nature of Islamic Fudamentalism* (Ithaca, NY: Cornell University Press, 1997); Aziz al-Azmeh, *Islams and Modernities* (London: Verso, 1993); and Aziz al-Azmeh, *Muslim Kingship: Power and the Sacred in Muslim, Christian and Pagan Politics* (London: I.B. Tauris, 1997), especially chapter 8, "Political Soteriology," pp. 189–219.

9. Attributed to the late-nineteenth and early twentieth-century American writer Elbert Hubbard (d. 1915).

10. I owe the idea for this analogy to Pastor Rich Nathan of the Vineyard Church, Columbus, Ohio, who originally used it in a sermon about Christian eschatology.

11. Ehuh Ya'ari, "Mahdi Now," "The Jerusalem Report.com," March 24, 2003, at http://www.jrep.com/Columnists/Article-87.html.

12. "The Coming of Mystery Imam al-Mahdi," at http://khidr.org/al-mahdi.htm.

13. See Daphne Habibis, "Millennarianism and Mahdism in Lebanon," *Archives Europennes de Sociologie* 30, no. 2 (1989), pp. 221–40.

14. See Richard Lyon, "Religion Is Not Withering Away" (November 2002), available at http://www.humanistsofutah.org/2002/ReligionIsNotWithering-Away%20_DiscGrp_11-02.html, for the 50 million figure. However, temper that with the observation of Habibis, pages 230ff, that there is a difference between Sufi *murid*s, the devoted practitioners, and *muhibb*s, those on the fringes of the organization (rather akin to part-timers). Lyon's high figure almost certainly incorporates the latter.

15. Habibis, p. 239.

16. "A Turkish man claimed to be the awaiting [*sic*] for Mahdi," October 26, 2001, at www.arabicnews.com.

17. The correct transliteration of the Arabic is al-Qa`idah, however.

18. Formerly available at www.tawhed.ws/r?i=657. Dr. Revuen Paz, director of PRISM (Project for the Research of Islamist Movements), Herzliya, Israel, was kind enough to provide me with the Arabic text. PRISM's website is www.e-prism.org.

19. Actual Mahdist movements throughout history, within the fold of Islam, have to my knowledge always been led by Muslim men. In more religiously pluralist environments such as India, with its Hindu majority, large Muslim minority,

and smaller groupings of Sikhs, Christians. Buddhists, Zoroastrians, and others, sometimes more synergistic types of Mahdism manifest. For example, currently there is a woman named Shri Mataji Nirmala Devi, born a Christian in Maharashtra, India, claiming to be the Mahdi, Maitreya (a Buddhist messianic figure), and Comforter (Christian terminology for the Holy Spirit), as well as a Hindu divine avatar. Needless to say, her following in the Muslim world is at best limited.

20. Max Weber, *On Charisma and Institution-Building: Selected Papers*, edited by S.N. Eisenstadt (Chicago: University of Chicago Press, 1968), p. 48. The entire chapter "The Nature of Charismatic Authority and Its Routinization," pp. 48–65, is germaine.

21. Ibid., p. 52.

22. See David Aberbach, *Charisma in Politics, Religion and the Media: Private Trauma, Public Ideals* (New York: New York University Press, 1996), p. 36.

23. See Len Oakes, *The Psychology of Revolutionary Religious Personalities* (Syracuse: Syracuse University Press, 1997).

24. Ibid., pp. 21–23, 42–43.

25. Ibid., pp. 183–84.

26. See "Detached Note: Some Common Features of Millenarianism," pp. 78–94.

27. Once again, the shoddily transliterated version of an Arabic name or term— in this case "Osama bin Laden" or "Usama bin Laden" has become the norm. In fact the correct rendering of the Arabic into English is *Usama[h] bin Ladin*. Furthermore, when dropping off his "first" name it should become *Ibn Ladin*.

28. *Hazrat* is the Persianized or Urdu-ized version of the Arabic *hadrah*, "(your) highness" or "eminence." I strongly suspect that this is an interpolation into Muhammad bin Ladin's quote by the Pakistani interviewing him, rather than the title he actually used with "Mahdi."

29. Anonymous, *Through Our Enemies' Eyes: Osama bin Laden, Radical Islam and the Future of America* (Dulles, VA: Brassey's, 2002), p. 82. The citations in the text are to Bassam al-Umash, "The Mentality of Osama bin Laden," *Al-Ra'y*, August 16, 1999, and Hamid Mir, "Interview with Osama bin Laden," *Pakistan*, March 18, 1997; and to my article "Bin Ladin: The Man Who Would Be Mahdi," *Middle East Quarterly* 9, no. 2 (spring 2002), pp. 52–59.

30. Anonymous, quoting an anonymous Arab intellectual, p. 170.

31. Ibid., p. 154, quoting a *Frontline* story on Usama bin Ladin.

32. Personal communication of the author with members of one U.S. intelligence agency.

33. See Reuven Paz, "Global Jihad and the United States: Interpretation of the New World Order of Usama bin Ladin," available at www.intelligence.org/il/eng/g_j/rp_a_11_03.htm.

34. Ravi Nessman, "Egyptian Diplomat Kidnapped," *The Atlanta Journal-Constitution*, July 24, 2004.

35. Daniel Pipes, "Bin Ladin Is a Fundamentalist," *National Review Online*, October 22, 2001.

36. Muhammad Jarbu`ah and Ramzi Dishum, *Usaman bin Ladin wa-Zahirah al-`Unf al-Dini fi al-`Alam. Limadha?* (Beirut: Dar al-Nida' lil-Nashr wa-al-Tawzi`, 2001).

37. Most French, I think it safe to say.

38. Jarbu`ah and Dishum, p. 99.

39. Ihyab al-Badawi and Hassan al-Zawam, *Usamah bin Laden: al-Mahdi al-Muntazar am al-Masikh al-Dajjal? Harb al-Fana' wa-Barunat al-CIA* (Cairo: Madbuli al-Saghir, 2002).

40. Ibid., p. 211.

41. See chapter 8, "Scenario for the Day of Judgment," and chapter 9, "The CIA: Cowards Who Incite the Volatile of the World."

42. *The Economist*, "Al-Qaeda: Amorphous but Alive," June 5, 2004.

43. One email I received from a denizen of the "MahdiUnite" website articulates the expectation that the Mahdi will come by the "2050's."

44. See Bernard Lewis, "License to Kill: Usama bin Ladin's Declaration of Jihad," *Foreign Affairs* 77, no. 96 (Nov./Dec. 1998).

45. For background see W. Ende, "Salafiyya," *EI2*.

46. Anonymous, quoting *Frontline*, pp. 87–88.

47. Ebru Bayrak, of Harun Yahya.com, personal email to the author, October 3, 2004.

48. Robert Leiken and Steven Brooke, "Who Is Abu Zarqawi? What We Know about the Terrorist Leader Who Murdered Nicholas Berg," *The Weekly Standard*, May 24, 2004.

49. On this phenomenon see Marvin Zonis and Daniel Brumberg, *Khomeini, the Islamic Republic of Iran, and the Arab World*, Harvard Middle East Papers Modern Series, no. 5 (Cambridge, MA: Harvard University Press, 1987); Graham E. Fuller and Rend Rahim Francke, *The Arab Shi`a: The Forgotten Muslims* (London: MacMillan Press, 1999); Hamid Enayat, *Modern Islamic Political Thought* (Austin: University of Texas Press, 1982), especially pp. 18–51, "Shi`ism and Sunnism: Conflict and Concord"; and Sivan, pp. 181–207, "In the Shadow of Khomeini."

50. Sabine Schmidtke, "Modern Modifications in the Shi`i Doctrine of the Expectation of the Mahdi (Intizar al-Mahdi): The Case of Khumaini [Khomeini]," *Orient* 28 (1987), pp. 389–406.

51. Ibid., p. 405, Zonis and Brumberg, p. 25.

52. The entire constitution of the Islamic Republic is available online at http://www.salamiran.org/IranInfo/State/Constitution/.

53. Al-Azmeh, *Muslim Kingship*, pp. 202 and 262.

54. Lapidus, p. 262.

55. See http://www.globalsecurity.org/military/world/para/al-sadr.htm.

56. See Manocher Dorraj, *From Zarathustra to Khomeini: Populism and Dissent in Iran* (Boulder, CO: Lynne Rienner Publishers, 1990). Although formerly "populist," the Islamic nature of Khomeini's movement and state is not very popular anymore in Iran, at least outside of the ranks of the ayatollahs.

57. Zonis and Brumberg, pp. 17ff.

58. Fuller and Francke, pp. 31, 45.

59. Leiken and Brooke, "Who Is Abu Zarqawi?"

60. Moni Basu first broached this idea in "Life after Death for Bin Laden?" *The Atlanta Journal-Constitution*, November 22, 2001.

61. Ebru Bayrak maintains that both the Mahdi and Jesus are already here on earth, but are "obliged to conceal [themselves] because of the terrorist and political attacks [they] would be exposed to." Personal email to author, October 3, 2004.

Also, I advanced such a counter-Mahdist agenda for the first time in "Bin Ladin: The Man Who Would Be Mahdi," *Middle East Quarterly*, 9, no. 2 (spring 2002), pp. 53–59.

62. Reuel Marc Gerecht, "Not a Diversion: The War in Iraq has Advanced the Campaign against Bin Ladenism," *The Weekly Standard*, April 12/19, 2004.

Subject Index

Note: The Arabic definite article *al–* has been ignored in alphabetization.

Abbas: 12

Abbasid(s): 12, 13, 17, 26 n.52, 30, 63 n.1, 104, 134, 139, 143,

Abd al–Aziz: 81

Abd al–Mu'min: 33–34, 36–37, 58, 75

Abd al–Muttalib: 138

Abd al–Qadir: 44, 52

Abdulaziz: 96

Abdulhamid II: 53, 55, 77–79

Abduh, Muhammad: 91

Afghanistan: 12, 35, 40, 88, 157–158, 163

Aga Khan: 5

Ahl al–Bayt: 15, 74,

Ahl al–Kitab: 18

Ahmad, Ghulam: 4, 102, 114, 139

Ahmad, Muhammad: 3, 45–46, 48–59, 67 n.81, 77–81, 83, 85 n.72, 102, 110, 118 n.5, 136, 139, 143, 151, 155

Ahmadis, Ahmadiyah: 3, 4, 23 n.14, 40, 102–3, 114, 139, 143

Ahriman: 8

Ahura-Mazda: 8

Alexander the Great: 19, 102, 136

Algeria: 13, 30, 43–45, 52, 67 n.73, 72, 77, 81, 131

Ali (caliph): 12, 26 n.51

Ali b. Yusuf: 33, 35

Ali, Muhammad: 45–46, 67 n.83, 78

Ali Shamil: 3

Allah: 1, 2, 17–19, 32–35, 56, 64 n.12, 80, 93, 106, 112, 114–116, 140, 143, 154, 156, 163

Amzian, Muhammad: 2, 44–45, 77

al–Andalus: 35, 72, 136

Angel(s), angelic: 8, 19, 101, 141,

Ansar: 52

Apocalypse, apocalypticism: 6–8, 44, 62, 98–99, 104, 118 n.5

al–Aqsa Mosque: 97, 106, 123 n.94

Arab(s): 2, 6, 8, 14, 16, 19, 27 nn.67 and 69, 29 n.103, 31, 48, 53, 58, 70 n.127, 72, 74, 77, 79–80, 87–89, 92, 94, 95, 105, 107, 108, 110, 111, 119 n.7, 120 nn.24 and 32, 122 nn.69 and 73, 125 n.139, 131, 133, 135, 138, 143, 145, 151–52, 158–59, 165 n.30

Arabia: 3, 13, 17, 19, 27 n.67, 30, 32, 41, 43, 46, 52–53, 60–62, 64 n.13, 70 n.127, 77, 79–81, 83, 87–88, 91, 101, 104, 107–08, 111, 114, 153, 162

Aragorn: 27 n.82

Ark of the Covenant: 108, 123 n.94

Armageddon: 97–99, 101, 109,

Assyrian(s): 2, 100, 148 n.72

Atatürk, Kemal: 58–59, 77, 100, 105, 125 n.130

Atlas Mountains: 33

al–Azhar: 31, 48, 79, 100

Baha'is, Baha'ism: 4, 23 n.14, 101–103, 139, 142–43, 149 n.107

Baha'ullah: 4, 102, 139, 149 n.107

Bahrain: 101, 106–07, 139
Balearic Islands: 36
Barelwi, Ahmad: 2, 42–43, 45, 58,
    76–77, 103, 162
Barnes, Fred: 24 n.23
Basrah: 13
Baz, Shaykh Abd al-Aziz: 82
Beast of the Qur'an: 17–18,
Beast of Revelation: 10, 18
Berbers: 33
Bible: 10, 93, 98–99, 133, 141
Bin Laden, Osama: 1, 5, 22 n.3,
    29 n.103, 76, 88, 111, 154, 156–59,
    162, 165 n.27
Bin Ladin, Usama: 165 n.31

Brits, Britain: 3, 38, 42–43, 45–46, 48,
    50, 53–54, 56–59, 70 n.136, 72, 76, 78,
    81, 114, 152, 158
Bu Ziyan: 44–45
Bukhara: 14
Bush, President (George W.): 24 n.23,
    62, 158–59
Byzantine Empire: 29 n.103, 105

Cairo: 30, 36, 48, 54, 72–73, 78–79, 81,
    89, 120 n.24, 131, 151, 160
Calendar, Christian/Western: 110
Calendar, Islamic/Muslim: 1, 22 n.2,
    39, 58, 65 n.44, 110
Caliphs, caliphate: 4, 12, 14–15, 17, 19,
    27, 30, 36–37, 39, 43–44, 50, 52,
    54–55, 58–59, 63 n.1, 77, 79–80,
    90–91, 95, 100, 103–05, 109–110, 114,
    134–35, 139, 154
Calvin, Jean: 35
Centennialism: 7, 8, 38, 40, 57, 62, 76
Charisma: 3, 5, 8, 52, 54, 88, 151,
    154–56, 159, 160, 162
Chechnya: 3
Chiliastic: 6, 7
China: 46, 109
Chishtiyah: 39
Christ: 2, 7, 9–10, 18, 28 n.102, 98, 116
Christianity: 1, 2, 8–10, 21, 22 n.107, 42,
    57, 65 n.39, 97, 130, 132, 150, 160
Churchill, Winston: 95
Committee on Public Safety: 34

Constantine: 130
Constantinople: 19, 95, 101, 105, 108,
Crusades, Crusaders: 31, 38, 73, 158

Dajjal: 17–19, 28 n.101, 59, 61, 73, 77,
    79, 92, 95–102, 106, 107, 109, 110,
    111, 114–117, 123 n.86, 124 n.107,
    128 n.214, 137, 141, 144, 158, 163
Damascus: 2, 4, 18, 91, 97
Darfur: 53
David, King: 2, 9
Day of Resurrection: 15
Deendar Anjuman: 3–4, 143
Demon(s): 8, 149 n.104
Don Fodio, Usman: 3, 52
Dönme: 101
Doppelganger: 19, 28 n.101
Druze: 135, 147 n.48

Egypt, Egyptians: 13, 26 n.51, 30, 32, 37,
    45–46, 48–57, 59, 61, 67 n.84, 68 n.99,
    70 n.127, 72–73, 77–78, 80, 85 n.20, 91,
    108, 111, 125 n.156, 131, 135, 139
Eschatology, Christian: 9, 18, 98–99,
    112–113, 133, 164 n.10
Eschatology, general: 6, 8, 163
Eschatology, Islamic/Muslim: 6–8, 17,
    19, 21, 27 n.74, 28 n.86, 29 n.103, 42,
    59, 79, 83, 89, 94–95, 98–99, 101–102,
    105, 108–113, 116–117, 124 n.107, 137,
    141, 147 n.48, 161
Eschatology, Jewish: 99
Eschatology, Zoroastrian: 8–9
Eurasia: 3, 102

False Prophet: 10, 18
Falwell, Jerry: 99
Fatimah: 14–16, 27 n.65, 35, 49, 95, 138
Fatimid Empire, Fatimids: 30–31, 35,
    38, 63 n.3, 73–74, 103, 135, 139
Fez: 37
The Four Feathers: 45
Fox News Channel: 24 n.23
Franciscan(s): 37
French Revolution: 34
Fukuyama, Francis: 92, 133
Fundamentalism, Muslim/Islamic: 6,
    25 n.34, 55, 62, 74, 152–53, 159, 162

Genghis Khan: 133, 146 n.32
al–Ghazali, Abu Hamid Muhammad:
    32–33, 49, 57
Gnosticism: 30
Gog and Magog: 10, 17–18, 99, 117
Gordon, Charles: 46, 54, 69 n.113, 79
Graham, Billy: 99
Granada: 36
Guantanamo: 157
Gujarat: 38–40, 65 n.41
Gujarati Sultantate: 39
Gulf War: 88

Hadith: 2, 6, 7, 11–15, 17–19, 21, 25 nn.
    47 and 49, 27 nn. 67–68, 74 and 81,
    28 n.85, 35–36, 39–40, 55, 79–80, 85
    n.26, 87, 90–92, 94, 97–98, 100–101,
    104, 111–114, 117, 127 n.194,
    128 n.210, 132, 137–39, 141, 144,
    148 n.79, 152, 154, 163
Hajj: 27 n.66, 42–43, 53, 72, 115
al–Hakim: 133,
Hamzah: 16
Hanafis: 64 n.15
Hanbalis: 64 n.15
al–Harith b. Harrath: 15
Hasan (son of Ali): 4, 16, 27 n.79, 95,
    107, 138
Hassan, Muhammad b. Abd Allah: 3,
    136
Heaven: 8–10, 18
Hell: 8, 115
Heston, Charlton: 45, 54
Hidden Imam: 4–5, 61, 93, 107, 118,
    128 n.220, 134–35, 160–61
Hijaz: 13, 53–55, 78–79, 163
Hindus, Hinduism: 4, 38, 40, 65 n.39,
    66 n.64, 133, 146 n.31, 155, 164 n.19,
    165 n.19
Huntington, Samuel: 92,
Husayn (son of Ali): 4, 16, 27 n.79,
    107, 138
Hussain, Siddiq: 4

Iberia: 33, 36–37, 41, 73, 75
Ibn Abu Mahallah: 2–3, 41–42, 45,
    66 n.56, 76
Ibn al–`Arabi, Muhyi al-Din: 136

Ibn Khaldun: 72–76, 84, 91–92, 134,
    138–139, 143
Ibn Taymiyah: 91, 125 n.142, 134, 138,
    159
Ibn Tumart al-Susi, Abu Abd Allah
    Muhammad: 2, 31–38, 40–42, 45, 49,
    52, 57–58, 63 n.6, 64 nn. 13 and 18,
    73–75, 83, 85 n.27, 96, 102–03, 114,
    139, 151, 155
India: 2–4, 13, 38, 39–40, 42–43, 45, 48,
    54, 57, 70 n.127, 72, 76, 113, 162,
    164 n.19, 165 n.19
Indiana Jones: 108
Iran: 4, 5, 8, 12–13, 23 n.18, 27 n.78, 30, 52,
    61, 84, 85 n.27, 86 n.32, 88, 94, 99–101,
    105–07, 113, 126 n.167, 126 n.169, 131,
    135, 149 n.107, 161–62, 166 n.56
Iran–Iraq War: 88, 106
Iraq, Iraqi(s): 1, 5, 13, 14, 23 n.18, 30,
    32, 52, 71 n.144, 80, 88, 96, 106–07,
    111, 157–58, 160, 161
`Isa: 2, 22 n.4
Ishtar: 132
Islamic Mahdiyah of Arabia: 162
Islamic Republic of Iran: 84, 94,
    100–01, 107, 161, 166 n.52
Islamic Union: 160
Isma'il (grandson of Muhammad Ali):
    46
Isma'il (Shi`i Imam): 5
Isma'il (son of Muhmmad Ali): 46
Isma'il Pasha (Turkish politician): 59
Isma'il, Shah: 85 n.27, 107

Isma'ili(s) ("Seveners"): 5, 23, n.18, 30,
    101, 135, 139
Israel: 2, 9, 88, 96, 98, 100–01, 106, 109,
    115, 133, 142, 149 n.107, 158, 164 n.18
Israfil: 19
Istanbul: 19, 29 n.103, 46, 53, 54, 77–78,
    80, 81, 95, 101, 104–05
Italy: 37

Ja`far: 16
Jawnpuri, Muhammad: 2–3, 38–42, 45,
    57–58, 65 n.44, 76, 143
Jaysh al-Mahdi: 1, 111, 161
al–Jazeerah: 87, 157, 160

Jerusalem: 19, 31, 88, 97, 101, 106–07,
    109–110, 115
Jesus: 1, 2, 4, 9–10, 17–19, 21, 22 n.6,
    28 nn.87, 88 and 102, 40, 61, 68
    n.104, 73, 76, 79, 91, 95, 97–102,
    107–110, 113–117, 122 n.76, 123 n.89,
    126 n.171, 128 n.215, 133, 137,
    141, 149 n.119, 151–152, 161, 163,
    166 n.61
Judah: 2, 133
Judaism: 2, 8, 9, 101, 121, 150, 160
Judas Iscariot: 18

Ka`bah: 14, 27 n.66, 139, 140
Karbala: 4
Kazakhstan: 27 n.69
al–Kazim, Musa: 39
Kerry, John: 24 n.23
Khariji(s), Kharijism: 12, 17, 26 n.51,
    39, 75, 104, 133
Khartoum: 48–49, 51, 53–54, 56,
    68 n.99, 78–79
Khartoum (movie): 45
Khatami, Muhammad: 101, 107
Khatmiyah: 48
Khomeini, Ayatollah Ruhollah: 61,
    94, 107, 126 n.167, 161,
    166 n.156
Khundmir, Sayyid: 39
Khurasan: 12
Kingdom of Heaven: 117
Kitchener, Horatio Herbert: 57
Krishna: 4
Kurdufan: 50, 53, 79

Lake of Fire: 10
Lamtuna Berbers: 33
Las Navas de Tolas: 37
Last Judgment: 7
Libya: 3, 37, 56, 136, 139
Lindsey, Hal: 99
London: 53, 78, 127 n.190
Lord of the Rings: 27 n.82
Luther, Martin: 51

Machiavelli, Niccolo: 133
Maghrib: 30, 36, 44, 73
Mahdavis, Mahdavism: 39–41

al–Mahdi, 2, 22 n.8, 22 n.9, 24 n.25, 29
    n.105, 61, 110, 112, 139, 149 n.117
Mahdism, Stages of: 40–41
Mahdists: 1–8, 12, 13, 17, 21, 30–31,
    33–46, 48, 50–62, 64 n.18, 66 n.56,
    70 n.132, 70 n.136, 72–78, 81–84, 85
    n.27, 86 n.32, 87–118, 119 n.5, 119
    nn.5 and 6, 122 nn.64 and 69, 125
    nn.142 and 149, 127 n.181, 128 n.198,
    130–132, 134–142, 145, 149 n.117,
    150–158, 160–163, 163 n.1, 164 n.19
Mahdiyah: 3, 42, 45, 56–57, 67 n.81,
    78, 80, 102, 135, 139, 145, 150,
    155, 162
Mali: 41, 52
Malikis: 64 n.15
Mamluk(s): 67 n.84, 72
Mani: 132
al–Mansur: 15, 37
Marrakesh: 33, 36–37, 41, 66 n.56
Marx, Marxism: 104, 106, 109,
Mashiakh: 2, 9, 22 n.5
al-Masih: 2, 8, 22 n.6
Masmuda Berbers: 34
Masons, Masonic order: 105, 151
Mauritania: 33
al–Mawdudi, Sayyid Abu Ala: 94,
    122 n.65
Mecca: 1, 13–14, 16, 27 nn.66 and 77,
    30, 34, 39, 43, 53, 56, 60, 62, 79–82,
    93, 101, 104, 138–140
Medina: 1, 13, 14, 16, 18, 34, 39, 52–53,
    60, 79, 101,151, 153
Mehmet: 3, 29 n.103, 58–59, 62, 77
Messiah: 1, 2, 8–10, 75, 116, 150, 155
Millenarianism: 6, 150, 155–56,
    160, 162
Millennialism: 6–10, 65 n.44, 76
Millennium: 3, 5, 6, 8–10, 13, 38–40, 42,
    62, 65 n.44, 85 n.7, 93, 99, 119 n.7,
    133, 135, 150
Mongolia: 133
Morocco: 3, 13, 30–33, 41, 45, 54, 62, 76,
    114
Mortensen, Viggo: 27 n.82
Moses: 2
Mossad: 142
Mughal Empire: 38–40

Muhammad, Ali ("the Bab"): 4
Muhammad, prophet: 1, 2, 4, 7, 10–12,
    14–16, 18, 27 nn. 65, 68, 70, 72, 75 and
    77, 34, 36–37, 39, 41, 44, 50–52, 56,
    58–59, 79–80, 90, 95, 97, 104, 108, 109,
    112, 119 n.10, 125 n.135, 126 nn.165
    and 171, 127 nn.181 and 194, 132–33,
    135, 137, 138, 141, 148 n.80, 156
Muharram: 4, 60
Murabit(s): 31–38, 64 n.15, 72, 75, 83, 155
Musaylimah: 104
Muslim World League: 87
Muwahhid(s): 31–38, 40–42, 57, 64
    nn.17 and 18, 72–75, 83, 96, 139, 151
Muzaffar II: 39

Naqshabandiyah: 42–43, 58,
Nation of Islam: 116
Neo-Babylonian(s): 2
Neoplatonism: 30
New Testament: 10, 98, 128 n.215
Nigeria: 3, 56
Nixon, Richard: 99
Noah (*Nuh*): 2, 93, 102, 106, 121 n.61,
    126 n.159
Nostradamus: 99
Nuclear: 1, 97–99, 101, 106–07, 109, 163

Occulted, occultation: 4, 8, 31, 42–43,
    76, 93, 119 n.9, 135, 161
Old Testament: 99, 133, 149 n.100
Olivier, Laurence: 45
Oman: 106
Orientalism: 92
Ottoman Empire, Ottomans: 45, 48,
    52–54, 57–58, 68 n.88, 69 n.122, 72,
    77–78, 80–81, 83, 104–05, 107, 126
    n.169, 149 n.107, 152, 155

Palestine: 73, 100, 107, 149 n.107, 158
Pan–Islam: 56, 91, 94, 106, 161
Persia, Persian(s): 5, 8, 13, 19, 39, 61, 67
    n.83, 107, 121 n.63, 132, 134, 161
Persian Gulf: 106, 107
Pisyotan: 8
Portugal: 37
Prophet (generic): 1, 2, 4, 7, 8–16, 18,
    27 n.72, 34, 36–37, 41, 44, 50, 52, 55,

59, 79–80, 82, 90, 93, 95, 97, 99, 102,
    104, 106, 108, 109, 112, 114, 125
    n.135, 126 n.159, 127 n.194, 132–33,
    137–38, 149 n.119, 150, 154–55, 160

Qadiyan, Qadiyanis: 3, 4,
al–Qahtani, Muhammad: 3, 86 n.31,
    155
Qahtani, the: 111
al–Qaeda (al-Qa`idah): 153–54, 157,
    159, 162, 164 n.17
Al–Qa'im: 30
Qarmatians: 139, 140
Qazvin: 13
Qur'an: 2, 7, 8, 10–13, 17–19, 21, 27
    n.75, 33, 35–36, 38–40, 43, 55–56, 58,
    70 nn.126 and 130, 80, 82, 92–94,
    96–98, 109, 112, 117, 120 n.22, 122
    n.64, 128 n.226, 135–137, 142, 144,
    148 n.72, 150, 152, 156
Quraysh: 15, 90
Qutb, Sayyid: 125 n.156, 161
Qutbaniyah: 41

Rahmaniyah: 45
Reagan, Ronald: 99
Red Sea: 46, 53, 78
Rida, Rashid: 91–92, 100, 138–139
Riyadh: 160
Robertson, Pat: 99
Robin Hood: 97
Roman Empire: 58, 108
Rome: 19, 95, 108
Russia: 3, 48, 99, 101–02, 105, 139

Sabbatai Sevi: 101
al–Sadr, Muqtada: 1, 111, 161
al–Sadiq, Ja`far: 27 n.78
Sa`diyan(s): 41–42, 72, 76, 83
Safavid Empire, Safavids: 30, 85 n.27,
    107, 126 n.169, 161
Said, Edward: 92, 126 n.158
Salah al-Din: 31, 37–38
Sammaniyah: 48–49
Sanhaja Berbers: 33
al–Sanusi, Sayyid Muhammad
    al-Mahdi: 3, 55, 103, 136, 139
Sanusiyah: 3, 55–56

Saoshyant: 8
Sargon: 132
Sasanian(s): 8, 132
Satan: 104
Sa`ud, Sa`udi Arabia: 43, 51, 60
Saul: 9
Saviour: 8
Scramble for Africa: 57
September 11 (9/11): 5–6, 24, 61, 84,
    163, 157–158
Seven Sleepers: 58–59
Shafi`is: 64 n.15
Shah: 61, 107
Shah-namah: 19
Shi`ah, Shi`ism: 3–6, 8, 12, 17, 21, 23
    nn. 16, 17 and 18, 25 n.49, 30–31, 35,
    38–40, 42–43, 61–62, 63 n.1, 74–76,
    84, 85 n.7, 87, 89–90, 92–95, 101,
    106–07, 109, 112–114, 119 nn.9 and
    10, 120 nn.24 and 25, 121 n.63, 122
    n.64, 125 n.135, 126 n.169, 128 nn.198
    and 220, 131–137, 140, 143–44, 150,
    159, 160–62
Si Muhammad Ben Bou Khentach: 44
Si Sadok Ben al-Hadj: 44
Siberia: 19
Sicily: 37
Signs of the End: 17, 19, 90, 92, 95,
    102, 108, 112–114, 117, 122 n.69,
    124 n.107, 126 n.171, 141, 144–45,
    153
Sijilmasa: 37, 41, 66 n.56
Sikhs, Sikhism: 42–43, 66 n.64, 76,
    165 n.19
Sinai: 88, 101,
Six Days' War: 84, 88, 151,
Slavery, Slave trade: 46, 50, 54, 56–57,
    68 n.88
Smallpox: 163
Sokoto Caliphate: 3, 52, 56
Somalis, Somalia: 3, 52, 136, 139
Son of Man: 98, 116, 117
St. Paul: 99, 127 n.73, 128 n.224
St. Peter's Basilica: 108
Sudan: 2–3, 13, 45–46, 48–54, 57–58, 68
    nn.93 and 95, 70 n.127, 72, 77–81,
    85 n.20, 107, 110, 136, 139, 143
Suez Canal: 46, 48, 57

Sufis, Sufism: 3, 32, 39, 42–43, 45,
    48–51, 53–59, 62, 65 n.43, 68 n.95,
    72–74, 76, 85 n.7, 91, 94, 122 n.64,
    132–136, 138, 141, 147 n.57, 153,
    164 n.14
Sufyan, Mu`awiyah b. Abi: 19, 27 n.67,
    141
Sufyani: 17–19, 28 nn.100 and 101, 79,
    95, 102, 107–110, 138, 141
Sunni(s), Sunnism: 2–6, 8, 11–14, 19,
    21, 30, 31, 35, 37, 38–41, 43, 45, 49,
    55, 61–62, 63 n.1, 76, 79, 85 n.27,
    87–89, 91–95, 101, 104, 107, 111–114,
    116, 119 nn. 9 and 10, 120 n.32,
    130–36, 140, 143, 144–45, 150, 153,
    156, 158, 160–162
al–Suyuti, Jalal al-Din: 91, 120 n.34,
    135, 138–39, 148 n.87
Swaggart, Jimmy: 99
Syria: 13–14, 16–17, 19, 26 n.51, 32,
    37–38, 52, 70 n.127, 73, 80, 88, 91,
    106, 108, 135

Tajikistan: 13
Taliban: 35, 64 n.26, 88
Tanzimat: 68 n.87
Temple of Solomon: 106, 123 n.94, 137
Thanesari, Muhammad: 42
The Passion of the Christ: 28 n.90
Timbuktu: 41
Trinity Broadcasting Network: 99
Trojan Horse: 60
Tunisia: 30, 37, 72
Turkey: 3, 13, 29 n.103, 58–60, 70 n.127,
    77, 83, 100
Turkmenistan: 101
Twelvers: 5, 23 n.18, 27 n.78, 39, 135

Ubayd Allah: 30, 103, 135
Uhud, Battle of: 27 n.77
Umayyad(s): 4, 12–13, 17, 19, 26 n.51,
    27 n.67, 28 n.100, 92, 104, 134,
    139–141
United Arab Emirates: 106
United Nations: 109
Usedar: 8
al–Utaybi, Juhayman: 3, 60, 83, 86 n.31,
    102, 139, 155

Utopia, utopian: 6–10, 156, 160
Uzbekistan: 14, 27 n.69, 101, 114

Valencia: 36
Vatican: 51, 107
Virgin Mary: 151
Vishnu: 133

al-Wahhab, Muhammad b. Abd: 43
Wahhabis, Wahhabism: 43, 53, 60–61,
    66 n.69, 77, 91, 138, 151, 157
Wara' al-Nahr: 15,
West Bank: 88, 106
Western Sahara: 33, 40
Wilson, Woodrow: 36
World Trade Center: 88, 120 n.22, 158
World Trade Organization: 158
World War I: 58, 105
World War II: 88, 100
World War III: 108

Ya`qub, Idris b.: 37
Ya`qub al-Mansur, Abu Yusuf: 37
Yahya, Harun: 112–113, 151, 163 n.1,
    166 n.47
Yajuj wa-Majuj: 17–19, 95, 101, 117, 137
Yasin, Abd Allah b.: 33
Yasin, Ahmad: 107
Yemen: 17, 19, 23 n.18, 27 (note 67), 95,
    135, 147 n.48

Zanata Berbers: 34
al–Zarqawi, Abu Masab: 96, 160, 162
Zayd, Zaydi(s): 5, 23 n.18, 135,
    147 n.48
Zaydan, Mawlay: 41
Zionism, Zionists: 9, 137, 142, 100–101,
    109
Zoroaster, Zoroastrianism: 8, 9, 21, 92,
    132–133, 135, 165 n.19

Index of Important Arabic Terms

Note: The Arabic definite article *al–* has been ignored in alphabetization.

`Adl: 17
`Asabiyah: 73–74

Batinis: 101

Da`wah: 50, 79
Dar al-Harb: 159
Dar al-Islam: 159
Dawlah Allah: 96
Dawlah Islamiyah: 96

Fatwa(s): 48, 79–81, 83, 87, 159, 163
Fitnah (Fitan): 15, 106, 132, 140

Ghaybah: 4, 135, 119 n.9

Hadrah(s): 34, 50, 165 n.28
Hajj: 27 (note 66), 42–43, 53, 72, 115
al–Harb al-Salibiyah: 158
Harmagiddun: 98
Hijrah: 1, 34, 37, 39, 52, 59, 75, 105

Ilham: 55
Imam(s): 4, 5, 17, 23 (note 16), 27 n.78,
   39, 42, 54, 60, 79, 90, 95, 106, 135,
   136, 141, 143, 147 n.48
`Ismah: 35
Isnad: 11, 15
"Isra'iliyyat": 100

Jihad: 3, 7, 37, 42–45, 52, 59, 62, 150
Jinn: 141, 149 n.104

Kufr: 33, 39, 123 n.86

al–Mahdi al-Muntazar: 5
al–Mahdi al-Sahyuni: 100
Malakut Allah: 97
al–Malhamah al-Kubra: 98
Matn: 11–12
Mufti(s): 48, 78, 79, 91, 100
Mujaddid: 3, 7, 38, 43–44, 52, 61, 136,
   138
Mutamahdi: 80

Na'ib al-Imam al-Mahdi: 94

Qutb: 134, 136, 146 n.42

Rashidun: 104
al–Rukn wa-al-Maqam: 27 n.66

Salafiyah: 159
Shi`at Ali: 4
Sunnah: 11, 15–16, 74, 80, 87, 114

Tadlis: 12, 90
Tadlis: 90
Takfir: 39
Tamyiz: 34
Tawhid: 31, 38, 43, 65, 96, 136, 161
Thawrah: 132, 140

Ulama: 41, 48, 51, 54, 60, 76, 78–81,
   91–92, 110, 118, 137–38, 163

Wad`: 12, 90

Zhikr: 58

Index of Qur'anic Citations

Note: The Arabic definite article *al–* has been omitted. A "p" for page numbers has been added to clarify the differentiation between Qur'an citations that use a colon and actual page references. In addition to spaces between alphabetical entries, a space has also been added between the different surahs of the Qur'an cited.

Ahzab [33]: p. 28 n.88

An`am [6]: p. 28 n.88
An`am [6]:36, 74: p. 24 n.31
An`am [6]:75: p. 123 n.102
An`am [6]:101, 113, 129: p. 149 n.104
An`am [6]:116: p. 147 n.69

Anbiya' [21]:47, 103: p. 24 n.31
Anbiya' [21]:96: p. 28 n.96

Ankabut [29]:25: p. 24 n.31

A`raf [7]:38, 179: p. 149 n.104
A`raf [7]:32, 167: p. 24 n.31
A`raf [7]:59: p. 126 n.159
A`raf [7]:185: p. 123 n.102

Bani Isra'il [17]:13: p. 24 n.31

Baqarah [2]: p. 28 n.88
Baqarah [2]:255: p. 64 n.12

Furqan [25]:22: p. 24 n.31, p. 127 n.180

Hadid [57]: p. 28 n.88

Hajj [22]:1, 9: p. 24 n.31

Hijr [15]:27: p. 149 n.104

Hud [11]:25: p. 126 n.159

Ibrahim [14]:44: p. 24 n.31

`Imran [3]: p. 28 n.88
`Imran [3]:26: p. 64 n.12
`Imran [3]:30, 45–55, 106, 161, 185:
    p. 22 n.2
`Imran [3]:73: p. 128 n.215

Infitar [82]:1: p. 127 n.180
Infitar [82]:1: p. 24 n.31

Inshiqaq [84]:1: p. 24 n.31

Isra' [17]:3–8: p. 148 n.72

Jathiyah [45]:26: p. 24 n.31

Kahf [18]: p. 70 n.125
Kahf [18]:48, 106: p. 24 n.31
Kahf [18]:51: p. 149 n.104
Kahf [18]:90: p. 148 n.70
Kahf [18]:95: p. 28 n.96

Ma`arij [70]:7: p. 127 n.180

Ma'idah [5]: p. 28 n.88
Ma'idah [5]:3: p. 147 n.68
Ma'idah [5]:52: p. 22 n.4
Ma'idah [5]:109: p. 128 n.215

Maryam [19]: p. 28 n.88
Maryam [19]:85: p. 24 n.31

Mu'min [40]:15: p. 24 n.31

Mu'minun [23]:88: p. 123 n.102

Mumtahanah [60]:3: p. 24 n.31

Mursalat [77]:2: p. 127 n.180

Muzammil [73]:12: p. 127 n.180

Naba' [78]:17: p. 24 n.31

Nahl [16]:25: p. 24 n.31

Naml [27]:17, 139: p. 149 n.104
Naml [27]:82: p. 28 n.92

Nisa' [4]: p. 28 n.88
Nisa' [4]:11: p. 69 n.119
Nisa' [4]:59: p. 69 n.105
Nisa' [4]:87, 109, 157, 159: p. 22 n.2

Nuh [71]: p. 126 n.159

Qari`ah [101]:1: p. 24 n.31
Qari`ah [101]:3: p. 68 n.101

Qasas [28]:41–42, 61: p. 24 n.31

Qiyamah [75]:34–36: p. 126 n.172
Qiyamah [75]:6: p. 24 n.31

Ra`d [111]:11: p. 147 n.67

Rum [30]:56–57: p. 24 n.31

Saba' [34]:12ff, 41: p. 149 n.104

Saff [61]: p. 28 n.88

Saffat [37]:20: p. 24 n.31
Saffat [37]:158: p. 149 n.104

Sajdah [32]:13: p. 149 n.104

Shura [42]: p. 28 n.88

Taha [20]: 100: p. 24 n.31

Takwir [81]:1: p. 24 n.31

Yasin [36]:83: p. 123 n.102

Zalzalah [99]:1: p. 24 n.31

Zukhruf [43]: p. 28 n.88

Zumar [39]:24, 47: p. 24 n.31

Index of Biblical Citations

Note: A "p" for page numbers has been added to clarify the differentiation between Scriptural citations that use a colon and actual page references. In addition to spaces between alphabetical entries, a space has also been added between the different books of the Bible cited.

Acts 7:56: p. 124 n.109

Daniel 7:13: p. 124 n.109
Daniel 9:25–26: p. 25 n.45
Daniel 11:5: p. 124 n.122
Daniel 11:31: p. 124 n.123
Daniel 12:9–10: p. 148 n.98

Ezekiel 38, 39: p. 28 n.95; p. 124 n.115

Genesis 6–9: p. 126 n.159

Isaiah 2:4: p. 146 n.126
Isaiah 9:2–7: p. 25 n.45

Jeremiah 23:3–8: p. 25 n.45

John 1:41, 4:25–26: p. 25 n.46
John 7:5: p. 68 n.104

Luke 1–23: p. 123 n.103
Luke 9:10: p. 123 n.89
Luke 9:18: p. 25 n.46
Luke 12:8: p. 124 n.109
Luke 18:8: p. 124 n.109
Luke 21: p. 124 n.119; p. 126 n.171
Luke 21:9: p. 122 n.76
Luke 21:11: p. 128 n.197

Mark 1–15: p. 123 n.103
Mark 3:33: p. 68 n.104

Mark 6:30: p. 123 n.89
Mark 8:27: p. 25 n.46
Mark 8:38: p. 124 n.109
Mark 13: p. 25 n.44, p. 28 n.87; p. 124 n.119; p. 126 n.171
Mark 13:7: p. 122 n.76
Mark 13:8: p. 128 n.197
Mark 13:22: p. 29 n.102
Mark 14:62: p. 124 n.109

Matthew 1:16, 16:13: p. 25 n.46
Matthew 3–26: p. 123 n.103
Matthew 12:8, 32; 13:41; 16:27; 19:28; 24:27, 30, 44; 25:31: p. 124 n.109
Matthew 12:46: p. 68 n.104
Matthew 14:13ff: p. 123 n.89
Matthew 20:1–16: p. 124 n.116
Matthew 24: p. 25 n.44; p. 28 n.87; p. 124 n.119; p. 126 n.171
Matthew 24:6: p. 122 n.76
Matthew 24:7: p. 128 n.197
Matthew 24:24: p. 28 n.102
Matthew 24:27: p. 128 n.218

Micah 5:2: p. 146 n.27

Revelation 1:13: p. 124 n.109
Revelation 8:10–11ff: p. 127 n.180
Revelation 13:11: p. 28 n.93
Revelation 14:14: p. 124 n.109

Revelation 16:16: p. 124 n.111
Revelation 19:11–22:21: p. 25 n.42
Revelation 20: p. 25 n.35
Revelation 20:7–9: p. 28 n.95
Revelation 20:8: p. 28 n.97

Romans 7:14–8:17: p. 128 n.224

I Thessalonians 4:13–18: p. 124 n.117
I Thessalonians 4:16–5:3: p. 25 n.43

I Timothy 3:1: p. 127 n.173

Zechariah 10:4: p. 146 n.28
Zechariah 14: p. 124 n.118

About The Author

TIM FURNISH teaches world history at Georgia Perimeter College. He learned Arabic while serving in U.S. Army Intelligence and received his doctorate in Islamic History from Ohio State University. His specialty is Islamic eschatology, particularly modern Mahdism—Islamic "messianism"—and how such beliefs have influenced revolutionary political thought in the Muslim world.